Electronic engineering materials and devices

Electronic engineering materials and devices

John Allison
Senior Lecturer
Department of Electronic and Electrical Engineering
University of Sheffield

McGRAW-HILL Book Company (UK) Limited

London · New York · St Louis · San Francisco · Auckland · Bogotá
Guatemala · Hamburg · Johannesburg · Lisbon · Madrid · Mexico · Montreal
New Delhi · Panama · Paris · San Juan · São Paulo · Singapore · Sydney
Tokyo · Toronto

Published by:
McGRAW-HILL Book Company (UK) Limited
MAIDENHEAD · BERKSHIRE · ENGLAND

---

07 094163 7

Preface

In the early days of electronic engineering the essentials of vacuum electronic devices could be understood without too much difficulty and many of their characteristics derived theoretically by classical methods. Today, not only is the physical nature of the transport of charge in modern electric devices more complicated, but many of the more recent devices have properties which cannot be explained without recourse to quantum electronics.

Many textbooks describe, for example, the theoretical physics of the solid state, often in great detail and not without some degree of mathematical complexity. Other engineering texts merely provide a cursory description of devices as a preliminary to a detailed discussion of their circuit application. This book is an attempt to close the gap between the two extremes. It provides a physical description of the properties of materials which is sufficiently detailed to allow complete characterization of the electrical performance of modern electronic devices in a manner that can be fully understood by the engineer.

The author is acutely aware of the rapid advances being made in electronic engineering. New devices are continually being developed and absorbed into the technology, causing some textbooks on the subject to become obsolete almost as soon as they are published. It is hoped that, by concentrating on fundamental processes occurring in materials and by discussing contemporary devices as specific examples of these processes, this book will avoid such a fate. Although lack of space prevents complete coverage of all devices, sufficient insight into the basic properties of elementary devices is given to enable the reader to progress to the study of whatever new or perhaps undeveloped device may be his own peculiar interest.

The text is based in the main on a series of lecture courses given to university undergraduates in their first, second, and final years. For this reason a choice had to be made between subdividing the subject matter so as to make the level of treatment progressively more difficult or arranging the material in a more logically acceptable way. The former method is usual in teaching, where the presentation has to be geared to the mathematical ability of the student, but it suffers the disadvantage of lack of continuity, each device being described on several occasions, each time with an increasing depth of treatment. In this book the latter course has been adopted in an attempt to provide a text which unifies much of the materials and device teaching over the complete subject range, so emphasizing the relevance of each topic. This arrangement need not be a disadvantage as few textbooks are read, in the first instance, straight through from beginning to end. The main advantage is that while the student is able to cover the contents by any one of many routes, dictated by his own ability or as directed by his tutor, he will at the same time possess a book which amalgamates all the material into a coherent whole.

It might be supposed that this textbook is aimed solely at electronic engineering students, but practising engineers who feel the need for retraining should also find it helpful, as well as students of associated disciplines in applied technology, physics, and chemistry.

I am grateful to my colleagues and friends at Sheffield for many enjoyable and useful discussions, in particular to Professor P. N. Robson for his advice on some of the subject matter and to Professor F. A. Benson for his patience and understanding during the preparation of this work. I am also deeply indebted to Professor A. L. Cullen, whose encouragement persuaded me that this project was worthwhile. Finally, I am most appreciative of the help of Mrs E. Byrne and her staff in typing the manuscript. That they managed to decipher my hieroglyphics with so few errors compares well with the wonders of modern electronics.

John Allison

Physical constants

	Symbol		Units
Permittivity of free space	ϵ_0	8.854×10^{-12}	F/m
Permeability of free space	μ_0	$4\pi \times 10^{-7}$	H/m
Electronic charge	e	1.602×10^{-19}	C
Electronic rest mass	m	9.108×10^{-31}	kg
Electronic charge/mass ratio	e/m	1.759×10^{11}	C/kg
Proton rest mass		$1836\ m$	
Planck's constant	h	6.625×10^{-34}	J s
Boltzmann's constant	k	1.380×10^{-23}	J/K
kT at room temperature		0.0259	eV

Properties of some common semiconductors at room temperature

	Si	Ge	GaAs	InSb
Atomic weight	28·09	72·59	–	–
Atomic density, m^{-3}	5·02 x 10^{28}	4·42 x 10^{28}	–	–
Lattice constant, a nm	0·543	0·565	0·563	0·645
Relative permittivity, ϵ_r	11·8	16·0	13·5	11·5
Energy gap, E_g eV	1·08	0·66	1·58	0·23
Electron mobility, μ_e m^2/V . s	0·13	0·38	0·85	7·0
Hole mobility, μ_h m^2/V . s	0·05	0·18	0·04	0·10
Intrinsic concentration, n_i m^{-3}	1·38 x 10^{16}	2·5 x 10^{19}	9 x 10^{12}	1·6 x 10^{22}
Electron diffusion const., D_e m^2 s^{-1}	0·0031	0·0093	0·020	0·0093
Hole diffusion const., D_h m^2 s^{-1}	0·0007	0·0044	–	–
Density of states at C.B. edge, N_c m^{-3}	2·8 x 10^{25}	1·0 x 10^{25}	4·7 x 10^{23}	–
Density of states at V.B. edge, N_v m^{-3}	1·0 x 10^{25}	6·0 x 10^{24}	7·0 x 10^{24}	–
Melting point, °C	1420	936	1250	523

Contents

x

1. The quantum behaviour of waves and particles

1.1 Introduction

Throughout our discussion of the electronic properties of materials and the application of these properties to a physical understanding of the operation of electronic devices we shall constantly be referring to the interaction of particles of atomic size, for example electrons, with other particles or with waves. We shall discover that in some instances elementary mechanics is no longer adequate to describe the dynamics of microscopic particles and that this theory has to be supplemented by one which is more generally applicable, the so-called *quantum* or *wave* mechanics.

Classical mechanics is based on laws developed by Newton. For example

$$F = \frac{dp}{dt} \tag{1.1}$$

Newton's laws, together with a classical electromagnetic theory as summarized by Maxwell's equations, proved adequate for the quantitative explanation of most experiments done before the beginning of the twentieth century. Equation (1.1) was found to be quite satisfactory for predicting the dynamics of large-scale systems. This is, of course, also true today. The term 'large-scale systems' in this context applies equally well to normal engineering laboratory experiments and to the more obviously large systems such as collections of planets.

A series of experiments conducted at the beginning of this century exposed a basic limitation of classical Newtonian mechanics, which is its inability to predict correctly events which take place on a microscopic or atomic scale. In the sections which follow we shall discuss the experiments which led to this failure in classical mechanics while at the same time we will attempt to lay a general foundation for later discussions of a more general quantum-mechanical theory. It should be stressed that quantum mechanics does not entirely supplant Newtonian mechanics but rather augments it in that it is more widely applicable. We shall show that within the limits of laboratory-sized objects, however, the newer mechanics reduces to the classical theory which, because it is simpler to apply, is still to be preferred.

1.2 Black-body radiation

One of the earliest experiments to defy analysis by classical methods was the determination of the frequency spectrum of emitted radiation of an incandescent radiator or 'black body'. In this experiment the intensity of emitted radiation is measured as a function of frequency or wavelength for a fixed temperature, with typical results as indicated diagrammatically in Fig. 1.1.

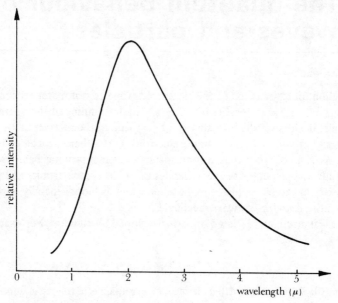

Fig. 1.1 Relative intensity of radiation emitted from a black body as a function of wavelength.

The various earlier theories attempting to explain this experimental evidence were based on classical mechanical ideas incorporated in thermodynamical theory. These theories were never successful in agreeing with the experiment, particularly in the short-wavelength limit. We know now that they broke down because of a fundamental misconception that atomic oscillators are capable of emitting or absorbing energy in continuously variable amounts. It was not until 1901 that Max Planck discredited this false notion by correctly predicting the intensity of radiation at all the frequencies. His theory involved the hypothesis that energy could only be absorbed or emitted by the black body in discrete amounts. He assumed that the energy of light waves, for example, is transported in packets or bundles, called *photons* or *quanta*. He further assumed the energy of a photon to be given by

$$E = hf \text{ joules} \tag{1.2}$$

where f is the frequency of the radiation. Planck's constant, h, is a universal constant which is found for the black-body radiator and other experiments to have a value $h = 6 \cdot 626 \cdot 10^{-34}$ joule-second. Equation (1.2) is sometimes more conveniently written as

$$E = \hbar\omega \qquad (1.3)$$

where ω is the angular frequency of the radiation, $2\pi f$, and $\hbar$ equals $h/2\pi$. Thus, the total energy of the black-body radiator was envisaged to exist only in discrete allowed energy states:

$$0, \hbar\omega, 2\hbar\omega, 3\hbar\omega, \ldots, n\hbar\omega$$

transition between these states being brought about by absorption or emission of one or more photons of radiation, each of energy $\hbar\omega$.

It is not surprising that such a theory, being completely opposed to the existing continuously variable energy theories, was not readily accepted, even though it explained the experimental findings most satisfactorily. However, Planck's quantum hypothesis, which forms the basis of modern quantum mechanics, was further vindicated by later experimental evidence, as will be discussed in subsequent sections.

1.3 The photoelectric effect

If light of sufficiently short wavelength impinges on the surface at certain solids then it is possible for electrons to be emitted from the solid. This is called the photoelectric effect. In the early twentieth century, Einstein reinforced Planck's photon concept of light by providing a satisfactory quantitative explanation of the effect.

The experimental evidence for the effect may be obtained using apparatus of the type shown diagrammatically in Fig. 1.2. Light of frequency f illuminates

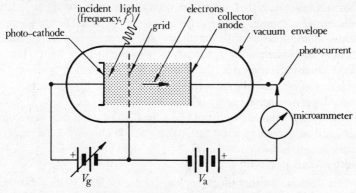

Fig. 1.2 A photoelectric experiment.

3

a cold cathode situated inside a vacuum envelope. If electrons are emitted, then, provided they have sufficient energy to overcome the retarding force field set up by the voltage V_g between grid and cathode, they will be swept to the positive collecting anode and a current will be registered on the micro-ammeter in series with it.

The first thing which would be noticed when carrying out such an experiment is that unless the frequency of the incident light is greater than some critical value, f_0, which is dependent on the material of the cathode, no emission is observed, *no matter how intense the light.* For constant light frequency, and provided f is greater than f_0, the photocurrent can be measured as a function of grid voltage V_g and light intensity, keeping the anode voltage constant, to give typical collector current data of the form shown in Fig. 1.3.

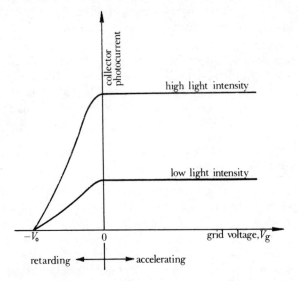

Fig. 1.3 Variation of photocurrent with grid voltage in the photoelectric experiment.

The surprising result is that, no matter what the intensity of the light, there is some constant retarding voltage, in this case $-V_0$, which entirely inhibits emission. This implies that the maximum kinetic energy of emitted electrons is constant and independent of the intensity of the incident light. However, as the light intensity is increased, the photocurrent increases in sympathy. Thus the number of emitted photoelectrons is a function of the intensity of the light but their maximum energy is constant.

Such experimental results cannot be explained by a classical wave theory of light and a satisfactory explanation can only be obtained by considering the light energy to be quantized. That is, the light energy is transported in discrete packets or photons.

Before discussing either theory we must digress a little to discuss briefly the reasons for the emission of electrons from a metal surface. We shall see

4

later that a metal contains many highly mobile electrons which can participate in the electrical conduction process, but these are confined to the interior of the metal by a binding energy. Thus, no conduction electrons can leave the surface of a metal unless they are in some way provided with additional energy to enable then to overcome this binding energy. The minimum energy required for an electron to be just emitted from a metal surface is called the *work function* of the particular metal and is usually designated $e\phi$ where ϕ is in volts.

In a classical theory of photoemission, conduction electrons in the cathode are accelerated by the electric field of the light wave and, if the light is bright enough, can gain sufficient energy to be emitted. Any surplus energy over and above the work function appears as kinetic energy of the emitted electron. Thus the brighter the light the more energy is left over after overcoming the binding energy and the greater the kinetic energy of the emitted electron. This result is clearly at variance with the experimental evidence that the emitted electrons have a constant maximum energy. Further, a classical wave theory would not predict a threshold frequency f_0, which again is contrary to the experimental results.

If now we turn to a quantum theory based on Planck's photon hypothesis we can give a simple explanation for the observed effects. We assume that the incident light is composed of discrete quanta or photons, each of energy hf. When the light impinges on the metal of the photocathode, each photon can transfer energy hf to a conduction electron. Some of the energy is used to overcome the binding forces and the remainder is converted to kinetic energy of the emitted electron. Thus

kinetic energy of emitted electron = photon energy − work function

or
$$\tfrac{1}{2}mv^2 = hf - e\phi \tag{1.4}$$

The limiting case occurs when an electron is just emitted with no kinetic energy. Then

$$f = f_0 = \frac{e\phi}{h} \tag{1.5}$$

At frequencies less than this critical value the photon's energy, hf, is not even sufficient to overcome the work function and no emission occurs. Further, if the intensity is increased the number of incident photons is increased but their energy remains constant, provided the frequency remains constant. Thus the kinetic energy of the emitted electrons, as given by eq. (1.4), stays constant, which is again borne out by experiment. Incidentally, eq. (1.4) gives the maximum kinetic energy at some particular frequency and in our experiment this is entirely converted to potential energy when the photo-current is reduced to zero by a retarding voltage $-V_0$.
Hence

$$eV_0 = hf - e\phi \tag{1.6}$$

We see that V_0 does not vary with light intensity, a fact we have already noted experimentally.

Thus, when considering the interaction of light with electrons, as in discussing the photoelectric effect, the quantum theory of light must be used in preference to the classical wave theory.

It will be useful to contrast this situation with the earlier experiments with light displaying such phenomena as diffraction, refraction, and so on. These effects could all be explained by a classical theory which relied on a wavelike description of the light radiation. As an example, let us remind ourselves of the situation when light is diffracted by a mirror diffraction grating. A schematic diagram of the essential elements of the experiment is shown in Fig. 1.4. A light wave, wavelength λ, is incident normally on to a reflecting

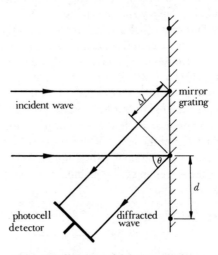

Fig. 1.4 Diffraction of light by a grating.

diffraction grating of the type used in optical spectrographs, which has a grating spacing d. The light wave is diffracted by the grating and the diffracted wave is detected at some angle θ to the normal. The detector might, for example, be a photocell similar to the one just described. Experimentally, what is observed is that as θ is varied the intensity at the detector varies cyclically from maximum to minimum values. These are the well-known diffraction fringes. A typical result might be as shown in Fig. 1.5. The appearance of the fringes can be explained quantitatively by invoking the wave description of light. The path length between light beams diffracted from adjacent rulings is indicated by Δl on Fig. 1.4. Whenever the angle θ is such that this length equals an integral number of wavelengths the diffracted waves interfere constructively and a bright fringe is observed. Thus, when

$$\Delta l = d \sin \theta = n\lambda$$

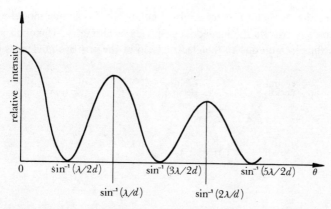

Fig. 1.5 Detected light intensity as a function of the angle of diffraction.

where n is an integer, there is constructive interference. This occurs at angles such that

$$\theta = \sin^{-1}\left(\frac{n\lambda}{d}\right) \tag{1.7}$$

Conversely, when the path difference Δl is equal to an odd number of half-wavelength, which is equivalent to a $180°$ phase difference, there is destructive interference and a dark band is observed. This occurs at angles given by

$$\theta = \sin^{-1}\left(\frac{2m+1}{2}\right)\lambda \tag{1.8}$$

Both these results agree with the experimental evidence and a wave theory is entirely adequate to explain this phenomenon.

We see, then, that light can in some circumstances be considered to possess wavelike properties but on other occasions it must be treated in a quantized manner, its energy being transported by discrete photons which are particle-like units each having energy hf. This wave–particle property of light radiation is sometimes referred to as the 'dual nature of light'.

If a light wave can behave as a particle, can a particle, say, for example, an electron, behave as a wave? The answer to this question will become apparent as we discuss further the historical development of quantum theory.

1.4 The Bohr atom

An excited hydrogen atom emits radiation at a discrete set of frequencies only. In 1913 Bohr produced a theoretical model which very accurately accounted for the observed sharp-line radiation spectrum from atomic hydrogen.

Let us consider the hydrogen atom to consist of a central nucleus with an electron travelling in a circular orbit round it, at some radius, r, as shown in Fig. 1.6(a). We shall see later that this description of an orbit is not very

7

precise, neither is the orbit necessarily circular, but this simple model will suffice to demonstrate the inadequacy of a classical theory. The coulomb force on the electron due to the electric field of the positive nucleus is just

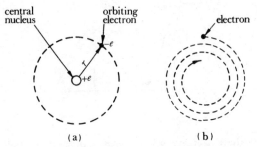

Fig. 1.6 (a) A possible model for a hydrogen atom, (b) spiral path due to radiated energy.

sufficient to provide inward acceleration for circular motion at a constant radius r. Thus:

$$F = -\frac{e^2}{4\pi\epsilon_0 r^2} = -\frac{mv^2}{r} \tag{1.9}$$

Now, the total energy of the electron, E, is the sum of its potential energy, V, and its kinetic energy, T. Further

$$V = -\frac{e^2}{4\pi\epsilon_0 r}$$

and from eq. (1.9)

$$T = \tfrac{1}{2}mv^2 = \frac{e^2}{8\pi\epsilon_0 r}$$

Therefore, the total electron energy is

$$E = -\frac{e^2}{8\pi\epsilon_0 r} \tag{1.10}$$

Now, the electron in the circular orbit is constantly being accelerated and it can be shown by electromagnetic theory that such an accelerated charge radiates electromagnetic energy, with a corresponding loss of energy. Classical theory thus indicates that radiation can occur, its frequency corresponding to the periodic frequency of the circular motion. This frequency can be shown to be plausible by observing the electron's motion in the plane of the orbit. The electron will be seen to oscillate sinusoidally about a central position where the nucleus is located. The resultant sinusoidally varying current can then be likened to that occurring in an ordinary radio transmitting aerial which radiates electromagnetic waves.

The frequency of the radiated wave from the classical atom is thus

$$f = \frac{v}{2\pi r}$$

which, using eq. (1.9), gives

$$f = \frac{e}{4(\pi^3 \epsilon_0 m r^2)^{1/2}} \tag{1.11}$$

Now, the conservation of energy indicates that as the electron radiates energy, its total energy, E, must decrease. Thus the radius of the orbit must also decrease, as shown by eq. (1.10). This would lead to a continual loss of energy and spiralling of the electron towards the nucleus, as shown in Fig. 1.6(b). This, in turn, would indicate that the frequency of the emitted radiation is continuously varying according to the dependence of f on the radius r as set out in eq. (1.11). This is clearly in complete disagreement with the experimentally observed discrete frequency spectrum.

To overcome this difficulty, Bohr postulated that the electron could only exist in discrete energy levels, corresponding in certain allowed stable orbits, without radiating any energy. He further argued that radiation from the atom occurs only when the electron makes a transition from one allowed energy level to another, when the energy lost by the atom is converted into the energy of a single photon. Thus, if the electron is transferred from one stable orbit, corresponding to a total energy E_1, to another allowed orbit with lower energy E_2, a photon of radiation is emitted whose frequency, f_{12}, is given by

$$E_1 - E_2 = h f_{12} \tag{1.12}$$

Thus, since only a discrete set of energy levels is postulated, only a discrete set of characteristic frequencies is present in the output spectrum.

In order to calculate the value of the discrete allowed energy levels, Bohr was obliged to postulate, in a rather intuitive way, that the angular momentum, L, associated with a gyrating electron is quantized such that

$$L = mvr = n\hbar \quad \text{where } n = 1, 2, 3, \ldots \tag{1.13}$$

We can now eliminate v from eqs. (1.9) and (1.13) to obtain an expression for the radii of allowed orbits. From (1.9) and (1.13):

$$v^2 = \frac{2e^2}{m8\pi\epsilon_0 r} = \frac{n^2 \hbar^2}{m^2 r^2}$$

or

$$r_n = \frac{4\pi n^2 \hbar^2 \epsilon_0}{e^2 m} = \frac{n^2 h^2 \epsilon_0}{\pi e^2 m} \simeq 0.05 \, n^2 \text{ nm} \tag{1.14}$$

Thus, the first possible orbit, when $n = 1$, has a radius of about 0.05 nm (1 nm $\equiv 10^{-9}$ m). Other possible orbits, corresponding to the various integer values of n, are 0.2 nm ($n = 2$), 0.45 nm ($n = 3$), and so on.

Each discrete orbit has a corresponding allowed energy level associated with it which is evaluated by substituting the values of r_n in eq. (1.10) to give:

$$E_n = -\frac{e^2}{8\pi\epsilon_0} \cdot \frac{\pi e^2 m}{n^2 h^2 \epsilon_0} = -\frac{me^4}{8\epsilon_0^2 h^2 n^2} \simeq -\frac{13\cdot6}{n^2} \text{ eV} \qquad (1.15)$$

Here the energy is expressed in electronvolts, a common practice in electronic engineering. One electronvolt corresponds to the energy acquired by an electron which has been accelerated through a potential difference of 1 V.

We see from eq. (1.15) that the system energy is restricted to discrete levels corresponding to the various values of n. The lowest energy level or *ground state* for hydrogen is $E_1 = -13\cdot6$ eV. Further allowed energy values are $E_2 = -3\cdot4$ eV, $E_3 = -1\cdot51$ eV, and so on. The allowed energy levels are usually represented in an energy level diagram, which for the hydrogen atom is shown in Fig. 1.7 (Note that in this representation the horizontal scale has

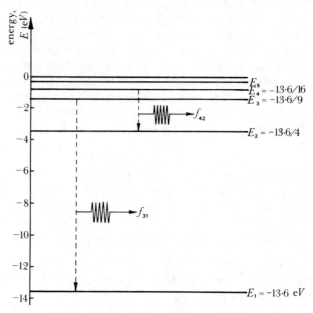

Fig. 1.7 Energy level diagram for the hydrogen atom.

no physical significance.) As explained previously, it is possible for an electron to undergo a transition between any of the allowed energy levels as indicated by arrows on the diagram. The corresponding frequency of the emitted or absorbed radiation for such an occurrence is given by eq. (1.12).

Although the characteristic emission frequencies predicted by the Bohr theory are very close to those observed for the hydrogen atom, the theory is only extendible to deal with hydrogen-like atoms and it fails for atoms with more than one orbiting electron. A further limitation is the *ad hoc* manner in which the assumptions of quantized angular momentum and the relationship between energy change and frequency are introduced. We shall see later that there are further fundamental inadequacies in the theory. Meanwhile, it is well to remember that the Bohr theory, in a historical context, was a great step forward, in that it not only accounted for the predicted hydrogen frequency spectrum but, more important, it also clearly demonstrated a certain discreteness in some of the physical properties of matter, which is quite at variance with previous classical theory. A further advantage of the theory is that it indicates the importance of Planck's constant, h, for determining details of atomic structure.

1.5 Particle–wave duality

Let us return to our discussion of the possible dual nature of matter, in which waves can sometimes behave as particles and conversely particles can in some circumstances be considered to have wavelike properties.

We will firstly consider a light photon, frequency f and energy hf. The photon travels at the velocity of light, c, which is related to frequency and wavelength, λ, by

$$c = f\lambda \tag{1.16}$$

Now, if energy E is transported with velocity c the momentum of the photon is given by

$$p = \frac{E}{c} \tag{1.17}$$

This expression could be derived by finding the radiation pressure on a plate caused by an incident electromagnetic light wave and equating to the photon flux, but this is clearly too difficult, at this stage. Instead, we offer the following somewhat crude argument. Suppose that photons are subjected to an external force F which acts over some distance dx. The change in photon energy is then

$$dE = F\,dx$$

Also, if the photon momentum is p, then, by Newton's law

$$F = \frac{dp}{dt}$$

and

$$dE = \frac{dp\,dx}{dt} = \frac{dx}{dt}\,.\,dp = c\,dp$$

Integrating we get

$$p = E/c$$

as before. Equations (1.16) and (1.17) can now be combined to give

$$p = \frac{E}{c} = \frac{E}{f\lambda} = \frac{hf}{f\lambda}$$

or

$$p = \frac{h}{\lambda} \qquad\qquad (1.18)$$

Now, in 1924 de Broglie argued that if light photons with wavelength λ have momentum $p = h/\lambda$, it might be possible for *particles* with momentum p to have some associated wavelength λ also and behave in a wavelike manner, under some circumstances. He further suggested that eq. (1.18) might also be the correct relationship between p and λ for a particle.

Let us assume for the moment that this hypothesis, which as we shall see later can be substantiated by experimental evidence, is correct, and calculate the wavelength associated with various bodies. Firstly, consider a classical Newtonian particle—an apple! If we let its mass be $m = 1/5$ kg, and its velocity $v = 10$ m/s, then its momentum

$$p = 10/5 = 2 \text{ kg m/s}$$

and its associated wavelength is

$$\lambda = \frac{h}{p} = \frac{6 \cdot 6 \, . \, 10^{-34}}{2} \approx 10^{-34} \text{ m}$$

Effects due to such a wavelength are much too small to be detected in ordinary laboratory experiments!

As a further example, consider an electron, mass m, charge $-e$, accelerated through a potential difference, V. Equating the gain in kinetic energy of the electron to its loss in potential energy:

$$\tfrac{1}{2}mv^2 = eV$$

where v is its final velocity, gives:

$$v = \sqrt{\frac{2eV}{m}}$$

The momentum of the electron is then

$$p = mv = \sqrt{2eVm}$$

and its associated wavelength is

$$\lambda = \frac{h}{p} = \frac{h}{\sqrt{2eVm}} = \frac{1 \cdot 225}{V^{\frac{1}{2}}} \text{ nm} \qquad\qquad (1.19)$$

For example, if V = 50 volts, λ = 1·7 . 10^{-7} mm, which again is small but, as we shall see, can produce measurable effects.

Soon after de Broglie suggested that particles could exhibit wavelike characteristics, Davisson and Germer provided experimental confirmation of his ideas by diffracting electrons and producing interference between electron waves. Their experiment is similar to the grating experiment with light, which we have already discussed, a beam of electrons rather than light being diffracted by a 'grating'. We have seen that the wavelengths, λ, associated with electrons are small and, for a reasonable angular spread of the diffracted wave, the periodicity of the grating, d, should be of the same order as λ. The regular array of atoms within a single crystal of a metal satisfies this condition and can behave as a grating for electron diffraction. The apparatus for such an experiment is shown diagrammatically in Fig. 1.8(a). An electron gun accelerates a beam of electrons through a potential V which impinges normally on to a plane single-crystal metal target. The detector is so biased as to provide a retarding field and only detects electrons which have been scattered with negligible loss of energy. It can be moved in angular direction, so as to measure the electron current diffracted by the target as a function of θ.

Let us now consider that electrons behave as waves which are diffracted by the regular array of atoms on the surface of the target, spaced distance d apart, as illustrated in Fig. 1.8(b). By analogy with the mirror grating experiment, we would expect a maximum detected electron current at an angle θ such that the path difference between adjacent waves is an integral number of wavelengths and the first maximum detected signal to be given by

$$\sin \theta_{\mathbf{max}} = \frac{\lambda}{d}$$

Now if de Broglie's hypothesis is correct, the wavelength of the electron is given by eq. (1.19). Thus:

$$\theta_{\mathbf{max}} = \sin^{-1}[h/(2emVd^2)^{\frac{1}{2}}] \qquad (1.20)$$

Clearly, our simple model is not complete since waves are also diffracted from atomic planes within the body of the crystal. Further, when these waves leave the crystal they are refracted at the crystal–vacuum interface. When eq. (1.20) is modified to account for these additional factors, as was done by Davisson and Germer, excellent agreement between theory and experiment is obtainable. In all their experiments, electrons were found to behave as waves with wavelength given by eq. (1.19). Incidentally, electron diffraction apparatus has since become an important analytical tool to study such things as interatomic spacing and the structure of molecules.

Suppose the experiment is now extended by replacing the detector with a cathode ray screen. In this way an average measurement of electron current over a long time can be taken by observing the intensity of illumination at the screen versus θ. A typical result would be as shown in Fig. 1.8(c). We see that there is a strong tendency for electrons to come off at angles near $\theta = 0$,

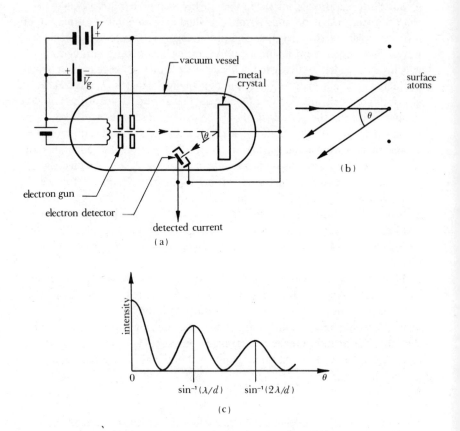

Fig. 1.8 An electron diffraction experiment.

$\sin^{-1}(\lambda/d)$, $\sin^{-1}(2\lambda/d)$, etc., and the probability of finding electrons at $\theta \approx \sin^{-1}(\lambda/2d)$, $\sin^{-1}(3\lambda/2d)$, etc., is very small. In this respect, the electrons behave like light waves.

A further experiment might be to replace the detector by an electron multiplier, connected via a high-gain amplifier to a loudspeaker. Each time a diffracted electron is detected a sharp 'click' is heard in the loudspeaker, each click being equally loud. Further, for a fixed value of θ, the number of electrons arriving when averaged over some time is constant, although the individual arrival times are erratic. Moving the detector alters the rate of clicks but their size, as measured by their loudness, remains constant. Lowering the cathode temperature or making the grid voltage in the electron gun more negative reduces the number of emitted electrons and hence alters the

14

click rate but the loudness of each still stays the same. Thus, whatever is being detected arrives in discrete amounts and in this respect the electrons are quantized and behave as particles.

We see, then, that the electrons are quantized but that they are in some way 'guided' by 'matter' waves, (sometimes called probability waves, de Broglie waves, or ψ-waves). Loosely speaking, wherever the matter waves have a large amplitude the probability of finding electrons is high, the converse being also true. Notice that we have had to abandon the absolute determinancy implicit in Newtonian mechanics since there is uncertainty as to where a particular electron will go after diffraction by the crystal lattice. We are forced to revert to discussing the probability of an electron being in a certain position at a given time.

The Davisson and Germer experiment, and a similar diffraction experiment carried out independently and almost concurrently by G. P. Thomson, clearly demonstrated the dual nature of matter and provide conclusive proof of the de Broglie wavelength relationship, $\lambda = h/p$. Whether a wave behaves as a particle or, conversely, whether a particle behaves as a wave is not only dependent on the type of experiment performed but also on the magnitude of the energies and momenta involved. Tables 1.1 and 1.2 are included to indicate under what conditions wave or particle properties become dominant.

Table 1.1 The electromagnetic spectrum of waves

Frequency (Hz)	Wavelength (m)	Typical wave type	Remarks
	10^{-12}		
10^{20}		gamma rays	photon energy ($\hbar\omega$)
		X-rays	and momentum (h/λ) increases—particle characteristics
	10^{-8}		become important
10^{16}		ultra-violet	
		visible	
	10^{-4}	infra-red	
10^{12}		millimetre waves	wave character-
		microwaves	istics dominant
	1		
10^{8}			
	10^{2}		
10^{6}		radiowaves	

Table 1.2 Particle spectrum

Mass (kg)	Typical particle	Remarks
10^{20}	star	
	planet	total energy increases; 'particle' behaviour predominates
1	car	
	football	
	dust grain	
10^{-20}	molecule	
	atom	wavelength (h/p) increases as p decreases; wave
10^{-40}	electron	characteristics become
	neutrino	important

1.6 Wavepackets: group and phase velocities of particles

It may be helpful to consider a geometric representation of how an object may simultaneously possess both wave and particle properties. We do this by studying the addition of waves of differing wavelength to produce a constructive interference pattern which has particle properties.

Firstly, consider two waves of slightly different wavelength travelling in the same direction. These add together and produce regions of constructive interference which are periodically positioned in space, as in Fig. 1.9(a). This phenomenon is analogous to the beating of two sound waves to produce interference in the time domain. If, now, three waves again slightly differing in frequency, are added, the interference maxima are not only larger but are spread at wider intervals, Fig. 1.9(b). The repetition in space of the regions of constructive interference is characteristic of the interference between finite numbers of waves. For an infinite number of waves, only one region of constructive interference exists; this is called a *wavepacket*, Fig. 1.9(c). The wavepacket geometrically represents an object with wave and particle properties. It obviously has wave properties since it is constructed from waves and has a wavelike form but it also behaves as a particle because of its localization in space. This is similar to the bow-wave of a ship, which has wave properties but travels with the ship and is always located relative to it. We have, so far, only considered waves travelling in the same direction but it is straightforward to extend the idea by describing a particle as consisting of an

16

infinite number of waves travelling in all directions and constructively interfering at some point in space where the particle is positioned.

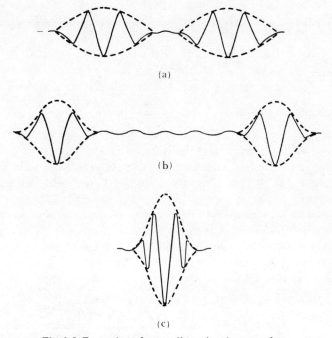

Fig. 1.9 Formation of a two-dimensional wavepacket.

What is the velocity of a wavepacket? In order to find this out, it will be necessary to digress slightly to summarize briefly the definitions and methods for calculating the various velocities associated with waves. A wave travelling in the positive x-direction may be represented by an expression

$$A_0 \cos (\omega t - \beta x) \tag{1.21}$$

where A_0 is the amplitude of the wave, ω is its angular frequency, and β is the phase constant, which is related to the wavelength by

$$\beta = 2\pi/\lambda \tag{1.22}$$

It is usually more convenient, mathematically, to represent the wave by an equivalent exponential function:

$$A_0 \, \mathrm{Re} \, e^{\, j(\omega t - \beta x)} \tag{1.23}$$

In most texts the Re is omitted but it is understood that only the real part of the result of any subsequent operation is valid.

The propagation of a wave is characterized by two velocities, the *phase velocity*, v_{ph}, and the *group velocity*, v_{g}. Phase velocity is defined as the velocity of planes of constant phase along the propagation direction of the wave. To obtain an expression for this velocity we must examine the motion of

17

a point of constant phase which is given from eq. (1.21) or (1.23) by the condition

$$\omega t - \beta x = \text{const.}$$

We obtain the phase velocity by differentiating this equation with respect to time:

$$\omega - \beta \frac{dx}{dt} = 0$$

or

$$v_{\text{ph}} = \frac{\omega}{\beta} \tag{1.24}$$

It is important to remember that this is the velocity at which some arbitrary phase propagates. Nothing material propagates at this velocity; indeed it is possible for v_{ph} to be greater than the speed of light without violating any physical laws.

Now, let us investigate what happens when two waves of equal amplitude but with slightly different wavelengths propagate simultaneously in the x-direction, as discussed qualitatively earlier. Let the small differences of frequency and phase constant be $\delta\omega$ and $\delta\beta$. The resultant wave can then be represented by the sum:

$$A_0 \cos(\omega t - \beta x) + A_0 \cos[(\omega + \delta\omega)t - (\beta + \delta\beta)t]$$

$$= 2A_0 \cos \tfrac{1}{2}[(2\omega + \delta\omega)t - (2\beta + \delta\beta)t] \cos \tfrac{1}{2}[\delta\omega t - \delta\beta x]$$

$$\simeq 2A_0 \cos \tfrac{1}{2}[\delta\omega t - \delta\beta x] \cos(\omega t - \beta x) \tag{1.25}$$

since $\delta\omega \ll 2\omega$ and $\delta\omega \ll 2\beta$ by our original assumption.

Thus, the resultant total wave consists of a high-frequency wave, varying as $\cos(\omega t - \beta x)$, whose amplitude varies at a much slower frequency rate represented by the other cosine term in (1.25); it is *modulated* by destructive and constructive interference effects, as shown in Fig. 1.10. The high-frequency wave has phase velocity ω/β as before. The variation of wave amplitude is called the envelope of the wavegroup; it varies sinusoidally with time and distance and is a travelling wave with the relatively long wavelength, $2\pi/\delta\beta$. Group velocity is defined as the velocity of propagation of a plane of constant phase on the envelope. It corresponds to the velocity of the group or packet of waves along the direction of propagation. A plane of constant phase on the envelope is given by

$$\delta\omega \cdot t - \delta\beta \cdot x = \text{const.}$$

Thus, using the same procedure used to evaluate the phase velocity, we see that the group velocity is given by

$$v_{\text{g}} = \frac{\partial\omega}{\partial\beta} \tag{1.26}$$

18

Furthermore, it can be shown that v_g is the velocity at which energy is transmitted along the direction of propagation.

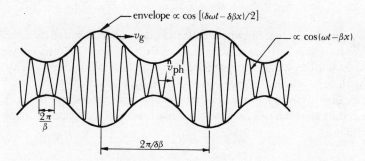

Fig. 1.10 Interaction of two waves of slightly different frequencies.

We can now return to the discussion of the velocities of particle waves. The hypotheses of de Broglie and Planck, corroborated by experiment, suggest that the momentum and kinetic energy of a particle are given by

$$p = mv = h/\lambda$$

and

$$T = \tfrac{1}{2}mv^2 = hf$$

$$(1.27)$$

Now, we know that an infinite plane wave travelling in the x-direction has the form $A_0 \exp[-j(\omega t - \beta x)]$. Equation (1.27) indicates that for a particle wave we might write the equivalent phase constant and frequency:

$$\beta = \frac{2\pi}{\lambda} = \frac{2\pi p}{h} = \frac{p}{\hbar}$$

and

$$\omega = \frac{2\pi T}{h} = \frac{T}{\hbar}$$

$$(1.28)$$

This suggests that it might be possible to represent a particle by a function ψ, called a *wave function*, where

$$\psi = A_0 \exp[-j(Tt - px)/\hbar] \qquad (1.29)$$

From (1.24) and (1.28) the phase velocity of such a wave is:

$$v_{ph} = \frac{\omega}{\beta} = \frac{T}{p} = \frac{\tfrac{1}{2}mv^2}{mv} = \frac{v}{2}$$

Note that this result is not valid for a single particle, however, since we have seen that this must be represented by a discrete wavepacket and the concept of phase velocity is applicable only to infinite wave trains.

A valid group velocity for the particle can, however, be found. From eqs. (1.27) and (1.28):

$$\partial \omega = \frac{mv}{\hbar} \partial v \quad \text{and} \quad \partial \beta = \frac{m}{\hbar} \partial v$$

19

which, using eq. (1.26), gives:

$$v_\mathbf{g} = \frac{\partial\omega}{\partial\beta} = v \qquad (1.30)$$

Thus, a single electron or bunch of electrons can be represented by a wave–packet travelling with the same velocity as the electron. This seems physically reasonable when we remember the alternate definition of group velocity as being the rate at which energy is transported by waves.

Our discussion so far on wave–particle duality is summarized in Fig. 1.11 where the behaviour of light waves and electrons is compared diagrammatically.

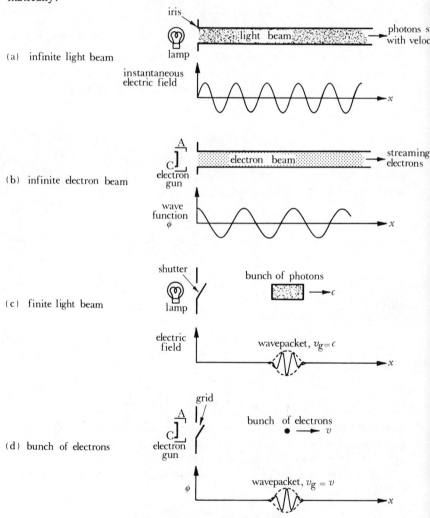

Fig. 1.11 Particle–wave duality.

20

1.7 The Schrödinger wave equation

So far, we have discussed experiments for which there exists no explanation based on classical concepts. However, if a series of assumptions is made, for instance the de Broglie hypothesis that $p = h/\lambda$, a quantitative description of the mechanism of each phenomenon can be provided. What is now required is some sort of unifying theory which will enable us to predict and explain other occurrences on the atomic scale. In 1926 Schrödinger provided a basis for such a theory by discovering an equation for predicting ψ, the wave function of a particle, in any particular circumstance. The equation he discovered is named after him; it replaces Newton's laws when atomic-sized particles are being considered. The theory based on Schrödinger's equation is called *wave* or *quantum mechanics*.

We have seen that particles can possess wavelike properties and that the probability waves associated with a beam of particles can be described in terms of a wave function, ψ, given by eq. (1.29). This expression includes the kinetic energy, T, associated with a particle. In general, however, a particle can also possess potential energy. For instance, it might be an electron moving in a solid; the electron not only has kinetic energy but it also moves in the field due to the lattice and thus has a space-dependent potential energy. In general the total energy, E, of a particle is therefore

$$E = \hbar\omega = T + V \tag{1.31}$$

where V denotes the potential energy. The one-dimensional wave function in the more general case then becomes:

$$\psi = A_0 \exp[-j(Et - px)/\hbar] \tag{1.32}$$

What equation does this generalized wave function satisfy? We would expect it to be some differential equation comparable to a one-dimensional wave equation, say

$$\frac{\partial^2 H}{\partial x^2} = \epsilon\mu \cdot \frac{\partial^2 H}{\partial t^2} \tag{1.33}$$

the solution of which,

$$H = H_0 \, e^{-j(\omega t - \beta x)} \tag{1.34}$$

gives in this instance the magnetic field of a plane wave propagating in a medium with permittivity ϵ and permeability μ.

Let us try to find a wave equation similar to (1.33) but which has ψ given by eq. (1.32) as its solution. Firstly, differentiate (1.32) with respect to t:

$$\frac{\partial\psi}{\partial t} = -\frac{j}{\hbar}E\psi = -j(V + \tfrac{1}{2}mv^2)\,\psi/\hbar \tag{1.35}$$

21

Also, let us differentiate ψ with respect to x, twice:

$$\frac{\partial^2 \psi}{\partial x^2} = -\frac{p^2}{\hbar^2} \cdot \psi = -\frac{m^2 v^2}{\hbar^2} \psi \qquad (1.36)$$

We may now compare the equations to give from (1.35),

$$-\tfrac{1}{2} m v^2 \psi = -j\hbar \frac{\partial \psi}{\partial t} + V\psi$$

from (1.36),

$$= \frac{1}{2m} \hbar^2 \frac{\partial^2 \psi}{\partial x^2}$$

Rearranging the equations gives:

$$\frac{\partial^2 \psi}{\partial x^2} - \frac{2m}{\hbar^2} V\psi + j\frac{2m}{\hbar} \frac{\partial \psi}{\partial t} = 0 \qquad (1.37)$$

This equation is called the one-dimensional, time-dependent, Schrödinger wave equation. It governs the behaviour in one dimension of all particles. Notice that we have not derived this equation rigorously, since for example the relationships $p = h/\lambda$ and $E = hf$ have been assumed in writing the wave functions, which was our starting point. The above steps are only an argument to demonstrate the plausibility of Schrödinger's equation. In fact, there is no proof of the equation. This situation is directly comparable to the lack of proof for Newton's laws. Agreement with experiment is the only check as to its validity; it has been found to be correct when applied to a wide number of circumstances concerning microscopic particles particularly in its relativistic form. A further test is that, in the classical limit of laboratory-sized experiments, Schrödinger's equation must provide results which agree with those derivable from Newton's laws. It can be shown that this is so and that eq. (1.37) is quite general and reduces to Newton's laws of motion for large-sized objects. Schrödinger's equation must always be used in preference to Newton's laws however, when considering the interaction of atomic-sized particles.

If three-dimensional motion is allowed, the wave function becomes a function of three space coordinates and time, $\psi(x,y,z,t)$ and is a solution of the three-dimensional, time-dependent, Schrödinger's equation:

$$\frac{\partial^2 \psi}{\partial x^2} + \frac{\partial^2 \psi}{\partial y^2} + \frac{\partial^2 \psi}{\partial x^2} - \frac{2m}{\hbar^2} V\psi + j\frac{2m}{\hbar} \frac{\partial \psi}{\partial t} = 0 \qquad (1.38)$$

It should be noted that although this equation or the simple one-dimensional version will be used predominantly to predict the wave function of electrons, it is applicable to *any* particle, provided the appropriate mass and potential energy are included.

22

For a large class of problems in which the total particle energy is constant, Schrödinger's equation can be simplified by separating out the time- and position-dependent parts. This can be achieved by the standard separation-of-variables procedure. Accordingly we consider the one-dimensional equation for simplicity and assume solutions of the form:

$$\psi = \Psi(x) . \Gamma(t) \tag{1.39}$$

where Ψ and Γ are functions of position and time only.

We substitute this in eq. (1.37) to obtain:

$$\frac{\hbar^2}{2m} \frac{1}{\Psi} \frac{\partial^2 \Psi}{dx^2} - V = -j \frac{\hbar}{\Gamma} \frac{d\Gamma}{dt} \tag{1.40}$$

Now the left-hand side is a function of space coordinates only, provided V is time-independent, and the right-hand expression is a function of time only. Thus each equation must independently equal some constant, say C.

$$\therefore \frac{d\Gamma}{dt} = \frac{jC}{\hbar} . \Gamma$$

or

$$\Gamma(t) = e^{jCt/\hbar}$$

Comparison of this expression with the time-dependent part of the one-dimensional wave function, given in (1.32), indicates that the constant in the expression is equal to $-E$. Thus, if the energy is constant, the time-dependent part of the wave function is

$$\Gamma(t) = e^{-jEt/\hbar} \tag{1.41}$$

and

$$\psi = \Psi(x) e^{-jEt/\hbar} \tag{1.42}$$

The left-hand side of eq. (1.40) is then equal to $-E$ to give:

$$\frac{d^2\Psi}{dx^2} + \frac{2m}{\hbar^2} (E - V) \Psi = 0 \tag{1.43}$$

This is the one-dimensional time-independent Schrödinger equation. It may be used to find the space-dependent part of the wave function whenever the system energy is constant, for example, when considering bound particles or a constant current of particles. In all other situations, for example, when discussing a varying current of particles, the more general time-dependent version of the equation must be employed. For most problems dealing with particles of constant energy, it is usually sufficient to solve the three-dimensional version of eq. (1.43) to find the dependence of the wave function on position $\Psi(x,y,z)$, but if the complete wave function $\psi(x,y,z,t)$ is required $\Psi(x,y,z)$ must be multiplied by $\Gamma(t)$, as indicated by eq. (1.42).

23

1.8 Interpretation of the wave function ψ

We have shown that it is possible to describe the wave characteristics of a particle in terms of a wave function ψ but we have not yet discussed precisely what property of the particle is behaving in a wavelike manner. There is little difficulty in this respect with other wave types; for example, it is the electric and magnetic field vectors which are oscillating in a radio wave and for sound waves the variable parameter is pressure. However, the physical significance of the wave function is not so readily apparent. Since $\psi(x,y,z,t)$ is a function of space and time coordinates we might expect that it represents the position of a particle at some time t. However, we will see later that in general it is impossible to locate a particle exactly in space without there being any uncertainty as to its position. We can only consider the probability of a particle being at a particular point in space. A further complication is that, since ψ is a solution of Schrödinger's equation, it is usually a complex quantity.

Max Born, in 1926, overcame the difficulty of being unable to attach physical significance to ψ itself by showing that the square of its absolute magnitude, $|\psi|^2$, is proportional to the probability of a particle being in unit volume of space, centred at the point where ψ is evaluated, at time t. Thus, although the exact position of a particle at a particular time cannot be predicted, it is possible to find its most probable location. It follows that $|\psi|^2 \Delta V$ is proportional to the probability that a particle will be found in the volume element ΔV. For example, the probability of finding a particle in the range $x \to x + dx$, $y \to y + dy$, and $z \to + dz$ is proportional to

$$|\psi(x, y, z)|^2 \, dx \, dy \, dz = \psi\psi^* \, dx \, dy \, dz \qquad (1.44)$$

where ψ^* is the complex conjugate of the wave function. Although the direct physical significance of particle waves in not clear, if we solve Schrödinger's equation in particular circumstances and obtain a wave function ψ, the *probability density*, $|\psi|^2$, can be used to predict accurately what the spatial distribution of particles will be at some time, t, provided that a sufficiently large number of experiments have been performed.

If a particle exists at all it is certainly located somewhere in space, and since the probability of its being in an elemental volume is proportional to $|\psi|^2 \, dx \, dy \, dz$, it is convenient to choose the constant of proportionality such that the integral of the probability density over all space equals unity or

$$\iiint_{-\infty}^{+\infty} \psi\psi^* \, dx \, dy \, dz = 1 \qquad (1.45)$$

A wave function which satisfies this condition is said to be *normalized*. Whenever wave functions are normalised, $|\psi|^2 \Delta V$ *equals* the probability that a particle will be found in a volume ΔV.

Before solving Schrödinger's equation in any particular set of circumstances, it is first necessary to know what boundary conditions must be set on ψ. Since answers to physical problems are obtainable from wave functions, they must

24

be well-behaved in a mathematical sense. Firstly, ψ must be a continuous and single-valued function of position. Supposing for the moment that this were not so, $\psi\psi^*$ would be discontinuous also, as indicated for the one-dimensional case shown in Fig. 1.12(a). This would imply that the probability of finding a

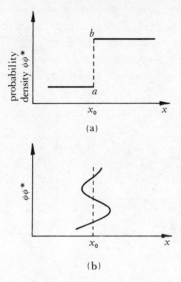

Fig. 1.12 (a) Discontinuous and (b) multivalued probability densities, which are not allowed.

particle is dependent on the direction from which the discontinuity is approached. Coming to x_0 from the left the probability density is a and from the right it is b, which in turn indicates that particles are instantaneously created or destroyed at x_0, which is clearly not allowable. Hence ψ must be continuous.

Consider now the possibility of ψ and hence $\psi\psi^*$ being multivalued, as shown in Fig. 1.12(b). This would imply that at some position, x_0, there are several probabilities of finding a particle, which is obviously not physically possible. Hence ψ must be single-valued. By similar reasoning, it is possible to show that the spatial derivatives of ψ, $\partial\psi/\partial x$, $\partial\psi/\partial y$, and $\partial\psi/\partial z$ must be continuous and single-valued across any boundary.

1.9 The uncertainty principle

In 1927, Heisenberg published the uncertainty principle, which was subsequently named after him. He showed that if an attempt is made to measure certain pairs of variables concerned with physical systems, then a lack of precision with which the two variables can be specified simultaneously becomes apparent. Such pairs of variables are momentum and position, energy and time. Suppose, for example, in a particular experiment, the energy

25

of a particle can be measured to some accuracy ΔE and the time at which the measurement is taken is known to some accuracy Δt; then a classical theory would indicate that the precision to which these parameters can be measured is limited only by the experimental apparatus and technique. The uncertainty principle shows, however, that if the particle's energy is determined very accurately, so that ΔE is small, there is a proportional increase in the lack of precision in the time measurement and Δt increases. This can be made to sound plausible by the following argument. We know that a single particle can be represented in one dimension by a wavepacket, as shown in Fig. 1.13(a).

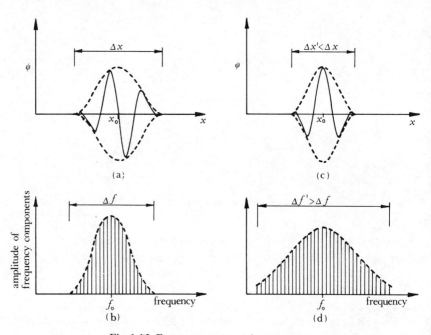

Fig. 1.13 **Frequency spectra of wavepackets.**

There is evidently some lack of precision in locating the wavepacket and hence the particle, since it is spread over some distance Δx in space. Since the particle can be assumed to be travelling at some velocity v, the time of arrival of the wavepacket at some particular location can only be measured to an accuracy Δt, related to Δx by

$$\Delta x = v\Delta t$$

We have discussed previously how the wavepacket can be synthesized from many waves, each of different frequency. The amplitudes of the various component waves can be obtained by Fourier analysis to give the frequency spectrum of the wavepacket as shown in Fig. 1.13(b). This indicates that the spread in frequency of the component waves is of order Δf, and since $E = hf$,

26

or $\Delta E = h\Delta f$, there is necessarily a corresponding uncertainty in the particle energy.

If, now, the accuracy in the location of x is increased somewhat, Δx and hence Δt decrease and the wavepacket is shorter, as shown in Fig. 1.13(c). This shortening can be achieved only by the addition of further frequency components, with a corresponding increase in the width of the frequency spectrum, as in Fig. 1.13(d). This leads, as we have seen, to an increased ΔE and a greater uncertainty as to the precise value of the energy of the particle. Thus, as Δt is decreased, ΔE is increased and vice versa. If the frequency spectra are obtained in a more quantitative way it can be shown that the best that can be done, no matter what the experimental apparatus, is that the product of the uncertainties to which each is known is equal to Planck's constant, or

$$\Delta E . \Delta t \geqslant h \tag{1.46}$$

Notice that there is no fundamental restriction on the accuracy with which either quantity can be determined individually, only on their product.

Now, the energy of a free particle, $E = hf = \frac{1}{2}mv^2$, from which we obtain

$$\Delta E = h\Delta f = mv\Delta v = v\Delta p$$

Thus, the momentum spectrum for a wavepacket shows similar characteristics to the frequency spectrum; for a short wavepacket, Δx is small but the width of the momentum spectrum Δp is large and if Δx is made bigger there is a corresponding decrease in Δp. Again, it can be shown that the product of the accuracies for a simultaneous measurement of momentum and position must be greater than $\hbar/2$, or

$$\Delta p . \Delta x \geqslant \hbar/2 \tag{1.47}$$

We might, for example, try to locate the exact position of a particle, thus specifying $\Delta x = 0$, but this would be possible only if all knowledge of its momentum were sacrificed since Δp to satisfy eq. (1.47) must become infinite.

Fortunately, the uncertainties implicit in Heisenberg's principle need not be too restricting for normal laboratory-scale experiments since h is very small, of order 10^{-34}. However the limitations to accuracy, as given in expressions (1.46) and (1.47), become critical for atomic-sized particles, when the magnitudes of the experimental variables can become minute.

1.10 Beams of particles and potential barriers

We shall now consider the interaction of beams of particles with potential barriers of various types. These problems are not only interesting in their own right but also serve as an introduction to discussions of the solution of Schrödinger's equation for particles confined in space, which begin in the next chapter. Interactions in one dimension only will be considered, mostly for mathematical convenience, but the solutions obtained are directly applicable to the motion of particles in devices with large dimensions transverse to the current flow.

Firstly, consider a beam of particles travelling in the x-direction with energy E, impinging on a potential barrier at $x = 0$, of height $V_2 - V_1$, such that $V_1 < E < V_2$, as shown in Fig. 1.14.

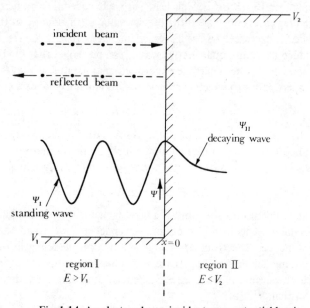

Fig. 1.14 An electron beam incident on a potential barrier.

Classically, we should expect particles in region I, where $E > V_1$, and none in region II, where $E < V_2$. We have deliberately chosen to investigate the motion of a beam of particles since, as we have seen, this can be represented by the simple wave function

$$\psi = A_0 \exp\left[-j(Et - px)/\hbar\right]$$

Strictly speaking, each particle in the beam should be represented by a wave-packet. However, for a small spread in phase constant, $\Delta\beta$, the reflection of a packet is similar to the reflection of an infinite wave.

Let us apply Schrödinger's stationary-state equation to regions I and II since E is constant. In region I:

$$\frac{d^2 \Psi}{dx^2} + \frac{2m}{\hbar^2}(E - V_1)\Psi = 0 \tag{1.48}$$

which, if we let

$$\frac{2m}{\hbar^2}(E - V_1) = \beta^2 \tag{1.49}$$

28

becomes

$$\frac{d^2 \Psi}{dx^2} + \beta^2 \Psi = 0 \qquad (1.50)$$

Solutions of this equation are of the form

$$\Psi_I = A e^{j\beta x} + B e^{-j\beta x} \qquad (1.51)$$

The complete wave function for the region, including time dependence, is obtained by multiplying Ψ by $\exp(-jEt/\hbar)$, giving

$$\psi_I = A \exp\left[-j\left(\frac{Et}{\hbar} - \beta x\right)\right] + B \exp\left[-j\left(\frac{Et}{\hbar} + \beta x\right)\right] \qquad (1.52)$$

The first term represents an incident probability wave travelling in the positive x-direction and the second term represents the wave reflected by the barrier, travelling in the negative x-direction.

In region II, $(E - V_2)$ is negative and we let

$$\frac{2m}{\hbar^2}(E - V_2) = -\alpha^2 \qquad (1.53)$$

so that, in this region, the stationary state equation becomes

$$\frac{d^2 \Psi}{dx^2} - \alpha^2 \Psi = 0 \qquad (1.54)$$

This has a general solution

$$\Psi_{II} = C e^{-\alpha x} + D e^{\alpha x} \qquad (1.55)$$

Arguing on physical grounds, we would not expect Ψ_{II} to become infinite at large x, so D evidently must be zero, which gives

$$\Psi_{II} = C e^{-\alpha x} \qquad (1.56)$$

We now find relationships between the magnitudes A, B, and C by applying the boundary conditions on ψ at the barrier, $x = 0$. That ψ and hence Ψ are continuous at the boundary gives

$$\Psi_I\big|_{x=0} = \Psi_{II}\big|_{x=0}$$

which, from eq. (1.51) and (1.56), gives

$$A + B = C \qquad (1.57)$$

Also, for continuity of the derivative of Ψ,

$$\frac{\partial \Psi_I}{\partial x}\bigg|_{x=0} = \frac{\partial \Psi_{II}}{\partial x}\bigg|_{x=0}$$

or

$$j\beta A - j\beta B = -\alpha C \qquad (1.58)$$

29

Equations (1.57) and (1.58) give

$$A = \frac{C}{2}\left(1 - \frac{\alpha}{j\beta}\right)$$
$$B = \frac{C}{2}\left(1 + \frac{\alpha}{j\beta}\right)$$
(1.59)

Notice that the amplitudes of incident and reflected waves are identical, i.e.,

$$|A| = |B|$$

but, because there is a phase difference between the forward- and backward-travelling waves, the total Ψ-wave or sum of incident and reflected waves is a standing wave. A further point of interest is that the solution Ψ_{II} given in eq. (1.56), which applies to the right of the barrier, represents a wave whose amplitude decays exponentially with increasing x. Both of these situations are illustrated diagrammatically in Fig. 1.14. It will be seen that there is a finite probability that the incident beam penetrates some distance into the classically forbidden region, since $|\Psi_{\text{II}}|^2$ is greater than zero there. However, if α is large, i.e. $V_2 \gg E$, few particles are found very far inside the boundary.

Now let us turn our attention to the situation where the barrier is not sufficiently high to cause complete reflection of the incident beam. In these circumstances, there is only partial reflection and part of the beam is transmitted through the barrier, as shown in Fig. 1.15. If, as before, we let

$$\beta_{1,2} = \frac{2m}{\hbar^2}(E - V_{1,2})$$
(1.60)

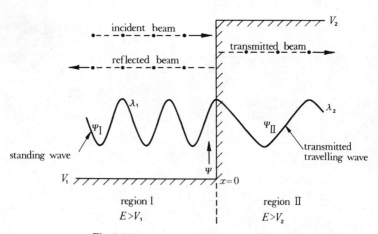

Fig. 1.15 An electron beam incident on a potential step.

then the solutions of Schrödinger's equation in the two regions are:

$$\Psi_I = A e^{j\beta_1 x} + B e^{-j\beta_1 x}$$

and

$$\Psi_{II} = C e^{j\beta_2 x}$$

$$(1.61)$$

if it is assumed that there is no reflected wave in region II. Matching Ψ and $\partial\Psi/\partial x$ at the boundary as before we have, from (1.61):

$$A + B = C$$

and

$$\beta_1(A - B) = \beta_2 C$$

$$(1.62)$$

C can be eliminated from these equations to give

$$\frac{B}{A} = \frac{1 - \beta_2/\beta_1}{1 + \beta_2/\beta_1} \qquad (1.63)$$

which is used to find a reflection coefficient:

$$\frac{\text{density of particles reflected}}{\text{density of particles incident}} = \frac{|\Psi_{ref}|^2}{|\Psi_{inc}|^2} = \frac{BB^*}{AA^*} = \frac{B^2}{A^2}$$

$$= \left[\frac{1 - \{(E - V_2)/(E - V_1)\}^{\frac{1}{2}}}{1 + \{(E - V_2)/(E - V_1)\}^{\frac{1}{2}}}\right]^2 \qquad (1.64)$$

where we have substituted for the β's from eq. (1.60).

Eliminating B from (1.62) gives the relative amplitude of the transmitted wave:

$$\frac{C}{A} = \frac{2}{1 + \beta_2/\beta_1} = \frac{2}{1 + \{(E - V_2)/(E - V_1)\}^{\frac{1}{2}}} \qquad (1.65)$$

We thus find the surprising result that the amplitude of the transmitted wave is bigger than that of the incident wave, or the probable density of particles in the transmitted electron beam is greater than that in the incident beam! This may be explained by noting that the transmitted particles are moving more slowly than the incident particles. Thus, although $C > A$, the *rate* of flow of particles in the transmitted beam is less than that in the incident beam. Notice also that since $\beta_2 < \beta_1$, the wavelength of the transmitted Ψ-wave is greater than that for the incident wave, as shown in Fig. 1.15.

Our final example in this series is the interaction of a constant-energy beam of particles incident on a classically inpenetrable potential barrier of finite width, d, as shown in Fig. 1.16. Applying Schrödinger's equation to the three regions gives wave functions of the form:

$$\Psi_I = A e^{j\beta x} + B e^{-j\beta x}$$

$$\Psi_{II} = C e^{-\alpha x} + D e^{\alpha x}$$

$$\Psi_{III} = F e^{j\beta x}$$

$$(1.66)$$

where

$$\beta^2 = \frac{2m}{\hbar^2}(E - V_1) \quad \text{and} \quad \alpha^2 = \frac{2m}{\hbar^2}(V_2 - E) \qquad (1.67)$$

as before. Notice that in order to satisfy the boundary conditions a highly attenuated reflected wave, magnitude D, has been included in the barrier region; also, it has been assumed that no reflection occurs in region III. We can now apply the usual boundary conditions at $x = 0$ and $x = d$ and hence find the relative values of the wave functions at various positions, as shown in Fig. 1.16. If, in particular, B, C, and D are eliminated the amplitude of the

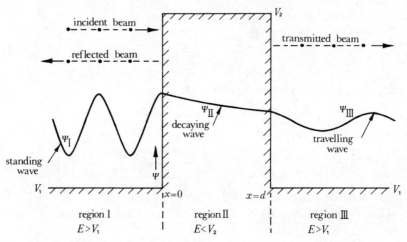

Fig. 1.16 Partial transmission of an electron beam through a narrow potential barrier.

Ψ-wave in region III in terms of the amplitude of the incident wave in region I can be obtained, thus

$$F = A e^{-j\beta d} \left[\cosh \alpha d + \tfrac{1}{2} \left(\frac{\alpha}{\beta} - \frac{\beta}{\alpha} \right) \sinh \alpha d \right]^{-1} \qquad (1.68)$$

Now, the probability of a particle passing through the barrier, $P_{\text{I-III}}$, is proportional to the ratio of the absolute square of ψ in region III, to the absolute square of ψ in the incident region, or:

$$P_{\text{I-III}} = |F|^2 / |A|^2 \qquad (1.69)$$

which can be evaluated using eq. (1.68).

In most practical cases, αd is large because of high attenuation of the Ψ-wave in the barrier region, and the hyperbolic functions in (1.68) can be simplified to give

$$P_{\text{I-III}} = \frac{|F|^2}{|A|^2} \simeq \frac{e^{-2\alpha d}}{1 + \tfrac{1}{4} \left(\frac{\alpha}{\beta} - \frac{\beta}{\alpha} \right)^2}$$

we can now substitute values for α and β as defined in eq. (1.67) to give

$$P_{I-III} \approx \exp\{-2(2m\,\overline{V_2 - E})^{\frac{1}{2}}d/\hbar\} \tag{1.70}$$

Thus, if the barrier is sufficiently thin, i.e., d is small, there is a small but finite probability that particles can penetrate the barrier, even though classically this would not seem possible. The particle is said to have *tunnelled* through the barrier. The effect has important physical applications as will be discovered later when, for example, tunnel diodes and electron emission from a cathode are discussed.

Notice that the probability of tunnelling falls off exponentially with increasing barrier height and thickness. As an example of the sort of figures involved, consider a 1 A electron beam approaching a barrier 1 V high $(V_2 - E = 1.6 \cdot 10^{-19}$ J) and 2 nm wide. The probability of tunnelling, using (1.70), is then of order e^{-20} and a current of about 10^{-9} A tunnels through the barrier. However, if the barrier thickness is reduced to 0.1 nm the tunnelling current is increased to almost $\frac{1}{3}$ A!

Problems

1   An electron in an atom drops from an excited state to the ground state in a time normally lasting about 10^{-8} seconds. If the energy emitted is 1 eV, find (a) the relative uncertainty in the energy (b) the relative uncertainty in the frequency of the emitted radiation and (c) the number of wavelengths in and the length of the wavepacket of emitted radiation.

   Ans. $4 \times 10^{-7}, 4 \times 10^{-7}, 2 \times 10^{6}$, 3 m.

2   What is the inherent uncertainty in the velocity of an electron confined in a crystalline solid of volume 10 mm cube?

   Ans. 0.07 m/s.

3   Show that the probability of reflection of a beam of electrons of energy E incident on an abrupt potential energy step of height V_0 is determined by a reflection coefficient r given by

$$r = \left(\frac{1 - \sqrt{1 - V_0/E}}{1 + \sqrt{1 - V_0/E}}\right)^2$$

Also show that the magnitude of the reflection coefficient is independent of whether the electrons are incident from the high or low potential energy side. How is its phase affected?

4   Find the probability of transmission of a 1 MeV proton through a 4 MeV high, 10^{-14} m thick rectangular potential energy barrier $(m_p/m = 1836)$.

   Ans. 5×10^{-4}.

2. The electronic structure of atoms

2.1 Introduction

In the previous chapter we showed that microscopic particles can be described in terms of waves and wavepackets and used such a description to discuss the interaction of particles with potential barriers of various shapes. In this section we confine our attention to particles which are constrained to remain localized in some part of space. We shall see that under these conditions the particle cannot have a continuous spectrum of possible energies and the system is such as only to allow the particle to have discrete values of energy; nor can the wave function of a confined particle take up any arbitrary value, and only a set of discrete wave functions is allowable.

The properties of particles confined to a finite region of space or *bound* can be studied by considering them to be trapped in a potential well with very steep sides. The shape of such containers which we are able to deal with is artificial in the extreme for reasons of mathematical simplicity and bears little resemblance to physical reality. However, the results obtained have general characteristics which are most relevant to the description of electrons bound to parent atoms and which form a basis for the categorization of atoms in terms of their electronic structure.

2.2 A particle in a one-dimensional potential well

Consider the situation depicted in Fig. 2.1. A particle of mass m and total energy E moves only in the x-direction and is constrained to remain in a region of length d by potential barriers which exist at $x = 0$ and d. The barriers are made artificially steep and high and are infinite in extent so that there is no possibility of the particle surmounting them and escaping. We assume that the potential energy of the particle inside the well is zero and apply Schrödinger's time-independent equation, (1.43), since the total energy E remains constant. Hence, for $0 \leqslant x \leqslant d$, $V = 0$ and

$$\frac{d^2 \Psi}{dx^2} + \frac{2m}{\hbar^2} E\Psi = 0 \qquad (2.1)$$

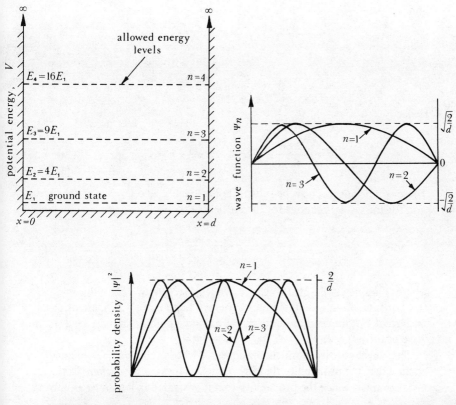

Fig. 2.1 Particle trapped in an infinitely deep, one-dimensional potential well.

We have seen that the general solution of this equation which gives the wave function of the particle inside the well is:

$$\Psi = A e^{j\beta x} + B e^{-j\beta x} \tag{2.2}$$

where

$$\beta^2 = \frac{2m}{\hbar^2} E$$

Now, since there is no possibility of the particle penetrating the containing walls and so gaining infinite potential energy, $\Psi\Psi^*$ and hence Ψ must be zero outside the well for $0 \geqslant x \geqslant d$. Thus for continuity of Ψ at the boundaries, the value of Ψ inside the well, given by (2.2), must become zero at $x = 0$ and $x = d$. Applying these boundary conditions to eq. (2.2) gives

$$B = -A$$

and

$$0 = A(e^{j\beta d} - e^{-j\beta d})$$

or

$$\sin \beta d = 0$$

Hence

$$\beta d = \frac{\sqrt{2mE}}{\hbar} d = n\pi \quad \text{where} \quad n = 1, 2, 3, \ldots \tag{2.3}$$

These conditions can now be substituted into eq. 2.2 to give a general expression for the wave functions for the particle in the well:

$$\Psi = C \sin\left(\frac{n\pi x}{d}\right) \tag{2.4}$$

where C is a newly defined constant. We see that the two travelling wave components of Ψ, as represented by the two parts of eq. (2.2), are of equal magnitude but move in opposite directions and combine to produce a standing wave in the usual way.

The constant C is a normalizing constant whose value can be obtained by arguing that the probability that the particle is located *somewhere* in the well must be unity. Since the probability that it is located in length dx is $\Psi\Psi^*dx$ then

$$\int_0^d \Psi\Psi^* \, dx = 1$$

or

$$\int_0^d C^2 \sin^2 (n\pi x/d) \, dx = 1$$

from which we find that $C = \sqrt{2/d}$ and the normalized solution for Ψ becomes:

$$\Psi = \sqrt{\frac{2}{d}} \sin\left(\frac{n\pi x}{d}\right) \qquad n = 1, 2, 3, \ldots \tag{2.5}$$

We see that the wave function for the bound particle is one of a set of discrete values, each corresponding to a different value of the integer n. This general conclusion is not confined to this particular example but applies to all bound particles. Each allowed value of the wave function, for instance for each value of the integer in eq. (2.5), is called an *eigenfunction,* which can be loosely translated from the German as 'particular function'.

Returning now to eq. (2.3), it is evident that the total energy of the bound particle also has only a discrete set of allowed values given by:

$$E = \frac{\hbar^2 n^2 \pi^2}{2md^2} = \frac{n^2 h^2}{8md^2} \qquad n = 1, 2, 3. \ldots \qquad (2.6)$$

Thus, the total energy of the particle in the well has particular allowed values, corresponding to the various integers; the energy is quantized and each particular energy level is called an eigenvalue. A set of possible energy levels are shown in Fig. 2.1. Notice that energy levels intermediate to those shown are forbidden and also that a particle in the lowest energy state or ground state, E_1, has a non-zero kinetic energy. Both of these general results are applicable to all bound particles and are at variance with classical mechanical ideas.

The probability per unit length that the particle is located at some particular position in the well, x, can be found in the usual way by forming $|\Psi|^2$ from the value of Ψ given in eq. (2.5). The eigenfunctions, Ψ_n, are plotted in Fig. 2.1 together with the corresponding probabilities of location per unit length, $|\Psi_n|^2$. Notice that the wavelength of the standing wave of Ψ, λ, is quantized, only having discrete values given by $\lambda = 2\pi/\beta = 2d/n$, and that n is the number of loops in the pattern. This result can be compared to the electrical resonances which occur in a transmission line which is short-circuited at each end; such resonances occur when the wavelength is equal to twice the line length divided by an integer. The analogy is valid and the results similar, since Schrödinger's equation is one of the same form as the electromagnetic wave equation and the boundary conditions are similar in each case.

The diagrams of $|\Psi|^2$ indicate that a particle in the ground state is most probably located at the centre of the well. For higher energy states, for example E_2, the particle may be located at some position removed from the centre of the well and there is zero probability of the particle being located at certain other positions. These conclusions do not agree with the classical picture of the particle being reflected elastically from the walls of the well, which results in a constant probability amplitude since the particle may be located anywhere in the well with equal probability. However, at higher energy levels, for large values of n, the agreement is better since the quantum probability oscillates rapidly with position about a mean value which is the classical probability and its average value taken over a short length is equal to the classically anticipated one.

The arguments for the infinitely deep well can be extended either theoretically or on a more intuitive basis, as we shall do here, to consider the case of a particle trapped in a one-dimensional potential well of finite depth. Although this problem is slightly more realistic in that it more closely resembles the situation of an electron bound to an atom, it is still somewhat artificial. The problem is illustrated in Fig. 2.2. Consider first the classically bound particle whose total energy, E, is less than V_0, the depth of the potential well. As we have seen earlier, there will be a small but finite probability that such particles can penetrate some way through the boundaries of the well before being reflected. The wave functions outside the well are attenuated and have the characteristic exponentially decaying form, much the same as that depicted in Fig. 1.14. The wave functions inside the well no longer fall to zero at the walls since there has to be smooth matching of wave functions across each boundary. Thus, although the wave functions have a shape generally similar to those for the infinite well, they are slightly modified in that they are no longer purely sinusoidal and their wavelength is increased. This leads to a set of eigenvalues slightly lower in value than the corresponding set for the infinite well, as shown in Fig. 2.2.

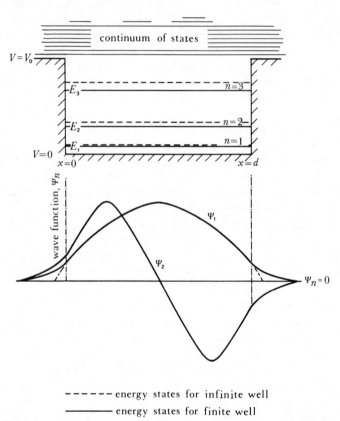

- - - - - energy states for infinite well
———— energy states for finite well

Fig. 2.2 Energy levels and wave functions for a particle in a finite one-dimensional potential well.

When the energy of the particle is greater than the depth of the well, $E > V_0$, then the particle is no longer classically bound and it can take up any level in a continuum of possible energy levels, as shown in the figure.

2.3 The hydrogen atom

We now turn our attention to a quantum-mechanical solution of the hydrogen atom. Not only is this a useful example of the application of Schrödinger's equation to a particle trapped in a more physically realistic potential well, but the results also explain much about the electronic structure of atoms, which lays the foundations for a logical classification of the elements.

The Bohr theory of the hydrogen atom, given in section 1.4, is unacceptable on several counts. Firstly, it assumes that the electron moves in a given orbit, which implies that its position is known precisely at any time, which violates the uncertainty principle. Second, the theory arbitrarily assumes that the angular momentum of the orbiting electron is quantized and has values given by eq. (1.13). Finally, the Bohr theory cannot be extended to treat atoms with more than one outer electron. These limitations are not present in a quantum-mechanical treatment and solutions can be obtained, in principle at least, for more complex atoms and molecules.

We assume that the hydrogen atom consists of a central nucleus of charge $+e$ surrounded by an electron. The nucleus is assumed fixed because of its relatively heavy mass but to relax this condition would make only a slight quantitative difference to the result. The potential energy of an electron located at a distance r from the nucleus was derived in section 1.4 and is

$$V = -\frac{e^2}{4\pi\epsilon_0 r} \tag{2.7}$$

This situation is shown diagrammatically in Fig. 2.3. The electron is trapped in the potential well created by the field of attraction set up by the positive

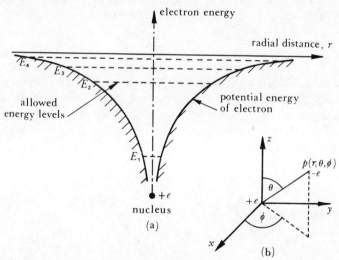

Fig. 2.3 (a) Section through the potential well of a hydrogen atom, (b) spherical polar coordinates.

39

nucleus; it is bound to the nucleus. The problem is more difficult than those encountered previously in that contours of the well are not so simple mathematically and, also, the geometry is now three-dimensional. It is convenient to define the problem in spherical polar coordinates, as shown in Fig. 2.3(b), because of a possible spherical symmetry in the solution. The three-dimensional time-independent Schrödinger equation given in eq. (1.38) is now written in the new coordinate system for the electron in the well and the potential energy function given in eq. (2.7) can be included at the same time to give:

$$\frac{1}{r^2}\frac{\partial}{\partial r}\left(r^2\frac{\partial \Psi}{\partial r}\right) + \frac{1}{r^2 \sin \theta}\frac{\partial}{\partial \theta}\left(\sin \theta \frac{\partial \Psi}{\partial \theta}\right) + \frac{1}{r^2 \sin^2 \theta}\frac{\partial^2 \Psi}{\partial \phi^2} + \frac{2m}{\hbar^2}$$

$$\times \left(E + \frac{e^2}{4\pi\epsilon_0 r}\right)\Psi = 0 \qquad (2.8)$$

Usually, this equation is solved completely by the separation-of-variables technique, but in order to simplify the problem we shall look for solutions which are independent of the angular coordinates θ and ϕ. The wave functions which are solutions of eq. (2.8) under these particular conditions will have spherical symmetry and will depend on the variable r only. Therefore, we let $\partial/\partial\theta$ and $\partial/\partial\phi$ be zero and carry out the differentiation implicit in the first term, to reduce eq. (2.8) to:

$$\frac{d^2 \Psi}{dr^2} + \frac{2}{r}\frac{d\Psi}{dr} + \frac{2m}{\hbar^2}\left(E + \frac{e^2}{4\pi\epsilon_0 r}\right)\Psi = 0 \qquad (2.9)$$

There is a set of spherically symmetrical or *radial* wave functions which satisfy this equation, but the simplest is of the form

$$\Psi_1 = A e^{-r/r_0} \qquad (2.10)$$

where r_0 is a constant and A is the usual normalizing constant. Once again, A is evaluated by arguing that the probability of locating the electron somewhere in space must be unity. Since the probability density is $\Psi\Psi^*$ and the volume of a spherical shell of radius r and thickness dr is $4\pi r^2/dr$, the probability that the electron is located inside such a shell is $\Psi\Psi^* . 4\pi r^2 dr$. Hence, using (2.10), we have:

$$\int_0^\infty \Psi\Psi^* . 4\pi r^2 \, dr = 4\pi A^2 \int_0^\infty r^2 e^{-2r/r_0} \, dr = 1$$

which can be integrated by parts to give

$$A = \pi^{-\frac{1}{2}} r_0^{-\frac{3}{2}}$$

and

$$\Psi_1 = \pi^{-\frac{1}{2}} r^{-\frac{3}{2}} . e^{-r/r_0} \qquad (2.11)$$

40

We can find the value of the constant r_0 by substituting this wave function into eq. (2.9), which gives:

$$\frac{1}{r_0{}^2} - \frac{2}{rr_0} + \frac{2m}{\hbar^2}\left(E + \frac{e^2}{4\pi\epsilon_0 r}\right) = 0 \qquad (2.12)$$

For this equation to be true for all values of r, the terms containing r must equate to zero or:

$$\frac{2}{rr_0} = \frac{2me^2}{4\pi\hbar^2 \epsilon_0 r}$$

which gives:

$$r_0 = \frac{4\pi\hbar^2 \epsilon_0}{me^2} = \frac{h^2 \epsilon_0}{\pi e^2 m} \qquad (2.13)$$

Comparing this result with eq. (1.14) we see that the constant r_0 is numerically equal to the radius of the lowest energy orbit of the Bohr atom; we will return to a discussion of the physical significance of this result later.

Meanwhile, if we now consider eq. (2.12) with the sum of the r-dependent terms equal to zero, the total energy of the electron in the lowest energy state:

$$E_1 = -\frac{\hbar^2}{2mr_0{}^2} = -\frac{me^4}{8\epsilon_0{}^2 h^2} \qquad (2.14)$$

where eq. (2.13) has been used to evaluate the constant r_0.

A more complete solution of the wave equation so as to include higher-order radial wave functions Ψ_2, Ψ_3, etc., leads to the following general expression for the allowed energy levels:

$$E_n = \frac{E_1}{n^2} = -\frac{1}{n^2} \cdot \frac{me^4}{8\epsilon_0{}^2 h^2} \qquad (2.15)$$

Again we see that the result of confining the electron to some localized portion of space is to quantize its possible energy levels, as shown in Fig. 2.3. The integer n is called the *radical* or *principal* quantum number. We shall see later that this is only one of several such numbers which are usually necessary to define the energy of a particular electron in an atom.

We may now use our knowledge of the wave function of the electron in the ground state, Ψ_1, to discuss the geometry of the hydrogen atom. We have shown that if the probability that an electron is located in a spherical shell of radius r and thickness dr is dP_r, then

$$dP_r = |\Psi_1|^2 \cdot 4\pi r^2 \, dr = \frac{4r^2}{r_0{}^3} \cdot e^{-2r/r_0} \, dr \qquad (2.16)$$

and the probability per unit radius for an electron in the ground state to be located at radius r is

$$\frac{dP_r}{dr} = \frac{4r^2}{r_0^3} \cdot e^{-2r/r_0} \tag{2.17}$$

This probability is plotted in Fig. 2.4(a). It can be shown by differentiation that the maximum value of dP_r/dr occurs when $r = r_0$ as shown.

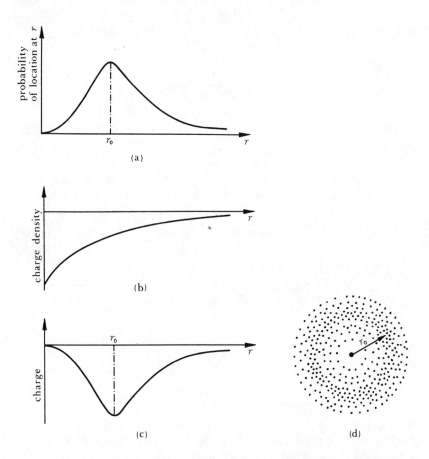

(a)

(b)

(c)

(d)

Fig. 2.4 (a)–(c) Geometry and charge configuration of the hydrogen atom in the ground state, (d) a two-dimensional representation of the smeared-out electronic charge.

Further, if we let $\rho_1(r)$ be the charge density due to the electron in the ground state, then

$$\rho_1(r) = |\Psi_1|^2 \cdot (-e) = -\frac{e}{\pi r_0^3} \cdot e^{-2r/r_0} \tag{2.18}$$

42

which is shown in Fig. 2.4(b). The charge contained in a spherical shell radius r and thickness dr is then q_r where

$$\frac{q_r}{dr} = -\frac{4er^2}{r_0{}^3} \cdot e^{-2r/r_0} \tag{2.19}$$

This expression is very similar to that in (2.17) and has a maximum value at $r = r_0$ again, as shown in Fig. 2.3(c). Hence a quantum-mechanical interpretation of the hydrogen atom indicates that the electron can no longer be considered as having a fixed orbit; it can be located at any distance from the nucleus, but when in the ground state its most probable location is at the Bohr radius. The charge associated with the electron is smeared out but there is a maximum in the probable charge distribution, again at the Bohr radius.

We have discussed so far those solutions of the three-dimensional Schrödinger equation which depends on radial distance from the nucleus only. A further series of wave functions is possible if this assumption of spherical symmetry is relaxed. When the wave function has angular dependence on θ and ϕ and neither $\partial/\partial\theta$ nor $\partial/\partial\phi$ is zero, eq. (2.8) is usually solved by the method of separation of the variables. This technique assumes a solution:

$$\Psi(r, \theta, \phi) = f_r(r) \cdot f_\theta(\theta) \cdot f_\phi(\phi) \tag{2.20}$$

where the functions $f_{r, \theta, \phi}$, are only dependent on r, θ, and ϕ, respectively. When this trial wave function is substituted into eq. 2.8, the three-dimensional equation r, θ, and ϕ, is subdivided into three separate differential equations, one in r only, one in θ only, and one in ϕ only.

The solution for the differential equation in r gives only the radial wave equations and a *principal quantum number, n* = 1, 2, 3, . . . , which defines the total energy of an electron in a particular state, as we have already discussed.

A further set of *quantum numbers, l* = 0, 1, 2, . . . , $(n - 1)$, arises from a solution of the separated differential equation in θ. Such *azimuthal quantum numbers* are associated with the angular momentum of an electron, which is itself quantized.

Finally, that part of Schrödinger's equation which is separated to provide an equation in ϕ can be solved to give a third set of possible quantum numbers, m, which vary from $m = -l$, including $m = 0$, to $m = +l$. These *magnetic orbital quantum numbers* are associated with the fact that an electron in an orbital constitutes a rotating charge and hence an electric current which has associated magnetic field and magnetic moment. The orientation of this inherent magnetic moment with an externally applied magnetic field is quantized and the quantum number, m, arises because of the discrete number of possible orientations.

We see that in general there exists a set of three possible quantum numbers, n, l, and m, and that a particular combination of these is necessary to specify an individual quantum state. In addition, a further quantum number is necessary to define completely a particular quantum state, which is not apparent from the solution to the three-dimensional Schrödinger equation. This was first introduced in an arbitrary manner to explain fine details of atomic spectra. The electron is assumed to spin about its axis in an either clockwise or anticlockwise direction. There are only two possible ways in which the inherent angular momentum vector due to the spin can be oriented with respect to an applied magnetic field. A *spin quantum number, s,* which can have only two values, accounts for this quantization. It has been shown more recently that the assumption of spin need not be introduced so arbitrarily since it arises directly as a solution of a more generalized form of the Schrödinger equation.

2.4 The exclusion principle and the periodic table of elements

We have seen that the particular quantum state of an electronic orbital can be specified by a set of quantum numbers, (n, l, m, s). Such numbers completely define the wave functions for a given electron and are usually quoted instead of the wave function because they are less cumbersome.

The Pauli exclusion principle provides a method of classifying atoms according to their electronic structure. It states that in a multi-electronic system, which in general can be an atom, a molecule, or a complete crystal, no more than one electron can exist in any one quantum state. For the particular case of an atom, the principle implies that no two electrons can be described by an identical set of quantum numbers. Physically what this means is that no more than two electrons can have the same distribution in space and even then they must have opposite spins. There is no proof of the exclusion statement but its validity is supported by an abundance of experimental evidence.

Consider now the electronic structure of different atoms containing an increasing number of electrons. Electrons will tend to fill the lowest available energy levels first. A consequence of the exclusion principle is that each additional electron must have a different set of quantum numbers and possess a higher energy than the preceeding electron. The energy levels are thus filled progressively and additional electrons always have quantum numbers which correspond to the lowest possible unoccupied energy state. A periodic table of elements based on their electronic structure can thus be constructed using this procedure in conjunction with the relationships between the various quantum numbers discussed in the previous section. Thus, for $n = 1$, l and m must both be zero and two electronic states exist, corresponding to the two spin quantum numbers. But for $n = 2$, l can equal 0 or 1, and for $l = 0$, m may have values -1, 0, $+1$; the various combinations of (n, l, m) are thus $(2, 0, 0), (2, 1, -1), (2, 1, 0), (2, 1, 1)$ and each of these is associated with two possible states because of spin, making a total of eight possible states with principle quantum number $n = 2$. This process can be repeated for $n = 3$, $l = 0, 1, 2$, and so on, and the periodic table shown in Table 2.1 results.

Electrons which have the same principle quantum number, n, are said to be in the same shell. It is evident from the table that the maximum number of electrons per shell is $2n^2$. Within a shell, each state corresponding to a particular integer value of l, the azimuthal quantum number, is given a letter designation, thus

$$
\begin{array}{cc}
l & letter \\
0 & s\text{-} \\
1 & p\text{-} \\
2 & d\text{-} \\
3 & f\text{-} \\
& etc.
\end{array} \left.\right\} \quad \text{state or subshell}
$$

(This peculiar nomenclature arises from the early spectroscopic identification of lines corresponding to various electronic transitions, namely, sharp, principal, diffused, fundamental, etc.) Thus, in the electronic classification of the lighter elements, given in the last column of Table 2.1, the integers refer to the principal quantum number of each shell, the letters correspond to the value of the azimuthal quantum number, and the indices give the number of electrons in such subshells.

Table 2.1 Electronic structure of the lighter elements

Element	Principal quantum number, n	Azimuthal quantum number $(l = 0, 1, 2, ..., n-1)$	Magnetic quantum number $(m = -l, ..., +l)$	Spectroscopic designation
H	1	0	0	$1s$
He	1	0	0	$1s^2$
Li	2	0	0	$1s^2 2s$
Be	2	0	0	$1s^2 2s^2$
Bo	2	1	-1	$1s^2 2s^2 2p$
C	2	1	-1	$1s^2 2s^2 2p^2$
N	2	1	0	$1s^2 2s^2 2p^3$
O	2	1	0	$1s^2 2s^2 2p^4$
Fl	2	1	1	$1s^2 2s^2 2p^5$
Ne	2	1	1	$1s^2 2s^2 2p^6$
Na	3	0	0	$1s^2 2s^2 2p^6 3s$
Mg	3	0	0	$1s^2 2s^2 2p^6 3s^2$
Al	3	1	-1	$1s^2 2s^2 2p^6 3s^2 3p$
Si	3	1	-1	$1s^2 2s^2 2p^6 3s^2 3p^2$
P	3	1	0	$1s^2 2s^2 2p^6 3s^2 3p^3$
etc.				

It should be noted that the periodic table does not progress continuously in such a numerically logical manner since for a group of the heavier elements the energy of some electrons in an outer shell is lower than that in an inner subshell and so these levels are filled before the inner subshells are fully occupied.

Problems

1   Compute the three lowest energy levels for electrons trapped in a one-dimensional well of length 0·1 nm.

   Ans. 6×10^{-18}, $2·4 \times 10^{-17}$, $5·4 \times 10^{-17}$ J.

2   An electron is confined in a one-dimensional potential energy well of length 0·3 nm. Find (a) the kinetic energy of the electron when in the ground state and (b) the spectral frequency resulting from a transition from the next highest state to the ground level.

   Ans. 16·6 eV, 3×10^{15} Hz.

3. Collections of particles in gases and solids

3.1 Introduction

We have so far discussed only properties of single, isolated particles. As soon as we turn our attention to whole collections of many such interacting particles, for example to consider molecules in a gas or electrons in a solid, it is no longer practicable to describe the detailed dynamics of the system by the application of Newton's laws to each particle. The detailed properties of individual microscopic components could be specified only at a particular time and would change continuously. Further, because of the vast numbers of particles involved in a typical gas or solid, a microscopic treatment would be too cumbersome to be readily solvable or physically meaningful.

Fortunately, we are usually more interested in the macroscopic or bulk behaviour of large numbers of particles, to predict such properties as currents, pressures, and so on. A statistical treatment which describes the average rather than detailed properties of a typical component of the complete assembly of particles is most useful, since the behaviour of the group of particles can then be deduced directly.

In order to determine the average value of, say, the velocity of a molecule in a gas or of the energy of an electron in a solid, it is necessary to know first of all how the velocities or energies are distributed throughout the collection of particles. The type of statistics developed to describe such distributions depends not only on the type of particle present but also on the possible interactions between them. For instance, in a neutral gas, molecules can interchange energy by collisions but there is no restriction on the energy of individual molecules. On the other hand, when electrons interact in a solid their allowed energies are restricted by the Pauli exclusion principle which permits only one electron to occupy a particular quantum state, and a different type of statistics applies.

We shall initially consider collections of neutral particles and develop a statistical method of treatment which not only will be useful in describing some of the properties of gases and plasmas but also is applicable to many other electronic materials. We shall then study the statistics of collections of interacting particles which obey the exclusion principle, since this is necessary for later discussion of the electrical and thermal properties of solids.

3.2 Assemblies of classical particles—ideal gases

Let us consider an ideal gas of neutral molecules containing N molecules per m^3. Individual molecules have a random motion and undergo many collisions with other molecules and container walls which result in changes in the magnitude and direction of their velocity. There is no restriction in the velocity of a particle at a particular time; it may be zero at one instant or relatively high at another and the energy of each molecule is independent of that of the others. We wish to find how the various velocities and hence energies are distributed between individual molecules.

At any instant, the position of a molecule can be specified by a set of coordinates, (x, y, z) say, and its velocity v can also be resolved into components, (v_x, v_y, v_z), in the x, y, and z directions, where

$$v^2 = v_x{}^2 + v_y{}^2 + v_z{}^2 \tag{3.1}$$

Hence, the velocity of each particle can be represented by a vector on a three-dimensional graph with axes v_x, v_y, and v_z. Such a *velocity space* is illustrated in Fig. 3.1. A few typical velocity vectors are shown and the dots represent the tips of the velocity vectors of the remaining molecules. The problem of finding the distribution of velocities among the particles is reduced to finding the density of such dots in velocity space. This dot density will have spherical symmetry, since there are no preferred velocity directions and it can be written $P(v^2)$. Thus, considering the elemental volume shown in

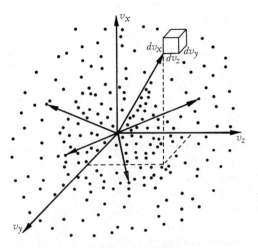

Fig. 3.1 Particles in velocity space.

Fig. 3.1, the number of molecules per unit volume, dN_{xyz}, with velocity components in the range $v_x \to v_x + dv_x, v_y \to v_y + dv_y$, and $v_z \to v_z + dv_z$ is

$$dN_{xyz} = P(v^2)\,dv_x dv_y dv_z \qquad (3.2)$$

Alternatively, the number of molecules per unit volume with *speeds* ranging from $v \to v + dv$, dN_v, is equal to the number of vector tips (points in Fig. 3.1) which lie in a spherical shell of radius v and thickness dv in velocity space or:

$$dN_v = P(v^2) \cdot 4\pi v^2\,dv \qquad (3.3)$$

The loosely termed dot density, $P(v^2)$, is called the distribution function for speeds; it gives the number density in velocity space of molecules with a certain speed, v. Notice that in all cases the number of particles in a given range equals the distribution function multiplied by the size of the range.

Since each particle must be represented somewhere in velocity space, the integral of the number in a given range over all velocity space must equal the total number of particles per unit volume. For example:

$$\int_0^\infty dN_v = \int_0^\infty P(v^2) \cdot 4\pi v^2\,dv = N \qquad (3.4)$$

3.2.1 The distribution function, $P(v^2)$. The method we use to determine $P(v^2)$ and hence the distribution of velocities in a neutral gas is not very rigorous but has the merit of not being mathematically complex.

Consider two molecules, each of mass M, with velocities v_1 and v_2 and which suffer an elastic collision which modifies their velocities to v_3 and v_4 respectively, as shown in Fig. 3.2(a). Since energy is assumed to be conserved in the collision:

$$v_1{}^2 + v_2{}^2 = v_3{}^2 + v_4{}^2 \qquad (3.5)$$

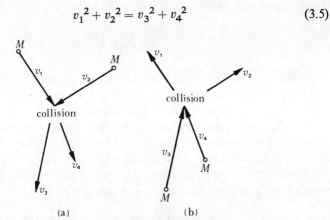

(a)   (b)

Fig. 3.2 Elastic collisions between gas molecules.

Now, the number of molecules having velocity v_1 is proportional to the distribution function evaluated at this velocity, $P(v_1{}^2)$. Similarly, the number of molecules with velocity v_2 is proportional to $P(v_2{}^2)$. Thus, the likelihood of two such particles colliding is proportional to the number in each class and

$$\text{collision probability} \propto P(v_1{}^2) P(v_2{}^2) \tag{3.6}$$

The probability of reverse collisions occurring between molecules with velocities v_3 and v_4 to produce particles with velocities v_1 and v_2 as depicted in Fig. 3.2(b) is, by similar argument, proportional to $P(v_3{}^2)P(v_4{}^2)$. Thus, provided the geometry remains constant and the system is in equilibrium, the probability of collisions of either type must be the same, and

$$P(v_1{}^2)P(v_2{}^2) = P(v_3{}^2)P(v_4{}^2) \tag{3.7}$$

Now the only type of solution which satisfies eq. (3.5) and (3.7) simultaneously is

$$P(v^2) = A\, e^{-\beta v^2} \tag{3.8}$$

which can be verified by substitution.

Equation (3.8) is the general form of the distribution function for speeds and all that remains is to find the values of the constants A and β. Firstly, the expression for $P(v^2)$ can be substituted in the normalizing equation (3.4) to obtain a relationship between A and β as follows:

$$N = 4\pi A \int_0^\infty e^{-\beta v^2}\, v^2\, dv \tag{3.9}$$

It may be verified from tables of definite integrals that:

$$\int_0^\infty e^{-\beta v^2}\, v^2\, dv = \pi^{\frac{1}{2}}/(4\beta^{\frac{3}{2}})$$

which can be substituted in eq. (3.9) to give:

$$A = \left(\frac{\beta}{\pi}\right)^{\frac{3}{2}} N \tag{3.10}$$

We now require a further relationship so that A and β can be obtained explicitly. We shall make use of the fact that the temperature of the gas, T, is defined in such a way that the mean particle energy per degree of freedom is $\frac{1}{2}kT$. Thus, since there are N molecule/m^3 in the gas, each having three degrees of freedom, the total energy per unit volume is $\frac{3}{2}NkT$. Now, the number of particles in the speed range between v and $v + dv$ is given by eq. (3.3), where $P(v^2)$ is now given by eq. (3.8), and each particle in the range has energy $\frac{1}{2}Mv^2$. Thus, the total energy per unit volume is:

$$\int_0^\infty (\tfrac{1}{2}Mv^2)(A\, e^{-\beta v^2})\, 4\pi v^2\, dv = \tfrac{3}{2}NkT \tag{3.11}$$

We again turn to tables of definite integrals to confirm that:

$$\int_0^\infty e^{-\beta v^2} v^4 \, dv = \frac{3}{8} \frac{\pi^{\frac{1}{2}}}{\beta^{\frac{5}{2}}} \tag{3.12}$$

Making use of this fact in eq. (3.11) and eliminating first A and then β from the resulting equation and eq. (3.10) gives:

$$\beta = \frac{M}{2kT} \tag{3.13}$$

and

$$A = N \left(\frac{M}{2\pi kT} \right)^{\frac{3}{2}} \tag{3.14}$$

which can be substituted in eq. (3.7) to give:

$$P(v^2) = N \left(\frac{M}{2\pi kT} \right)^{\frac{3}{2}} \exp\left(-\frac{Mv^2}{2kT} \right) \tag{3.15}$$

3.2.2 Maxwell–Boltzmann distribution function. The number of molecules in the speed range v to $v + dv$ is given by eq. (3.3). We can now be more explicit and include the expression for $P(v^2)$ given in eq. (3.15), to obtain:

$$dN_v = 4\pi N \left(\frac{M}{2\pi kT} \right)^{\frac{3}{2}} \exp\left(-\frac{Mv^2}{2kT} \right) v^2 \, dv \tag{3.16}$$

This can be simplified by writing

$$dN_v = Nf(v) \, dv \tag{3.17}$$

where

$$f(v) = 4\pi \left(\frac{M}{2\pi kT} \right)^{\frac{3}{2}} \exp\left(-\frac{Mv^2}{2kT} \right) v^2 \tag{3.18}$$

The function $f(v)$ is called the normalized Maxwell–Boltzmann distribution function for speeds. It is evident from the defining eq. (3.17) that $f(v)$ is the fraction of the total number of molecules per unit volume in a given speed range, per unit range of speed.

A graph of $f(v)$ versus v is shown in Fig. 3.3(a). Areas under such a graph represent fractional numbers of molecules in given speed ranges. For example, the area of the region of length dv shown is $f(v)$, dv, which, by referring to eq. (3.17), is seen to be equal to dN_v/N, the fraction of the total number of molecules per unit volume in the speed range dv. As a further example, the fraction of the total number of molecules with speeds less than v' shown on Fig. 3.3(a) is equal to the area under the curve to the left of v'.

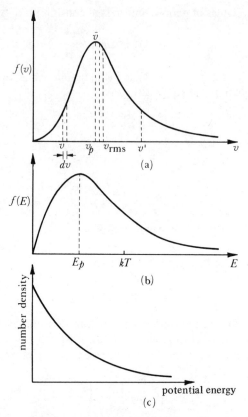

Fig. 3.3 (a) and (b). Maxwell–Boltzmann distributions for speed and energy. (c) Boltzmann
distribution of particles in a field of force.

3.2.3 Use of distribution functions to calculate average values. We have
determined the distribution of speeds amongst the constituent molecules of
an ideal gas, in terms of a normalized distribution function $f(v)$ and are now
able to use this to evaluate average values of speeds and velocities which in
turn can describe bulk properties of the gas, as discussed earlier. It should be
pointed out that the averaging procedures developed are quite general and can
be applied to *any* distribution function, even though we shall be specifically
concerned with the speed distribution function.

What is the most probable speed of a molecule, v_p, in a gas obeying Maxwell–
Boltzmann statistics? The defining equation (3.17) indicates that this occurs
when $f(v)$ is maximum, as shown in Fig. 3.3(a). Hence v_p can be found by
differentiation of eq. (3.18), which gives:

$$v_p = (2kT/M)^{\frac{1}{2}} \qquad (3.19)$$

We next turn our attention to the average speed of a molecule in the gas, $\bar{v}$.
This may be obtained by finding the number of molecules with a given speed,

52

multiplying by the speed, summing all such contributions, and dividing by the total number of molecules. Thus, by definition,

$$\bar{v} = \frac{\int_0^\infty dN_v \cdot v}{N} = \int_0^\infty vf(v)\,dv \tag{3.20}$$

For the particular case of a Maxwell–Boltzmann distribution, eq. (3.18) can be substituted in this expression and the integration carried out to give

$$\bar{v} = 2\sqrt{\frac{2kT}{\pi m}} = \frac{2}{\sqrt{\pi}} \cdot v_p \tag{3.21}$$

Thus, although $\bar{v}$ and v_p are nearly equal, $\bar{v}$ is slightly higher than v_p, as shown in Fig. 3.3(a), because in the averaging process the higher speeds are weighted more heavily than the lower.

The mean square and root mean square speed, v_{rms}, is often required, for instance, for calculating the average kinetic energy of gas molecules. We can use the same averaging process as described previously to define a mean square speed, then:

$$\overline{v^2} = \frac{\int_0^\infty v^2 \cdot dN_v}{N} = \int_0^\infty v^2 f(v)\,dv \tag{3.22}$$

This can be evaluated for the distribution function defined by eq. (3.18), again making use of tables of definite integrals to give:

$$\overline{v^2} = 3kT/M \tag{3.23}$$

and the root mean square speed is then:

$$v_{rms} = \sqrt{\overline{v^2}} = \sqrt{3kT/M} = \sqrt{\tfrac{3}{2}}\,v_p \tag{3.24}$$

as shown on Fig. 3.3(a).

It will be noticed in passing that eq. (3.23) can be rearranged to show that the average value of the kinetic energy of a molecule, $M\overline{v^2}/2$, is equal to $3kT/2$, which is consistent with our earlier assumption.

3.2.4 Energy distribution function. We now study how the energy of molecules is distributed throughout the ensemble. We make use of the fact that the translational kinetic energy of a particular molecule, designated E, is given by:

$$E = Mv^2/2 \tag{3.25}$$

We consider energies in the range between E and $E + dE$ and require an expression for the number of molecules per unit volume with energies in this range, dN_E. Differentiating eq. (3.25) gives:

$$dv = \frac{dE}{Mv} = \frac{dE}{M}\sqrt{\frac{M}{2E}} = \frac{dE}{\sqrt{2EM}} \tag{3.26}$$

Equations (3.25) and (3.26) are substituted in eq. (3.16) to give:

$$dN_E = 4\pi N \left(\frac{M}{2\pi kT}\right)^{\frac{3}{2}} \exp\left(-\frac{E}{kT}\right) \frac{2E}{M} \frac{dE}{\sqrt{2EM}}$$

or

$$dN_E = Nf(E)\,dE \qquad (3.27)$$

where $f(E)$, the distribution function for energies, is given by:

$$f(E) = \frac{2}{\sqrt{\pi}} \left(\frac{1}{kT}\right)^{\frac{3}{2}} E^{\frac{1}{2}} \exp(-E/kT) \qquad (3.28)$$

The distribution function, $f(E)$, as defined by eq. (3.27), gives the fraction of the total number of molecules per unit volume in the unit energy range centred on energy E. It can be seen from eq. (3.28) that the shape of the $f(E)$ versus E curve is dominated by the $E^{\frac{1}{2}}$ term at low energies, rises to a maximum value, and then has an exponentially decaying tail at higher energies when the exp $(-E/kT)$ term takes over, as shown in Fig. 3.3(b). It is left as an exercise to show that the most probable energy, which occurs when $f(E)$ is maximum, is

$$E_p = kT/2$$

3.2.5 Boltzmann distribution. We have assumed previously that the gas molecules are not acted on by any external forces. Under these conditions, the energy E refers to the kinetic energy of a molecule; also, the density of the gas does not vary from point to point.

We now relax this assumption and consider the assembly of molecules to be in a field which causes each molecule to experience a force which, although it may vary spatially, is identical for each constituent. For example, the molecular gas may be in a gravitational field or the ensemble may be electrons under the influence of an electric field. In either case, a more general theory shows that eq. (3.28) is still applicable, provided E is the total energy and includes a potential energy term. The distribution function is then:

$$f(E) \propto \exp(-E/kT) \propto \exp[-(\text{K.E.} + \text{P.E.})/kT] \qquad (3.29)$$

This expression is quite general and applies to any assembly of particles which interact infrequently. For example, consider a collection of electrons which originally has a Maxwellian distribution, say. When it is subjected to an electric field, applied such that the potential energy, eV, varies with position, the electron distribution everywhere still remains Maxwellian but the energy distribution function has an additional multiplying factor, exp $(-eV/kT)$, which affects the local electron density. The electron densities n_1 and n_2,

54

at two parts where the potential energies are eV_1 and eV_2, respectively, are
then related by:

$$\frac{n_2}{n_1} = \exp\left[-\frac{e(V_2 - V_1)}{kT}\right] \tag{3.30}$$

Hence, the electron density decreases exponentially with increasing potential
energy. Such a relationship between particle density and potential energy is
called a *Boltzmann distribution* and is of the form shown in Fig. 3.3(c). It
has general applicability to many systems other than the ones mentioned.

3.3 Collections of particles which obey the exclusion principle

We have discussed assemblies of particles in which each constituent is independent of any other in the sense that it can take up any energy value; in
other words, several molecules can exist in the same quantum state. We now
turn our attention to collections of particles, electrons in particular, which
interact quantum-mechanically with each other in such a way that the occupancy
of a particular state is restricted by the Pauli exclusion principle, i.e., no two
electrons are allowed to occupy the same state. The ensemble must again be
treated statistically, but the additional restriction leads to distribution
functions of a form different from that of those encountered previously. The
distribution function to be derived is most important, since it is applicable to
free electrons in metals and semiconductors and allows many electrical
phenomena in such materials to be understood which otherwise could not be
explained using classical concepts.

The arguments leading to a distribution function are similar to those
followed previously, but this time, since we are dealing with quantum-
mechanical systems, the uncertainty principle suggests that, rather than assign
definite energy values to each particle, the probability that an energy state
is occupied should be considered. Accordingly, let us consider a particular
state, E_1, and let the probability of this level being occupied be $p(E_1)$. As a
consequence, the probability that there are electrons at two different levels,
E_1 and E_2, *simultaneously* is $p(E_1)\,p(E_2)$. Now, suppose two such electrons
interact in such a way that they are transferred to two other energy levels,
E_3 and E_4. The precise nature of the interaction will be discussed in later
chapters. Energy will be assumed to be conserved by this process, and:

$$E_1 + E_2 = E_3 + E_4 \tag{3.31}$$

The exclusion principle implies that such an interaction is permissible only if
vacant energy levels exist at E_3 and E_4. Now, the probability that level E_3 is
not occupied is $1 - p(E_3)$ and the probability that states E_3 and E_4 are vacant
simultaneously is $[1 - p(E_3)]\,[1 - p(E_4)]$. Thus, the probability that two

55

electrons in states E_1 and E_2 interact and are transferred to states E_3 and E_4 is

$$p(E_1)p(E_2)[1 - p(E_3)][1 - p(E_4)]$$

Since the system is assumed to be in thermal equilibrium, the probability of the reverse process, that is, two electrons in the E_3 and E_4 states interact and are transferred to E_1 and E_2 states, must be the same and hence:

$$p(E_1)p(E_2)[1 - p(E_3)][1 - p(E_4)] = p(E_3)p(E_4)[1 - p(E_1)][1 - p(E_2)]$$

or

$$\left[\frac{1}{p(E_1)} - 1\right]\left[\frac{1}{p(E_2)} - 1\right] = \left[\frac{1}{p(E_3)} - 1\right]\left[\frac{1}{p(E_4)} - 1\right] \tag{3.32}$$

The solution which satisfies both this equation and the energy conservation condition, eq. (3.31), is of the form

$$\frac{1}{p(E)} - 1 = A e^{\beta E} \tag{3.33}$$

where A and β are constants. That this function simultaneously satisfies both equations can be verified by substitution.

Equation (3.33) can be rearranged to give:

$$p(E) = \frac{1}{1 + A e^{\beta E}} \tag{3.34}$$

For high-energy states, the exponential term dominates the denominator and

$$p(E) \simeq A e^{-\beta E} \tag{3.35}$$

Thus, at high energies the distribution approaches the Boltzmann distribution of eq. (3.29) and hence the constant β can be identified with $1/kT$. That the two distribution functions become almost identical for high energy states, even though one system (Boltzmann) allows multiple occupancy of states and that at present being discussed does not, is plausible on physical grounds. At high energies the number of electrons distributed over many available states is small and there are many more energy levels than electrons to occupy them. Under these conditions there is little chance of two or more electrons occupying the same state and whether the exclusion principle is included in the statistics or not becomes irrelevant to the form of the distribution function.

Equation (3.34) therefore becomes:

$$p(E) = \frac{1}{1 + A e^{E/kT}} \tag{3.36}$$

Finally, it is customary to assume, without any loss of generality, that the constant A is redefined such that

$$A = \exp(-E_F/kT)$$

where the new constant, E_F, is called the *Fermi energy*; the physical significance of this constant energy will become apparent later. Meanwhile, eq. (3.36) becomes:

$$p(E) = \frac{1}{1 + \exp\left[(E - E_F)/kT\right]} \tag{3.37}$$

This is the *Fermi–Dirac function*; it gives, for any ensemble obeying the exclusion principle, the probability that a particular state E is occupied. That the form of the function is consistent with the exclusion principle is apparent from (3.37); $p(E)$ can never exceed unity since the exponential term is always positive; hence the probability of occupancy of a particular state cannot exceed unity and no more than one electron per quantum state is allowed.

The nature of the probability function is best appreciated by plotting $p(E)$ versus E at various temperatures, as in Fig. 3.4. At 0 K the exponential

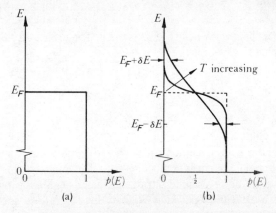

Fig. 3.4 Fermi–Dirac probability function (a) at 0 K and (b) at T K.

in eq. (3.37) has a value of 0 or ∞, depending on the sign of $(E - E_F)$. Thus, if $E < E_F$, the probability function is equal to unity and for $E > E_F$, the function equals zero, as shown in Fig. 3.4(a). Physically, what this implies is that at 0 K all available states up to an energy level E_F are filled, whereas all levels above E_F are empty, i.e., no electrons can possibly have energy greater than E_F. This serves as a preliminary definition of E_F and explains why it is alternatively called the *Fermi brim*.

When the temperature is increased to T K, there is a possibility that electrons which were originally at levels near to the maximum possible energy at 0 K, namely the Fermi level E_F, can now occupy states for which E is greater than E_F. However, energy cannot be transferred to those electrons in low-energy states because there are no unoccupied energy levels immediately above for them to move into and the probability function at these energies remains substantially as it was for $T = 0$ K. These arguments are substantiated by the shape of the probability function for $T > 0$ K, as shown in Fig. 3.4(b).

It will be seen that at low temperatures there is a small but finite probability that electrons will occupy available states for which $E > E_F$ but the probability rapidly decreases with increasing energy. As the temperature is increased, this *tail* of the probability function becomes more pronounced and the probability of occupancy of higher energy states is correspondingly increased.

Notice that the probability that an electron occupies the Fermi level, i.e., $E = E_F$, is always 50%, independent of the temperature. Another interesting fact is that the probability function is symmetrical about the value ($E = E_F$, $p(E) = \frac{1}{2}$). This can be shown as follows. Consider an energy level which is δE above the Fermi level, as shown in Fig. 3.4(b). The probability that the level is occupied is, using eq. 3.37

$$p(E_F + \delta E) = \frac{1}{1 + \exp\left[(E_F + \delta E - E_F)/kT\right]} = \frac{1}{1 + \exp(\delta E/kT)} \quad (3.38)$$

Now consider the level which is δE *below* E_F. The probability that this level is *not* occupied is

$$1 - p(E_F - \delta E) = 1 - \frac{1}{1 + \exp(-\delta E/kT)} = \frac{1}{1 + \exp(\delta E/kT)} \quad (3.39)$$

Comparison of eqs. (3.38) and (3.39) demonstrates the symmetry of the probability about E_F, since the probability that a level at a particular energy increment above E_F is occupied equals the probability that a level below E_F by same energy increment is empty.

Finally, it should be pointed out that in many solids E_F is typically of the order of a few electronvolts and at ordinary temperature kT is only a fraction of an electronvolt. Thus, since the probability function goes from nearly unity to nearly zero over an energy range near E_F of only a few kT, the ordinate of the probability curve in Fig. 3.4(b) has been artificially compressed so that details of the variation of $p(E)$ near to $E = E_F$ are not lost.

Problems

1   For a hypothetical gas the number of molecules per unit volume dN_v in the speed range from v to $v + dv$ is given by

$$dN_v = Kv \, dv \qquad v_0 > v > 0$$
$$dN_v = 0 \qquad v > v_0$$

where K is a constant. The total number of molecules per unit volume is N. Draw a graph of the distribution function and find the constant K in terms of v_0 and N. Compute the average, r.m.s., and most probable speeds in terms of v_0.

   Ans. $2N/v_0^2$, $2v_0/3$, $v_0/\sqrt{2}$, v_0.

2   A hypothetical gas with N molecules/m^3 has a speed distribution function

$$f(v) = Cv^2 \quad \text{for } v_0 > v > 0$$
$$= 0 \qquad \text{for } v > v_0$$

Find the mean-square fluctuation of the speeds which is defined as the mean-square speed minus the square of the mean speed.

   Ans. $0\cdot04v_0{}^2$.

3   Show that the Maxwell–Bolzmann distribution function for the speeds of molecules in a gas can be written in terms of a most probable speed v_p, thus

$$f(v) = \frac{4}{\sqrt{\pi}} \frac{v^2}{v_p{}^3} \exp\left(-\frac{v^2}{v_p{}^2}\right)$$

Use this expression to find the mean speed and the r.m.s. speed in terms of v_p.

   Assume $\displaystyle\int_0^\infty e^{-ax^2} x^{2k+1}\, dx = \frac{k!}{2a^{k+1}}$ and $\displaystyle\int_0^\infty e^{-ax^2} x^{2k}\, dx$

$$= \frac{1.3.5\ldots\overline{2k-1}}{2^{k+1}} \sqrt{\frac{\pi}{a^{2k+1}}}$$

   Ans. $2v_p/\sqrt{\pi}, \sqrt{\tfrac{3}{2}}\, v_p$

4   In a Maxwellian gas the number of particles colliding with unit surface area of its container per second is

$$\frac{N}{4}\left(\frac{8kT}{\pi M}\right)$$

Caesium atoms are contained within a furnace at temperature T K. There is also a hot tungsten wire radius r, length l, inside the furnace and caesium atoms striking this wire became singly ionized. The resulting ions are collected on a nearby negative electrode. Show that the ion current I to this electrode, I is given by

$$I = erlp(2\pi/kTM)^{\frac{1}{2}}$$

where p is the vapour pressure of the caesium at temperature T and M the mass of the caesium atom. Can you suggest a practical use for this device?

5   A gas possesses a Maxwellian velocity distribution. Show that the fraction of molecules in a given volume that possess a velocity component v_x whose magnitude is greater than some selected value v_{0x} is given by

$$\exp\left(\tfrac{1}{2} - \pi^{-\frac{1}{2}}\right) \int_0^{\left(\frac{mv_{0x}^2}{2kT}\right)} \exp\left(\frac{-mv_{0x}^2}{2kT}\right) d\left(\frac{mv_{0x}^2}{2kT}\right)^{\frac{1}{2}}$$

The definite integral $\int_0^\infty e^{-\beta s^2}\, ds = \dfrac{1}{2}\sqrt{\dfrac{\pi}{\beta}}$ will be required.

6   Show that the most probable energy of a molecule in a Maxwellian gas is $kT/2$.

7   Show that the number of molecules, N_0, in a Maxwellian gas whose energies lie between zero and E_0 where $E_0 \ll kT$ is given approximately by

$$\frac{N_0}{N} = \frac{4}{3\sqrt{\pi}}\left(\frac{E_0}{kT}\right)^{\frac{3}{2}}$$

Hence calculate approximately the percentage of molecules whose energies are less than 1% of kT.

8   At $T = 0$ K the electron energy levels in a metal are all occupied for $E < E_F$ and are empty for $E > E_F$. The energy distribution is then of the form

$$\frac{\Delta N}{N} = CE^{\frac{1}{2}}\Delta E \text{ for } E < E_F$$

$$= 0 \text{ for } E > E_F$$

where C is a constant. Find (a) the average electron energy under these conditions and (b) the percentage of the total number of electrons with energies between $0\cdot1E_F$ and $0\cdot2E_F$.

   Ans. $0\cdot6E_F$, $5\cdot8\%$.

4. Conduction in metals

4.1 Introduction

In this chapter we shall be considering the conduction of electricity in good conductors, typically metals. We shall see that in such materials the valence electrons are no longer associated with any one particular ion core but are free to wander about the lattice under the influence of external forces. The metal is then considered simply as a 'container' of free electrons which are only trapped within the boundaries of the metal. Earlier arguments about bound particles would suggest that confining the electrons in this manner leads to a set of discrete energy eigenvalues, much the same as for electrons trapped in the one-dimensional well of section 2.2. Further, since electrons in the metal will be subject to the exclusion principle, Fermi rather than Maxwell–Boltzmann statistics will be applicable to them.

4.2 A simple model of a conductor

The potential energy of an electron located at some distance r from the nucleus of a single, isolated metal atom will be of the general form shown in Fig. 2.3(a). Consequently, there will be a set of allowed electron energy levels associated with the atom, each specified by a particular set of quantum numbers, similar to that shown in Fig. 2.3(a). Electrons are trapped within the potential energy well and are thus bound to the atom; not even the outermost valence electrons usually have sufficient energy to escape.

When such atoms are incorporated in the lattice of a metal, the potential energy distribution between neighbouring atoms is different from that of the individual atoms, as shown in Fig. 4.1. Since potential energy is a scalar quantity, the potential energies of the individual atoms add and the net energy profile is depressed, i.e., is made more negative, as shown in the figure. This causes some of the less tightly bound electrons, lying in the outermost levels of the individual atoms, for example those in E_4 of Fig. 4.1, to have energies higher than the binding energies of atoms in the lattice. Such valence electrons can no longer be associated with a particular atom and are free to move about the lattice in the vicinity of any ion core. Notice that electrons occupying the

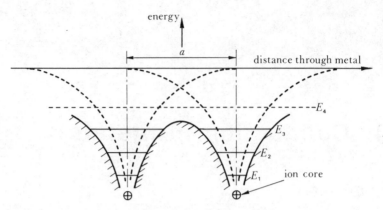

Fig. 4.1 Potential energy and energy levels of neighbouring atoms in a metal lattice.

lower energy states are unaffected by the atoms being incorporated into the metal and remain bound to the parent nucleus. We can estimate the number density of free electrons by assuming, conservatively, that each atom provides only one such electron. A typical lattice constant of 0.1 nm then suggests a number density of $(10^{-10})^3 = 10^{30}$ atoms per metre cube and a similar minimum number of free electrons in the same volume.

The situation is somewhat different near the surface of the metal. Consider a section of the metal lattice shown in Fig. 4.2(a). The nearest atom to a

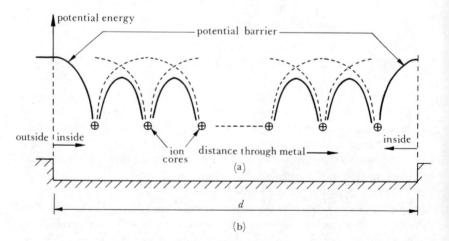

Fig. 4.2 (a) Section through a metal lattice, (b) potential box model.

particular surface obviously has no neighbouring atom outside the metal and the potential energy is not depressed as in the interior of the metal. Hence, potential barriers exist at each surface, as shown, which are normally unsurmountable by electrons. Thus, although electrons are considered to be free to wander unimpeded about the inside of the metal, they are reflected by the potential barriers at each surface and are effectively trapped inside the material in this way.

A simple model for a metal might then be as shown in Fig. 4.2(b). It consists of a three-dimensional container or box in which electrons are free to move without hindrance, but under normal conditions electrons are prevented from penetrating outside the walls by assuming the potential energy outside to be very high. Such a box will have dimensions which are the same as those of the metal being considered. Notice that there is some slight ambiguity about the position of the surface of the metal. All that can be said is that a surface is located within a distance of order of one lattice constant away from the last nucleus in a section through the lattice, as shown in Fig. 4.2(a).

4.3 Electrons trapped in a three-dimensional potential box

If the free-electron model of a metal is assumed, the electron energy states will be the same as those for electrons trapped in a three-dimensional potential box. Consider a box with dimensions shown in Fig. 4.3. Electrons are free

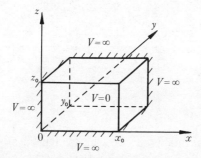

Fig. 4.3 Dimensions of a three-dimensional potential box model of a conductor.

to move inside the box since the potential energy there, V, is assumed to be zero. Everywhere else V is assumed to be infinite, in order to confine the electrons to the box. By reasoning similar to that given for the one-dimensional well problem (section 2.2), ψ must vanish at the walls to ensure that there is zero probability of an electron acquiring infinite energy by penetrating outside the box. Schrödinger's equation applied to electrons with constant total energy, E, inside the box, where $V = 0$, and stated in the coordinate system shown is, from eq. 1.43(b):

$$\frac{\partial^2 \Psi}{\partial x^2} + \frac{\partial^2 \Psi}{\partial y^2} + \frac{\partial^2 \Psi}{\partial z^2} + \frac{2m}{\hbar^2} E \Psi = 0 \qquad (4.1)$$

This equation can be solved by the separation-of-variables technique by assuming:

$$\Psi = f_x(x) f_y(y) f_z(z) \tag{4.2}$$

where the f's are functions only of the variable used as a subscript. This trial solution can be substituted in eq. (4.1) to give:

$$\frac{1}{f_x} \frac{d^2 f_x}{dx^2} + \frac{1}{f_y} \frac{d^2 f_y}{dy^2} + \frac{1}{f_z} \frac{d^2 f_z}{dz^2} = -\frac{2mE}{\hbar^2} \tag{4.3}$$

Then, by the usual arguments, since E is a constant making the right-hand side of the equation constant, each of the left-hand terms must individually equal constants, $C_{1,2,3}^2$, say, and

$$\frac{d^2 f_x}{dx^2} = C_1^2 f_x, \quad \frac{d^2 f_y}{dy^2} = C_2^2 f_y, \quad \frac{d^2 f_z}{dz^2} = C_3^2 f_z \tag{4.4}$$

As has been established already, the boundary conditions on the wave functions require that $\Psi = 0$ at the walls of the box. Hence:

$$\Psi = 0 \quad \text{at} \quad x = 0 \text{ and } x = x_0$$
$$y = 0 \text{ and } y = y_0 \tag{4.5}$$
$$z = 0 \text{ and } z = z_0$$

Possible solutions to Schrödinger's equation, given by eq. (4.4) and also satisfying the boundary conditions (4.5), are then:

$$f_x = A \sin(n_x \pi x / x_0)$$
$$f_y = B \sin(n_y \pi y / y_0) \tag{4.6}$$
$$f_z = C \sin(n_z \pi z / z_0)$$

where the n's are quantum numbers which independently have integer values 1, 2, 3, 4, ... and A, B, C are newly defined constants. That these functions are solutions of eq. (4.4) and also satisfy conditions (4.5) can be verified by substitution.

The complete expression for the wave functions can now be obtained by substituting the x-, y-, and z-dependent parts back into eq. (4.3). This expression is then normalized, using much the same technique as for the one-dimensional potential well in section 2.2, to give finally:

$$\Psi_{n_x n_y n_z} = \sqrt{\frac{2}{x_0}} \sin\left(\frac{n_x \pi x}{x_0}\right) \sqrt{\frac{2}{y_0}} \sin\left(\frac{n_y \pi y}{y_0}\right) \sqrt{\frac{2}{z_0}} \sin\left(\frac{n_z \pi z}{z_0}\right) \tag{4.7}$$

Notice that this wave function is the product of three one-dimensional wave functions of the type encountered in section 2.2 (This result may come as no surprise to readers familiar with electromagnetic theory, since as the one-dimensional potential well is analogous to a short-circuited resonant transmission line, the three-dimensional potential box has its electromagnetic equivalent in a short-circuited resonant cavity.)

The wave function expression of eq. (4.7) is next substituted back into Schrödinger's equation to obtain the permitted quantized energy levels of electrons in the box, to give:

$$E_{n_x n_y n_z} = \frac{\hbar^2}{2m}\left[\left(\frac{n_x \pi}{x_0}\right)^2 + \left(\frac{n_y \pi}{y_0}\right)^2 + \left(\frac{n_z \pi}{z_0}\right)^2\right]^2 \tag{4.8}$$

where $n_{x,y,z}$ are three quantum numbers which specify a particular electronic energy state.

The problem is simplified if the containing volume is considered to be a cube of side d. The expression for the energy eigenvalues given by eq. (4.8) then simplifies to:

$$E = \frac{h^2}{8md^2}(n_x^2 + n_y^2 + n_z^2) \tag{4.9}$$

Finally, if we write:

$$n^2 = n_x^2 + n_y^2 + n_z^2 \tag{4.10}$$

the expression for eigenvalues of electrons in a cubical potential box is

$$E = \frac{h^2}{8md^2} \cdot n^2 \tag{4.11}$$

which is of the same form as that obtained for the one-dimensional potential well (eq. (2.6)).

4.4 Maximum number of possible energy states

It is instructive to find the maximum number of possible energy states for which n, as defined by eq. (4.10), is less than some maximum value, n_F say. The discussion and result will be most pertinent to later consideration of the distribution of electron energies on a metal.

A particular value of n, which has components n_x, n_y, and n_z, all positive integers, can be visualized in n-space as shown in Fig. 4.4(a). In order to count the number of possible combinations of (n_x, n_y, n_z) up to the maximum value n_F, which will then automatically specify the possible energy levels via eq. (4.9), it is easiest to first of all assume n_x fixed at some value, n_{x_0} say, and consider a plane which is a section through n-space as shown in Fig. 4.4(b). Each point in the diagram represents a particular combination of quantum numbers n_y and n_z. Notice that any area on this plane is numerically equal to the number of possible combinations of n's enclosed by the area. For example, the section indicated by dashed lines is twelve units of area in

65

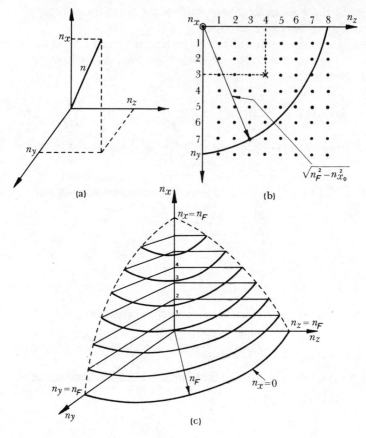

Fig. 4.4 Diagrams illustrating the evaluation of the maximum number of energy states of electrons trapped in a potential box.

extent and encloses twelve combinations of n_y and n_z. Now, for the fixed quantum number n_{x_0}, the other quantum numbers are related by

$$n^2 - n_{x_0}^2 = n_y^2 + n_z^2$$

and thus the maximum number of possible combinations of n_y and n_z for n less than or equal to n_F must lie within a circle centred at the origin and of radius $(n_F^2 - n_{x_0}^2)^{\frac{1}{2}}$ as shown; by our previous argument this number of combinations must be numerically equal to the area of the circle in the first quadrant.

If n_x is now allowed to assume other values the total number of possible combinations of (n_x, n_y, n_z) is included in a series of slices through n-space, each corresponding to different integer values of n_x, as shown diagrammatically in Fig. 4.4(c). It follows that the total number of possible combinations of the quantum numbers for $n \leqslant n_F$ is numerically equal to that volume of a sphere of radius n_F which is contained in the first quadrant of n-space. This latter condition is necessary since the n's are always positive integers. Hence

$$\text{Total number of combinations of } (n_x, n_y, n_z) = \tfrac{1}{8}(\tfrac{4}{3}\pi n_F^3) = \frac{\pi n_F^3}{6} \quad (4.12)$$

Now, in general, each electron energy state is characterized by four quantum numbers; in addition to n_x, n_y, n_z there is a spin quantum number which can have either of two values. Thus, there are two spin states for any particular combination of the n-quantum numbers which gives, from eq. (4.12):

$$\text{Total number of possible energy states} = 2\left(\frac{\pi n_F^3}{6}\right) = \frac{\pi n_F^3}{3} \quad (4.13)$$

This gives the total number of available energy levels. These are not in general necessarily all occupied by electrons. We shall assume, however, that in some circumstances, the physical significance of which will be discussed later, all states are occupied up to some maximum energy state characterized by n_F. If the number density of electrons in the box is N, we can then equate the total number of electrons to the total number of available states, since no more than one electron can occupy a particular state, by the exclusion principle. Hence

$$Nd^3 = \pi n_F^3/3$$

or

$$n_F = \left(\frac{3N}{\pi}\right)^{\frac{1}{3}} d \quad (4.14)$$

The energy of the highest occupied state can then be obtained by substituting this value of n_F into eq. (4.11) to give:

$$E_{F_0} = \frac{h^2}{8m}\left(\frac{3N}{\pi}\right)^{\frac{2}{3}} \quad (4.15)$$

The subscripts to E anticipate later discussions of the physical implications of the result, when this maximum energy will be seen to correspond to the Fermi energy of a metal at 0 K.

4.5 The energy distribution of electrons in a metal

In order to find out the manner in which energy is distributed among the free electrons in a metal it is first necessary to determine the energy distribution of allowed energy levels which are available for occupation by the electrons. In other words, the number of available energy states lying in a range of energies, say between E and $E + dE$, is required.

It is found convenient to define a function $S(E)$, called the *density distribution of available states*, which is defined in such a way that $S(E)dE$ is the number of available states per unit volume in the energy range considered; the problem is then modified to that of finding the form of $S(E)$.

The relationship between the energy of a state, E, and its quantum number designation, n, for a metal cube of side d is given in eq. (4.11). In the energy range dE there will be a corresponding range of quantum numbers, dn say. We can evaluate the number of states in the range by finding the volume that the range dn occupies in n-space, as was explained in the previous section. Thus, considering a spherical shell in n-space of radius n and thickness dn, as shown in Fig. 4.5(a), the number of states with quantum numbers between n and $n + dn$ is numerically equal to the volume of the shell in the first quadrant, multiplied by two; the additional factor accounts for the two possible spin states corresponding to each value of n. Thus the number of available states in the range is

$$2(4\pi n^2 \, dn)/8 = \pi n^2 \, dn \tag{4.16}$$

which by definition of the density distribution of available states function, $S(E)$, is equal to

$$S(E)dE.d^3$$

Hence

$$S(E) = \frac{\pi n^2}{d^3} \cdot \frac{dn}{dE} \tag{4.17}$$

Equation (4.11) can be differentiated to give

$$n^2 \frac{dn}{dE} = \frac{8\sqrt{2}m^{\frac{3}{2}}d^3 E^{\frac{1}{2}}}{h^3}$$

which can be substituted in eq. (4.17) to provide the following expression for the density distribution of available states:

$$S(E) = \frac{8\sqrt{2}\pi m^{\frac{3}{2}}}{h^3} \cdot E^{\frac{1}{2}} \tag{4.18}$$

To reiterate, the total number of *available* energy levels per unit volume in a given energy range, dE, is obtained by multiplying this distribution function, $S(E)$, by the size of the range. Thus an alternative definition of $S(E)$ is that it is the number of available states per unit volume, per unit of energy centred at E. Notice that eq. (4.18) is independent of d; the expression for $S(E)$ is quite general and is independent of dimensions.

The distribution function, $S(E)$, is plotted as a function of energy in Fig. 4.5(b). It will be seen that the number of available energy levels increases parabolically with increasing energy.

However, in general, not all the available energy states are filled, since, for example, it is extremely unlikely that an electron can gain sufficient energy

68

to occupy one of the relatively very high levels. What determines whether a particular energy level, E say, is filled or not is the probability that an electron can possess energy E. We have seen that for particles which obey the exclusion principle, as electrons in a metal do, such a probability is given

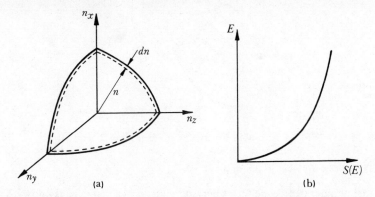

Fig. 4.5 (a) Spherical shell used to evaluate $S(E)$, (b) variation of $S(E)$ with energy.

by the Fermi–Dirac function, $p(E)$. Hence, the number of electrons per unit volume which are in a given energy range depends not only on the number of available states in the range but also on the probability that electrons can acquire sufficient energy to occupy the states, or

number of electrons per unit volume with energies between E and $E + dE$ = (number of available states/unit volume in the range E to $E + dE$) × (the probability that a state of energy E is occupied)

and

$$N(E)\,dE = S(E)\,dE\,.\,p(E)$$

where $N(E)$ is the number of electrons per unit volume per unit of energy centred at E. Thus, the number density of electrons in a unit energy range is obtainable from the distribution function of available states and the probability function since

$$\boxed{N(E) = S(E)\,p(E)} \tag{4.19}$$

The number density of electrons as a function of energy can thus be deduced from eq. (4.19) and Figs. 3.4 and 4.5(b) and is plotted at 0 K and some higher temperature in Fig. 4.6. At 0 K, $N(E)$ increases parabolically with E, following the $S(E)$ curve and all levels are filled up to the Fermi level, E_F; all levels above the Fermi levels are empty. At higher temperatures some electrons in the levels near to the Fermi brim can gain sufficient energy to have energies greater than E_F. Thus as the temperature is increased the number of electrons just below the Fermi level decreases and there is a corresponding increase in the number of electrons in the high-energy tail with energies greater than E_F.

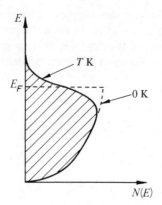

Fig. 4.6 Number density of free electrons in a metal.

4.6 The Fermi level in a metal

If the number of free electrons per unit volume in a metal, n, is known, it is then possible in principle to calculate the value of the Fermi energy, E_F. This can be done by normalizing by summing the number density per unit energy, $N(E)$, over all possible energies and equating to n, thus:

$$n = \int_0^\infty N(E)\, dE \tag{4.20}$$

Writing $N(E)$ in terms of the density of states function, $S(E)$, and the probability function, $p(E)$, using eq. (4.19), and including the more specific expressions of eq. (4.18) and (3.37) gives:

$$n = \int_0^\infty S(E)p(E)\, dE = \frac{8\sqrt{2}\pi m^{\frac{3}{2}}}{h^3} \int_0^\infty \frac{E^{\frac{1}{2}}\, dE}{1 + \exp[(E - E_F)/kT]} \tag{4.21}$$

This integral is difficult to evaluate except when $T = 0$ K; then $p(E)$ equals unity for all $E \leqslant E_{F_0}$ and is zero elsewhere and:

$$n = \frac{8\sqrt{2}\pi m^{\frac{3}{2}}}{h^3} \int_0^{E_{F_0}} E^{\frac{1}{2}}\, dE$$

The Fermi energy at 0 K is thus given by

$$E_{F_0} = \frac{h^2}{8m} \left(\frac{3n}{8\pi}\right)^{\frac{2}{3}} = 3\cdot 65 \cdot 10^{-19}\, n^{\frac{2}{3}}\, \text{eV} \tag{4.22}$$

a result which was anticipated in eq. (4.15).

Typical values for the Fermi energy at 0 K as calculated from eq. (4.22) and a knowledge of n are: for silver $E_{F_0} = 5\cdot5$ eV, for copper $E_{F_0} = 7\cdot0$ eV, and for aluminium $E_{F_0} = 11\cdot7$ eV. Thus, the Fermi energy for a good conductor is of the order of a few electronvolts. This emphasizes an essential

70

difference between a classical gas and the electron gas model of a metal at 0 K; in the former all particles have zero energy while in the latter all electron energies up to the Fermi energy are possible.

At temperatures other than 0 K, the Fermi energy can be obtained from eq. (4.21) by numerical integration. At room temperature it can be shown that a reasonably good approximation for E_F is:

$$E_F = E_{F_0}\left[1 - \frac{\pi^2}{12}\cdot\left(\frac{kT}{E_{F_0}}\right)^2\right]$$
(4.23)

This equation shows that whereas E_F decreases with increasing temperature, since kT is usually much smaller than E_{F_0}, E_F is not far removed from E_{F_0} and is fairly insensitive to temperature changes.

4.7 Conduction processes in metals

We shall first examine electrical conduction in terms of the free-electron model of a metal. Although there are drawbacks to the treatment, which will be discussed subsequently, what follows will serve as a simple introduction to the essential features of conduction processes.

Conduction in electrical conductors is governed by a fundamental experimental law, Ohm's law, which in its most general form may be written:

$$J = \sigma \mathscr{E}$$
(4.24)

where J is the current density, in a material of conductivity σ, produced by the application of an electric field $\mathscr{E}$. If we assume that the current flow is due to the movement of n free electrons per unit volume, each of charge $-e$ and travelling with velocity v, we can write:

$$J = -nev$$
(4.25)

Now, an electron subjected to an electric field, $\mathscr{E}$, by definition experiences an accelerating force, $-e\mathscr{E}$. Thus, in the absence of any restraining force the free electrons in a metal with an externally applied electric field accelerate progressively and as a consequence of eq. (4.25) the current density increases with time. This is clearly at variance with Ohm's law, which requires the current to be constant for a particular applied field. It is evident that, for the two expressions for current density to be compatible, the electron velocity must remain constant for any particular applied field. The constant velocity can be explained in terms of 'collisions' of the electrons with the crystal structure in which they move. The precise mechanism of the collision will be discussed more fully later. Meanwhile, it is sufficient to say that a free electron can be accelerated from rest by the application of an external electric field, acquires a linearly increasing velocity for a short time, but then undergoes some form of collision which reduces its velocity to zero; the process then repeats itself. As a consequence, the electron acquires a constant

71

average drift velocity in the direction of the accelerating force, which is superimposed on to its random thermal motion. This situation is shown diagrammatically in Figs. 4.7(a), (b), and (c).

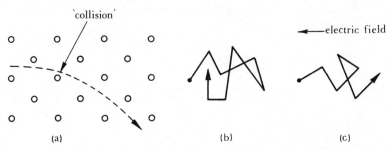

Fig. 4.7 (a) Random motion of an electron through the crystal lattice, (b) as for (a) but on a larger scale, and (c) drift motion of an electron under the influence of an external electric field.

The effect of collisions in this case, and, incidentally, for similar processes in semiconductors and plasmas which are considered in following chapters, is thus to introduce a viscous or frictional force which inhibits the continual acceleration of the carriers by the field and limits the velocity to some average drift velocity, v_D.

If the average time between collisions is τ_r, then the number of collisions per second is $1/\tau_r$ and the average rate of change of momentum or the frictional force on the carriers due to collision is $m v_D/\tau_r$. The equation of motion of an electron subject to an applied field in the x-direction $\mathscr{E}_x$ is then:

$$-e\,\mathscr{E}_x = m\frac{d}{dt}(v_{Dx}) + \frac{m(v_{Dx})}{\tau_r} \tag{4.26}$$

The solution of this equation is:

$$v_{Dx} = \frac{-e\tau_r\,\mathscr{E}_x}{m}\,(1 - e^{-t/\tau_r}) \tag{4.27}$$

which may be verified by substitution. We can now substitute this value of v_{Dx} in eq. (4.25) to obtain the current density:

$$J = n(-e)\cdot v_{Dx} = \frac{ne^2\,\tau_r\,\mathscr{E}_x}{m}\,(1 - e^{-t/\tau_r}) \tag{4.28}$$

We see that the electron drift velocity and the current density both rise exponentially with time to become constant in a time comparable to τ_r.

We can understand the significance of τ_r further if we suppose that after some initial application of field it is suddenly reduced to zero. Equation (4.26) indicates that the decay of drift velocity from its initial value at $t = 0$, v_{D_0}, back to the thermal equilibrium state when $v_D = 0$ is then governed by the equation

$$v_D = v_{D_0} e^{-t/\tau_r} \tag{4.29}$$

The time constant, τ_r, is often referred to as the electron relaxation time, since it controls the exponential way in which electron drift velocity and hence current relaxes back to zero when the field is suddenly removed. It is typically of order 10^{-14} s and so for any time after the application of an electric field which is long compared to this, the mean drift velocity and current density are constant, their steady-state values being:

$$v_{D_x} = -\frac{e\tau_r}{m} \mathscr{E}_x \tag{4.30}$$

and

$$J_x = \frac{ne^2 \tau_r}{m} \mathscr{E}_x \tag{4.31}$$

The negative sign in the former equation indicates that the electrons drift in the negative x-direction, in the opposite direction to the field. This corresponds to a conventional current flow in the opposite direction, so J_x remains positive.

Equations (4.30) and (4.31) can be somewhat simplified if we assume that τ_r is independent of $\mathscr{E}_x$, which is usually permissible. We then notice that the drift velocity of electrons is directly proportional to the applied field. The constant of proportionality, usually designated μ, is called the *mobility*.

Thus:

$$v_D = -\mu \mathscr{E}_x \tag{4.32}$$

where the electron mobility

$$\mu = \frac{e\tau_r}{m} \tag{4.33}$$

The mobility is thus defined as the incremental average electron velocity per unit of electric field.

We can now rewrite the current equation in terms of the mobility and eq. (4.31) becomes:

$$J_x = ne\mu \mathscr{E}_x \tag{4.34}$$

Comparing this equation with eq. (4.24), it is seen that the conductivity of the metal, σ, can be expressed as:

$$\sigma = ne\mu = \frac{ne^2 \tau_r}{m} \tag{4.35}$$

This expression is quite general and holds for any conduction process, provided μ, n, and m are specified for the particular process.

73

The discussion so far has excluded any mention of the distribution of allowed electron energy levels or the exclusion principle which must apply to electrons in a metal. A graphical representation of the statistical distribution of the energies of conduction electrons will now be considered since it gives more physical insight into the conduction process.

Each conduction electron occupies a particular energy state which has an associated velocity which can be represented as a point in the three-dimensional velocity space shown in Fig. 4.8(a). In the absence of applied electric field,

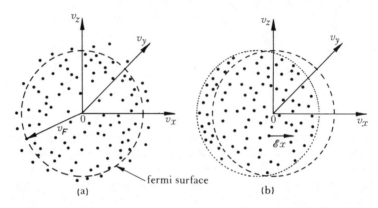

Fig. 4.8 Distribution of electrons in velocity space (a) with no applied field and (b) with field $\mathscr{E}_x$ applied.

the electron velocities are random; for every group of electrons travelling with a particular velocity, there will be a similar number travelling with the same speed but in the opposite direction and the distribution in velocity space will have spherical symmetry. At zero temperature the distribution will be most compact and all levels will be occupied out to a velocity, v_F, corresponding to the Fermi energy. Moreover, since $E_F = \frac{1}{2} m v_F{}^2$, the outermost boundary containing all possible velocities will be a sphere, shown dashed in Fig. 4.8(a). Such a boundary is called a *Fermi surface*, even when it is not spherical as it is in this case.

At more elevated temperatures the boundary of the distribution in velocity space becomes more diffuse since a small proportion of electrons now have velocities greater than v_F. This 'fuzzing' of the edges of the sphere is not very pronounced because the corresponding range of energies is only a few kT which is much less than E_F generally.

When an electric field $\mathscr{E}_x$ is applied as shown in Fig. 4.8(b), all electrons in the distribution are subjected to a force $e\mathscr{E}_x$ in the $-x$-direction. Only those electrons near to the Fermi brim can move since only they have unoccupied energy levels immediately adjacent to move into. Suppose for the moment that all electrons suffer a randomizing collision simultaneously at time $t = 0$ and that at this instant the electrons have the equilibrium velocity distribution shown in Fig. 4.8(a). At some time t later the distribution as a whole moves in the negative x-direction by a velocity increment $e\mathscr{E}t/m$. After a further series of collisions the distribution will tend to revert to its equilibrium position. Of course, in a more realistic situation, collisions occur in a more random manner; some electrons are returning to their equilibrium position in velocity space after a collision while others are being accelerated by the field. Hence, on average, application of an electric field causes the entire equilibrium velocity distribution to be shifted slightly by an amount $e\mathscr{E}_x\tau_r/m$ in the opposite direction to the field as shown in Fig. 4.8(b). The velocity distribution is no longer symmetrical about the origin and the precise cancellation of electron velocity components in the direction of the field does not occur. There is now a slightly preferred electron velocity direction in the opposite direction to the field which results in a drift velocity:

$$v_D = -\frac{e\mathscr{E}_x\tau_r}{m}$$

Thus, it is the difference between the equilibrium and the shifted steady-state distributions which accounts for the drift velocity and resulting current flow on the application of a field. Of course, as soon as the field is removed, the steady distribution relaxes to the symmetrical equilibrium form.

A further point to note is that the distribution is affected only by the applied field near to the Fermi surface and so the most significant relaxation time is not the average for the whole distribution but that of electrons near to E_F, τ_{rF} say. Equations (4.20) and (4.31), which give the drift velocity and current density, are seen to be still applicable provided τ_r is interpreted as τ_{rF}.

Finally, it should be emphasized that only a very slight shift for the equilibrium distribution is necessary to account for the flow of current in a metal, and that depicted in Fig. 4.8(b) is very much exaggerated for the sake of clarity.

The free-electron model has been used successfully to explain many aspects of electronic conduction in metals, particularly when Fermi statistics is employed. There are, however, some details of the properties of electrical conductors which cannot be accounted for quantitatively by the simple model. For example, in order that the electron velocity be limited to a drift velocity, it has been found necessary to postulate some sort of collision mechanism followed by energy randomization. Early theories assumed that the collisions were between electrons and ion cores which occupy most of the volume of a metal. That such a theory is unacceptable can be seen by estimating the mean free path or average distance between collisions, $\bar{l}$. For electrons near the Fermi level

$$\bar{l}_F = \tau_{rF}\,v_F \tag{4.36}$$

75

where v_F is the velocity of an electron with the Fermi energy. Since the Fermi energy is relatively insensitive to temperature, v_F is given approximately by

$$v_F \approx \sqrt{2E_{F_0} e/m}$$

If, for example, we consider copper, $E_{F_0} \approx 7$ eV and $v_F \approx 10^6$ m/s. The relaxation time for copper can be estimated using eq. (4.35); if a measured conductivity of $6 \cdot 10^7$ S/m and a free electron density of 10^{29} are assumed, then τ_{rF} is of order 10^{-14} s. Hence the mean free path from eq. (4.36) is of the order of tens of nanometres. This is very much longer than the lattice constant, which is of order of $0 \cdot 1$ nm. Clearly, collisions are not occurring between electrons and metallic ions since this would inevitably lead to mean free paths of the same order as the lattice constant. A more accurate description of the nature of the collision process will be deferred until the next chapter.

Another property of conductors which the simple model does not account for quantitatively is the temperature dependence of resistivity. It is well known experimentally that the resistance of a metal increases almost linearly with temperature. Thus, since:

$$\sigma = \frac{ne^2 \, \tau_{rF}}{m} = \frac{ne^2 \, \bar{l}_F}{mv_F}$$

and since v_F is almost independent of temperature, $\bar{l}_F$ would be expected to decrease almost linearly with increasing temperature; this is at variance with a free-electron theory which suggests a $T^{-\frac{1}{2}}$-dependence of the mean free path and the conductivity. The discrepancy will be accounted for in the next chapter.

Problems

1   A particular metal contains 10^{28} free electrons per cubic metre. Find the number density of electrons in the energy interval $2 \cdot 795$ eV to $2 \cdot 805$ eV at $T = 300$ K.

   Ans. 8×10^6 m^{-3}.

2   The Fermi level in copper at 0 K is $7 \cdot 0$ eV. Estimate the number of free electrons per unit volume in copper at this temperature.

   Ans. $8 \cdot 4 \times 10^{28}$ m^{-3}.

3   Calculate the Fermi energy at 0 K in copper given that there is one conduction electron per atom, that the density of copper is 8920 kg m^{-3} and its atomic weight is $63 \cdot 54$.

   Ans. $7 \cdot 06$ eV.

4   Use the equation of motion of an electron in a metal under the influence of an electric field $\mathscr{E}$, eq. (4.26), to show that if an alternating field $\mathscr{E}_0 e^{j\omega t}$ is applied the effective conductivity of a metal may be written

$$\sigma = \frac{\sigma_0}{1 + j\omega\tau_r}$$

where σ_0 is the low frequency conductivity. (Hint: write $Ce^{j\omega t}$ as a solution of the equation, where C is to be found.) What do you infer from the result?

5. Electrons in solids— an introduction to band theory

5.1 Introduction

The conduction theory presented in the previous chapter assumes that many free electrons are available within the body of the material which behave as classical particles. In a metal the free valence electrons are shared by all atoms in the solid; hence there is a tendency for the periodic potential of the crystal lattice as seen by the conduction electrons to be smeared out and appear almost constant. This accounts for the success of the free-electron model in explaining most, if not all, of the conduction phenomena in metals. However, for materials with different crystal structures, for example in the important case of covalent bonded solids such as some semiconductors, valence electrons are located much nearer to the parent atoms and cannot be associated with the entire collection of atoms as in a metal. The free-electron model fails for such materials since the potential seen by valence electrons can no longer be regarded as constant since it varies rapidly, particularly near to ion cores in the lattice.

A quantum-mechanical model which overcomes this difficulty assumes that the conduction electrons as well as being subject to the restriction of the exclusion principle as before are not entirely free but move in the perfectly periodic potential of a crystal. Such a distribution of potential arises because of the regular spacing of ion cores in the lattice and its periodicity is equal to the lattice constant. We shall see that in this situation the energy of electrons can be situated only in allowed bands, which are separated by forbidden energy regions. Within a particular allowed band, electrons behave in much the same way as the free electrons; they can again interact with externally applied fields to produce conduction effects but the interaction parameters have to be modified to account for the presence of the lattice.

The so-called band theory of solids which is developed from the periodic potential model has been most successful in explaining some of the anomalies predicted by the free-electron model and also can account for the differing electrical properties of conductors, semiconductors and insulators. What determines the conduction properties of a particular material is whether the electronic states within an allowed energy band are empty or full.

The more complete model also accounts for apparent changes in effective electron mass with position in an energy band. Further, it will be shown that the properties of a material with an almost filled band are identical with those of a material containing a few positive charge carriers in an otherwise empty band; this is a quantum-mechanical justification of the concept of a *hole* which will be used extensively when discussing semiconductors later.

Finally, departures from the assumed perfect periodicity of potential will be shown to account for resistive effects in a practical material.

5.2 Allowed energy bands of electrons in solids

5.2.1. General concepts. It was shown in chapter 2 that the electrons in an isolated atom are only allowed to possess discrete values of energy. The exclusion principle also stipulates that each energy level, which is defined by a set of three quantum numbers, can only be occupied by at most two electrons, provided they have opposite spins.

When atoms are packed closely together in a solid such that the electronic orbitals of neighbouring atoms tend to overlap, the allowed electron energy levels are modified from those of the individual constituent atoms. Consider, for example, two identical atoms which are gradually brought together. As the outermost orbitals overlap, electrons which originally had the same energy in the isolated atoms each have their energies slightly modified so that the exclusion principle is not violated for the two-atom systems; each allowed energy level is split into two closely spaced levels. If the atoms are brought still closer together such that the electrons in inner orbitals of each atom interact the lower energy levels split in a similar manner.

Energy level splitting of atoms in close proximity can be explained in terms of a simple quantum-mechanical model, as follows. Consider, for example, two hydrogen atoms separated by an initially large distance, r. The electronic energy structure of each atom will be as shown in Fig. 2.3(a) and for the two atoms is as shown in Fig. 5.1(a). To a first approximation each atom can be represented by a one-dimensional rectangular potential well of width δ, as shown in Fig. 5.1(b). We have seen that the wave functions of bound electrons in such a potential well are nearly sinusoidal (or exactly sinusoidal if the well is infinitely deep) and that the corresponding energies are discrete eigenvalues. For example, the possible wave functions of the lowest energy state ($n = 1$) are as shown in Fig. 5.1(c). Notice that the negative ψ solution, shown dotted, is included since it is equally possible because it is only the quantity $|\psi|^2$ which has any physical significance. The general expression for the energy

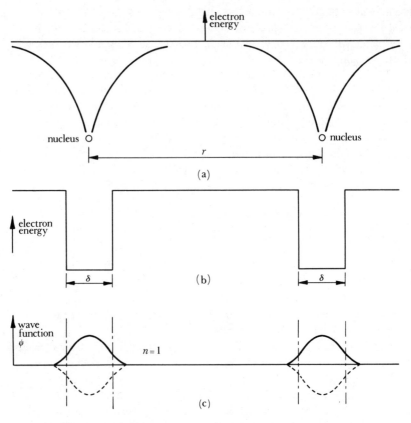

Fig. 5.1 (a) Potential energy of electrons in two isolated hydrogen atoms, (b) one-dimensional potential well equivalent, (c) wave functions of trapped electrons in the lowest energy state.

eigenvalues of a trapped electron is given in eq. (2.6), hence the lowest energy state for an individual well is:

$$E_1 = h^2/(8m\delta^2) \tag{5.1}$$

Now, consider the atoms when they are brought more closely together such that $r > \delta$, as shown in Fig. 5.2(a). The boundary conditions stipulate that both the wave function, ψ, and its gradient, $\partial\psi/\partial x$, must always remain continuous. It would appear that there are two possible configurations for the wave function of the complete system, as shown, one in which ψ is symmetrical about the centre line dividing the atoms and one in which ψ is antisymmetrical. When the atoms are brought even nearer, such that $r = \delta$, the wave functions of the lowest energy electrons merge into the symmetrical and antisymmetrical forms shown in Fig. 5.2(b) The electron energies corresponding to each wave

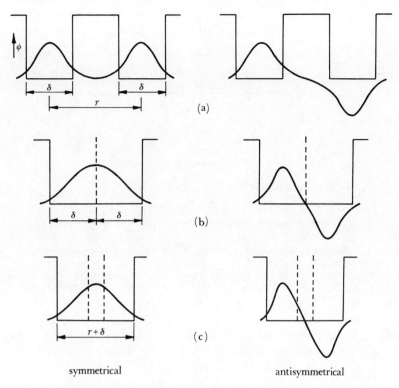

Fig. 5.2 Possible wave functions for the lowest energy states of a two-hydrogen-atom system as the separation is changed.

function of the complete system can again be obtained from eq. (2.6) and are

$$E_{1\,\text{sym}} = \frac{h^2}{8m(2\delta)^2} = \frac{1}{4} \cdot \frac{h^2}{8m\delta^2}$$ (5.2)

and

$$E_{1\,\text{antisym}} = \frac{2^2 h^2}{8m(2\delta)^2} = \frac{h^2}{8m\delta^2}$$ (5.3)

For even closer separation such that $r < \delta$, the possible wave functions for the system are shown in Fig. 5.2(c) and the corresponding electron energy values are:

$$E_{1\,\text{sym}} = \frac{h^2}{8m(r + \delta)^2}$$ (5.4)

and

$$E_{1\,\text{antisym}} = \frac{4h^2}{8m(r + \delta)^2}$$ (5.5)

These possible energy states of the system for various spacings r are collected together in Fig. 5.3. It will be seen that as soon as the spacing between the

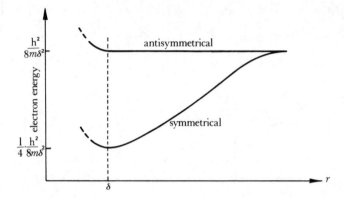

Fig. 5.3 Energy of lowest states in a system of two hydrogen atoms separated by distance r.

atoms is such that $r \approx \delta$ two definite energy states exist for the system where for the individual atoms there was only one.

It may be helpful to consider the electrical circuit analogue of closely coupled resonant circuits. The simple series LRC circuit depicted in Fig. 5.4(a) has a single current maximum when the frequency of the applied sinusoidal voltage is equal to the resonant frequency, f_0, as shown. When two such

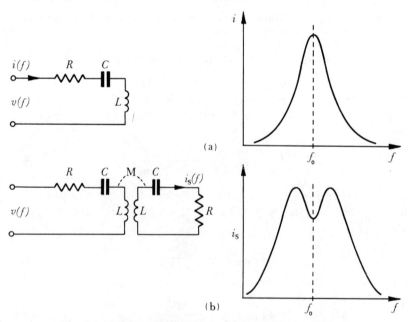

Fig. 5.4 (a) Series resonant circuit, (b) coupled resonant circuits.

82

circuits are tightly coupled via mutual inductance as shown in Fig. 5.4(b), two current maxima occur at frequencies displaced slightly to either side of f_0. Such frequency splitting can be compared to energy level splitting in atomic systems, particularly when it is remembered that energy and frequency are related quantities in quantum-mechanical systems.

Now let us consider briefly the case of three atoms brought into close proximity. For a particular separation there will now be three possible configurations for the wavefunctions, as shown in Fig. 5.5(a). The corresponding

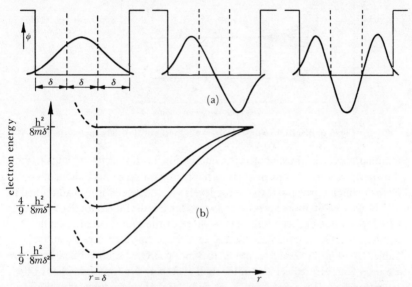

Fig. 5.5 Three-atom system: (a) possible wave functions for the lowest energy states, (b) electron energy as a function of atomic separation.

energies associated with the particular wave functions shown are as depicted in Fig. 5.5(b). Again, we see that each level of an individual atom is split into the same number of levels as the number of atoms in the system.

The extension of this argument is straightforward and it is reasonable to expect that in a system of n interacting atoms each discrete energy level of an individual atom is split into n closely spaced levels as the atoms are brought together. A system containing seven atoms is shown diagrammatically in Fig. 5.6; notice that the higher energy levels split at larger separations. This is because the electrons at these levels are on average further from the nucleus and interact with neighbouring atoms more readily.

Of course, in a more realistic system such as a solid the number of interacting atoms is much higher than seven; a typical figure may be, for example, 10^{22}. Also the total width of each band of allowed energy levels is of order 1 eV and depends not on the number of atoms grouped together but on their interatomic spacing. Since in this instance 10^{22} discrete levels have to be accommodated in an energy range which is only 1 eV in extent, individual levels in a band are of necessity very closely spaced together; the allowed energy levels within a band are therefore said to be *quasicontinuous*.

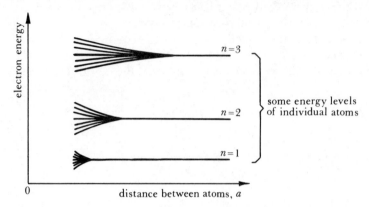

Fig. 5.6 Electron energy levels of a hypothetical seven atom system.

Summarizing, the allowed electron energies in a solid occur in bands in which the energy is *almost* continuously variable, separated by forbidden energy regions which correspond to energy levels which the electrons cannot attain.

Let us now be more specific and consider the useful example of carbon, which possesses properties similar to those of the more common semiconductors. The electronic structure of a single carbon atom is seen from Table 2.1 to be $1s^2 2s^2 2p^2$; that is, its inner principal shell is filled but there are only four electrons in its outer shell and there are four vacancies in the outer subshell. If we first of all consider a 'gas' of such atoms with the interatomic spacing or *lattice constant, a,* so large that no interaction occurs between them, then the energy levels of each atom are as shown at (i) in Fig. 5.7. As the carbon atoms are brought into closer proximity (i.e., a is reduced), level splitting occurs as described, which results in bands of allowed energies, as for example at (ii). For even closer spacings, as at (iii), the bands can overlap. Eventually, as a is reduced still further, the energies of the outer shell electrons can lie in one of two bands, separated by a forbidden gap, as at (iv).

Of course, it is not possible to vary continuously the interatomic spacing as we have assumed for convenience, since for a particular crystalline solid the lattice constant is fixed. The band structure of a particular allotropic form of carbon will then correspond to a vertical slice through Fig. 5.7; for example, carbon in the diamond form has a band structure similar to that at (iv). We shall see later that it is the magnitude and form of the band structure of a particular solid which completely specify its peculiar electrical conducting properties. Before doing so we will consider a more quantitative approach to the investigation of the band structure of solids.

84

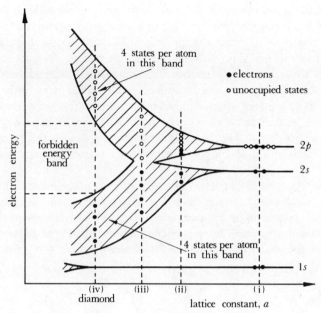

Fig. 5.7 Energy bands for carbon with varying interatomic spacing.

5.2.2. Mathematical model of a solid.

In an ideal solid, the ion cores of the crystal are spaced with perfect regularity and the potential experienced by an electron in the solid, V, is periodic in space; in any given direction, V repeats itself after distances equal to the lattice constant in that particular direction, a say. Thus:

$$V(x) = V(x + a) = V(x + 2a) \ldots$$

Of course, the precise nature of $V(x)$ is complex and the solution of Schrödinger's equation including such a function is difficult. The problem is considerably simplified if a simpler mathematical model of the solid is assumed in which the potential in a given direction, as seen by electrons in higher lying energy bands, changes abruptly from some value V_0 to zero with a periodicity a, as shown in Fig. 5.8. The model, which was proposed by Kronig and Penney, thus consists

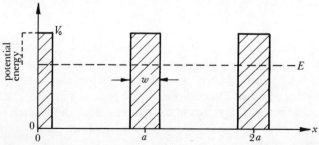

Fig. 5.8 One-dimensional idealized model of an array of atoms in a solid.

of a regular one-dimensional array of square-well potentials. Such a variation in potential is roughly similar to that of a linear array of atoms, as shown for example in Fig. 4.2(a), but the approximation is most crude; the chief merit of the model is that it predicts qualitatively the effects which are seen in real solids while retaining some mathematical simplicity. Furthermore, the discussion is limited to a one-dimensional model; while many of the results are qualitatively representative of those obtainable for a three-dimensional model, complete generalization is not always possible. Note also that the regions of low and high potential in the model alternate periodically; this property will be shown to be responsible for the allowed and forbidden electron energy bands.

Even when the simple model of a solid is assumed the mathematical treatment is involved and the analysis will only be outlined. An analogous electrical system will be discussed later which will explain some of the properties of the model. Applying Schrödinger's equation to the potential variation shown in Fig. 5.8 we have that, inside the wells, $V = 0$ and

$$\frac{\partial^2 \Psi}{\partial x^2} + \beta^2 \Psi = 0 \tag{5.6}$$

where
$$\beta^2 = 2mE/\hbar^2$$

and in the barriers, where $V_0 > E$,

$$\frac{\partial^2 \Psi}{\partial x^2} - \alpha^2 \Psi = 0 \tag{5.7}$$

where
$$\alpha^2 = 2m(V_0 - E)/\hbar^2$$

Equations (5.6) and (5.7) can be solved using the appropriate boundary conditions. It is usual at this stage, however, to make a further simplification to the model so that the problem becomes more tractable. This consists of letting the width of the barriers, w, go to zero and their height to infinity, in such a way that the 'strength' of the barrier, wV_0, remains constant; in other words, the potential is considered to be a periodic delta function. One type of solution which satisfies eqs. (5.6) and (5.7) is then found to be of the form

$$\Psi = U_k(x)\, e^{jkx} \tag{5.8}$$

When the normal exponential time dependence is included, the exponential part of the solution represents a plane wave of wavelength $\lambda = 2\pi/k$ which is travelling in the positive or negative x-direction, depending on the sign of k. The factor $U_k(x)$, called a Bloch function, is a periodic function which varies with the same periodicity as that of the lattice, a. Thus the solution to Schrödinger's equation consists of travelling waves which are modulated periodically in space.

86

When the usual boundary conditions of continuity of Ψ and $\partial\Psi/\partial x$ are applied it is found that eq. (5.8) is only a solution for particular values of electron energy, E, which satisfy the equation:

$$\left(\frac{maw V_0}{\hbar^2}\right)\frac{\sin(\beta a)}{\beta a} + \cos(\beta a) = \cos ka \qquad (5.9)$$

where β is as defined in eq. (5.6). Notice that the left-hand side is a function of the electron energy and the strength of the potential barriers, whereas the right-hand side consists of a wavelength term.

It will be noticed that whereas the $\cos ka$ term lies in the range between -1 and $+1$, there is no such limitation on the left-hand side of the equation, which can assume values outside this range, depending on the value of $w V_0$; this is illustrated graphically in Fig. 5.9(a). Whenever the left-hand side is greater than 1 or less than -1, no travelling-wave solution of the type described by eq. (5.8) exists for that particular value of electron energy, E. Such values of E lie in the forbidden bands.

The relationship between E and the wave number, k, for the travelling-wave solution in allowed bands can be derived from eq. (5.9) if a particular value of $w V_0$ is assumed and is typically as shown in Fig. (5.9). The resulting band structure of allowed electron energy bands separated by forbidden energy gaps is also included in the diagram.

It will be noticed from eq. (5.9) and Fig. 5.9(a) that if the barrier strength is increased, i.e., $w V_0$ is made larger, the allowed bands become much narrower and the forbidden bands are correspondingly widened. At the other extreme, as $w V_0$ is reduced to zero, eq. (5.9) reduces to $\beta = k$ and hence from eq. (5.6)

$$\beta = k = \frac{2\pi}{\lambda} = \frac{\sqrt{2mE}}{\hbar}$$

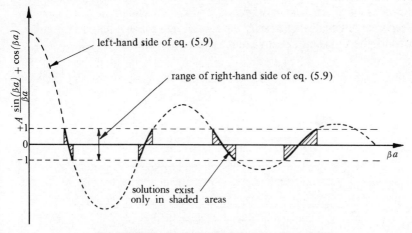

Fig. 5.9 (a) Range of possible solutions of eq. (5.9)

87

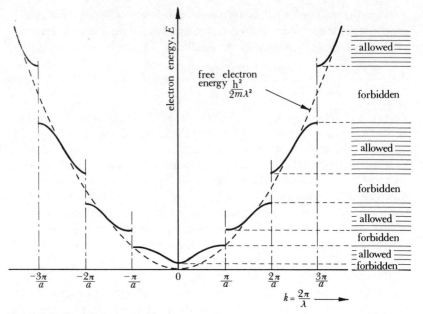

Fig. 5.9 (b) Electronic energy as a function of wavelength and the energy-band structure of a hypothetical solid.

or

$$E = \frac{h^2}{2m\lambda^2} \tag{5.10}$$

This energy expression is identical to that for the free electron, eq. (4.11); the result is not surprising, since as wV_0 becomes zero the potential barriers are removed and electrons can move freely inside the solid.

Let us now try to gain some physical insight into the striking behaviour shown in the $E - k$ diagram whenever $k = n\pi/a$, by employing the following electric circuit analogy. Consider the coaxial transmission line shown in Fig. 5.10(a); the voltage, V, at any point x on the line is given by

$$\frac{d^2 V}{dx^2} + \omega^2 \mu_0 \epsilon_r \epsilon_0 V = 0 \tag{5.11}$$

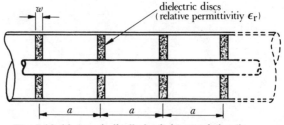

Fig. 5.10 (a) A periodically loaded transmission line.

If the line is air-filled but periodically loaded at intervals of a with dielectric discs of relative permittivity ϵ_r and thickness w, as shown, then the voltage equation becomes similar in form to eq. (5.6) and (5.7), provided $\omega^2 \mu_0 \epsilon_0 \equiv \beta^2$ and $\omega^2 \mu_0 \epsilon_r \epsilon_0 \equiv -\alpha^2$. Hence, in the circuit analogy, voltage V is equivalent to electron energy E and frequency bands are analogous to electron energy bands. The ω–k diagram for the loaded line can be obtained by solving eq. (5.11) using the appropriate boundary conditions and results in series of pass bands of frequency and stop bands which occur when $ka = \pi, 2\pi, 3\pi, n\pi$, as shown in Fig. 5.10(b). The stop bands arise because when $ka = n\pi$ the discs are

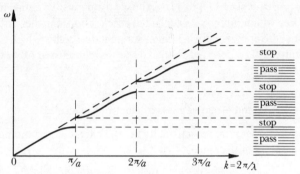

Fig. 5.10 (b) ω–k diagram of the loaded line.

are spaced an integral number of half-wavelengths apart and reflections from successive discs add in phase as shown diagrammatically in Fig. 5.10(c). Then, even if individual reflections are weak, their combined effect is to produce

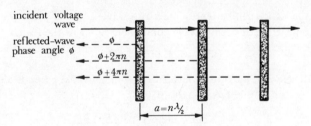

Fig. 5.10 (c) Total reflection occurring when $ka = n\pi$.

total reflection; hence, for this condition, no travelling-wave solution exists for the voltage and only standing-wave solutions are possible.

The situation in the stop bands is analogous to what occurs at the forbidden energy levels in a solid; at some critical wavelength (or k-value) the partial reflections of travelling electron waves from successive potential barriers add constructively to produce a reflected wave of the same amplitude as the incident wave and only a standing-wave solution occurs. This may be confirmed by putting $k = \pm n\pi/a$ into eq. (5.8); then, since $U_k(x)$ is periodic with periodicity a, ψ is also periodic, which suggests that ψ has a standing wave-form around these particular k-values.

We have seen it is impossible for an electron to possess energy corresponding to that in a forbidden band. However, an interesting consequence of the analysis is that, within the allowed energy bands, travelling-wave solutions exist which are unattenuated, since $\alpha = 0$; this implies there is no electron scattering in the uniform lattice of a perfect crystal and within an allowed band an electron can move in a completely unrestricted manner. This statement has to be reconciled with the fact that in a practical solid we have seen that, as a consequence of Ohm's law, the electron must be subjected to a viscous force which inhibits its continual acceleration. Further discussion of the essential differences between ideal and practical solids which can resolve this difficulty will be deferred until after we have discussed other consequences of the $E–k$ diagram.

5.3 The velocity and effective mass of electrons in a solid

Let us first consider a free electron; its kinetic energy E and momentum p are related parabolically since

$$p = mv \quad \text{and} \quad E = p^2/2m \tag{5.12}$$

which is identical to eq. 5.10.

However, electrons in a solid are not free; they move under the combined influence of an external field plus that of a periodic potential due to atom cores in the lattice. As a result the electron energy is no longer continuous and the energy–momentum relationship, since $p = \hbar k$, will be similar in shape to that shown in Fig. 5.9(b), as depicted in Fig. 5.11(a). Now, an electron moving through the lattice can be represented by a wavepacket of plane waves grouped around some value of k, each wave component being of the form

$$e^{-j(Et/\hbar \ -kx)}$$

The group velocity, v_g, of the wavepacket, which we have seen is identical to the electron velocity is, from eq. (1.30):

$$v_g = \frac{\partial \omega}{\partial k} = \frac{\partial(E/\hbar)}{\partial k} = \frac{1}{\hbar}\frac{\partial E}{\partial k} = \frac{\partial E}{\partial p} \tag{5.13}$$

Thus, the velocity of an electron which is represented by a packet of waves centred near to a particular value of $k = k_0$, say, is proportional to the slope of the $E–p$ or the $E–k$ curve evaluated at k_0. The slope of the $E–p$ curve in Fig. 5.11(a) is shown in Fig. 5.11(b) and gives the relative electron velocity over the lowest energy band. Notice that the electron velocity falls to zero at each band edge; this is in keeping with our finding that electronic wave functions become standing waves at the top and botton of a band, i.e., $v_g = 0$ there. It is evident that because of interaction with the lattice the

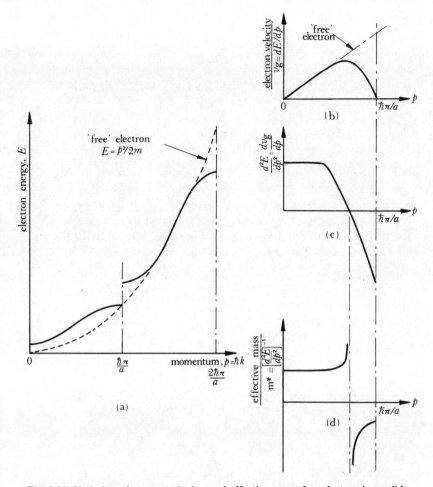

Fig. 5.11 Variation of energy, velocity, and effective mass of an electron in a solid.

momentum of an electron in a solid is no longer simply related to either its energy or its velocity and the classical eq. (5.12) is no longer applicable.

Now, consider an electronic wavepacket moving in a crystal lattice under the influence of an externally applied uniform electric field. If the electron has an instantaneous velocity, v_g, and moves a distance δx in the direction of an accelerating force, F, in time δt, it acquires energy, δE, where

$$\delta E = F\delta x = Fv_g\delta t$$

$$= \frac{F}{\hbar}\frac{\delta E}{\delta k}\cdot \delta t$$

91

which, in the limit of small increments in k, can be rearranged to give

$$\frac{dk}{dt} = \frac{F}{\hbar}$$

(5.14)

Digressing for a moment we see that for a classically free electron this equation reduces to Newton's second law:

$$F = \frac{d}{dt}(\hbar k) = \frac{dp}{dt} = m\frac{dv}{dt}$$

(5.15)

But this is not the case for the electron in a solid. This is not to say that Newton's laws no longer hold but is a consequence of the fact that the externally applied force is not the only force acting on the electrons; as we have seen, forces associated with the periodic lattice potential are also present. The acceleration of an electronic wavepacket in a solid is equal to the time rate of charge of its velocity, thus:

$$\text{acceleration} = \frac{dv_g}{dt} = \frac{d}{dt}\left(\frac{dE}{dp}\right) = \frac{d^2 E}{dt\, dp}$$

or, using eq. (5.14)

$$\frac{dv_g}{dt} = \frac{dp}{dt} \cdot \frac{d^2 E}{dp^2} = F\frac{d^2 E}{dp^2}$$

which can be rearranged to give:

$$F = \left(\frac{d^2 E}{dp^2}\right)^{-1} \cdot \frac{dv_g}{dt}$$

(5.16)

Comparing this equation with the classical equation of motion for a particle, eq. (5.15), we see that the quantity $(d^2 E/dp^2)^{-1}$ is equivalent to the mass of the free electron. Thus if, for an electron moving in the periodic lattice of a solid, we define an *effective mass, m**, where

$$m^* = \left(\frac{d^2 E}{dp^2}\right)^{-1} = \hbar^2\left(\frac{d^2 E}{dk^2}\right)^{-1}$$

(5.17)

then

$$F = m^* dv_g/dt$$

(5.18)

By this means it is possible to treat electrons in a solid in a semi-classical manner since quantum-mechanical interactions are included in the equivalent mass term; an electron mass, m, when placed in a crystal lattice responds to applied fields as if it were of mass m^*, interaction with the lattice being responsible for the difference between m and m^*. That it is possible using the device of an equivalent mass to treat an electron in a solid as a classical

particle should not be allowed to mask the fact that the electron lattice interaction is essentially quantum-mechanical. This is emphasized by the fact that m^*
can vary over a range from a few per cent of m to much greater than m, which
cannot be explained by classical arguments. A further point is that m^* is not
a constant but is a function of energy. We can see how it varies typically
over an energy band by noting the definition implicit in eq. (5.17) and
forming the reciprocal of the second derivation of energy with respect to
momentum; these steps are shown graphically in Figs. 5.11(c) and (d). It will
be seen that m^* can vary appreciably with position in the band; at the
minimum-energy edges of the band electrons have positive effective mass but
at the top end of a band their effective mass can, surprisingly, become
negative!

The changing sign of the effective mass of an electron can be explained
physically, as follows. Suppose an electron is situated at a point a on the
E-p diagram of Fig. 5.12. If an electric field, $\mathscr{E}$, is impressed in the direction

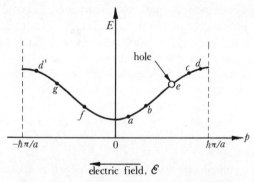

electric field, $\mathscr{E}$

Fig. 5.12 E–p diagram of a hypothetical solid.

shown the electron will accelerate and moves to the right on the diagram to
some point b where both its energy and its velocity have increased; this conventional behaviour corresponds to a positive effective mass. Now, consider
an electron at the upper end of a band, at c say. When the field is applied again
the electron moves to d where its energy is increased but its velocity has
decreased (see for example Fig. 5.11(b)). The electron appears to have been
decelerated by the previously accelerating force and since eq. (5.18) applies
always this can be accounted for by the electron having a negative effective
mass. It will be apparent from Fig. 5.11 that negative effective masses occur
whenever the E–p curve is concave downwards and that the electron mass is
positive whenever the curve is concave upwards. Now, the direction of
acceleration of an electron is determined by the sign of both its effective
mass and its charge, so an alternative way of accounting for the properties of
an electron with negative mass is to consider it as a particle with positive
mass but having a *positive* charge e (since acceleration $= -e\mathscr{E}/-m^* = +e\mathscr{E}/+m^*$).

Thus, when electrons at the top of a band are acted on by an applied field the resulting currents correspond to the movement of electrons with a positive charge $+e$ and a positive effective mass m^*.

In most materials, at least one band is only partly filled. For example, we have seen that in a metal conduction electrons occupy all levels up to around the Fermi energy, E_F. If, as is often the case with other materials, a band is almost entirely filled, it is often convenient to discuss its properties in terms of the relatively few unfilled states rather than those occupied by the many remaining electrons. An unfilled energy state providing a vacancy which can be occupied by an electron wavepacket is called a *hole*. Consider the hole shown diagrammatically in Fig. 5.12 at e. Because of the symmetry of the E–p diagram an electron with positive momentum, say at b, will be cancelled by another electron, in this case at f, with the same magnitude of momentum but oppositely direct. This cancellation of momentum by pairs applies to all electrons except the one at g, which is at the corresponding energy level to the hole; this electron has a negative velocity, v_g, (from eq. (5.13)), and so the hole at e must have a corresponding positive velocity, which can be accounted for by attributing a positive charge to the hole. Hence an electron moving in one direction results in a current flow which is equivalent to a hole or vacancy moving in the opposite direction. In general, the effective mass of a hole is again dependent on its location in the band and the sign of the mass can be found by arguments similar to those used previously. However, since holes are often located at the top of a band, if they are designated a positive charge and moreover move in the opposite direction to electrons, in this case they are accelerated in the same direction as the field, and they must usually possess a positive effective mass.

We see that conduction in a nearly filled band can be accounted for by considering the motion of a small number of positive particles of charge $+e$, possessing positive effective mass, m_h^*, which are called holes and correspond to the number of unoccupied electron states in the band. This concept is vital to an understanding of the details of conduction processes in semiconductors, which will be discussed later.

5.4 Conductors, semiconductors, and insulators

The band structure of a solid is a convenient method of classifying its conduction properties. Of course, electrical engineering materials can readily be characterized experimentally by means of their conductivities but the band theory explains the essential differences between materials with widely differing conductivities.

The conduction process in any material is dependent on the availability of charge carriers. Clearly, if a given energy band is unoccupied it can make no contribution to electronic conduction. What is not quite so obvious is the fact that there can be no net conduction effects if all the bands are completely full either. Consider, for example, a completely full band with E–p diagram as in Fig. 5.12 (disregarding the hole now). We have seen that because of symmetry of the graph there can be no net electron momentum when no external field is applied; obviously, no current flows when the field is zero. When the field, $\mathscr{E}$, is applied, electrons at a or b, say, are accelerated by the field and their momentum is increased. However, an electron at d, say, can have its momentum so increased that it reaches the boundary of the band edge, is reflected and reappears at d' with oppositely directed momentum. Thus, since all levels remain filled before and after the application of field, and since the distribution of electron momenta is unaltered, there is still no net flow of current.

In order for conduction to occur there must be empty available states in a particular band. Then, when an electric field is applied as shown in Fig. 5.13

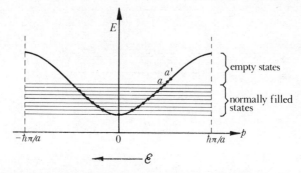

Fig. 5.13 Partially filled energy band with an applied field.

electrons at levels just below the empty ones can gain energy from the field and move into the available levels, for example from a to a' and all other electrons move to the right in momentum space as shown. This results in a net electron momentum in the opposite direction to the field which is no longer zero and an electron current flows.

In a good conductor, the essential requirement of many carriers being available in a partially filled energy band is achieved by the two outermost bands, one of which is completely empty and one full, overlapping; this situation is demonstrated diagrammatically in Fig. 5.7, where the section at (iii) represents the band structure of a metal. It is conventional to draw the band structure of a particular material with fixed lattice constant as shown in Fig. 5.14. While the extremities of each band are, in fact, dependent on crystal orientation, usually the maximum and minimum possible values for the band edges, regardless of direction, are chosen. A further point is that the abscissa on such diagrams have no significance. It is only usually necessary to show the outermost *filled* band and the next highest empty band, since lower bands are usually completely occupied and play no part in the conduction process. The band diagram of a metal is as shown in Fig. 5.14(a), then. All levels are filled

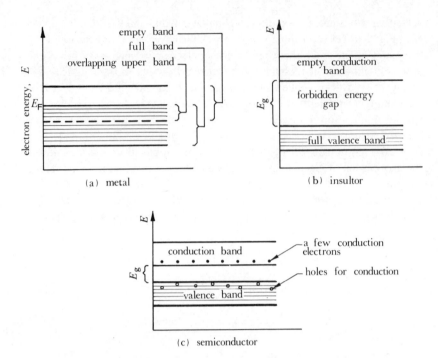

Fig. 5.14 Typical band structure of metals, insulators, and semiconductors.

in the band up to some level approaching E_F, above which are many empty states. Only electrons near the Fermi brim participate in conduction and they behave as if they had an effective mass, m^*, evaluated at $E = E_F$. Since E is not located near a band edge, m^* is nearly equal to m, as shown in Fig. 5.9(b); this accounts for the success of the free-electron model of a conductor.

At the other conductivity extreme, insulators are characterized by a band structure consisting of a completely full band, the *valence* band, separated from an empty band, the *conduction* band, by a wide forbidden energy gap of several eV, as shown in Fig. 5.14(b). At all ordinary temperatures, the statistical probability of electrons from the full band gaining sufficient energy to surmount the energy gap and becoming available for conduction in the conduction band is slight. This very limited number of free conduction electrons at all but very elevated temperatures accounts for the high resistivity of insulators.

Semiconductors, as their name suggests, have conduction properties which are intermediate between those of metals and insulators. They have a band structure as shown in Fig. 5.14(c) which is basically similar to that of insulators, except that the gap energies are very much smaller, being typically of order 1 eV. Since the gap is appreciably smaller than for insulators, it is statistically more probable at ordinary temperatures for electrons in the otherwise full valence band to be elevated across the forbidden gap to the empty

96

conduction band where they are available for conduction. An essential difference between conduction in metals and conduction in semiconductors is that when electrons in a semiconductor gain sufficient energy to occupy the conduction band they automatically create vacancies in the valence band due to their absence. Thus, additional current flow is possible due to charge motion in the now partially empty valence band; such currents can be described in terms of the motion of holes as discussed in the previous section. The relatively low conductivities of semiconductors, compared with metals is, of course, a consequence of the relatively small number of charge carriers, both electrons and holes, available for conduction.

5.5 Electrical resistance of solids

We have seen that for a perfect solid there is no attenuation of electrons in an allowed energy band; i.e., there are no electron 'collisions' and the solid is transparent to the electron; in this situation the mean free path for collisions is infinite. In the previous discussion of electrical conduction in metals it was found necessary to postulate some sort of collision mechanism to provide a frictional force to account for the terminal drift velocity of electrons which ensures that Ohm's law is obeyed. Since conduction processes in other solids are similar, with the added complication of hole conduction in some materials, it is again clearly necessary for some kind of collisional damping to be present. An electron in an allowed band can then gain energy from an applied field and move higher in the band, but then can suffer a collision (more usually it is said to be *scattered*), give up its energy in the form of Joule heating of the lattice, and return to lower down in the energy band. The conductivity of the solid can again be expressed using equations similar to (4.35), except that since the carriers are no longer necessarily free, their effective mass must be included to account for interaction of carrier and lattice.

But what are electrons colliding with? What are they scattered by? It was shown in section 4.7 that electrons colliding with ion cores cannot account for the electrical resistance of a solid. It is the interaction of electrons with the slightly aperiodic potential fields experienced in real solids which can cause scattering effects and hence account for electrical resistance effects. Such deviations from the perfect periodicity in potential, which was assumed for an ideal solid, can be due to thermal latice vibrations, lattice defects, or the presence of impurity atoms and boundaries, some or all of which are normally present in practical materials.

The most important scattering process at ordinary temperatures can occur in crystals where impurity atom or structural imperfections are negligible. The departure from periodicity necessary to produce scattering is in this case brought about by thermal vibration of the lattice atoms about their equilibrium

97

position. Such a displacement alters the local potential, hence its regular periodicity, and an electron travelling in this field can have both the magnitude and direction of its momentum altered. Such an event constitutes what we have thought of as a collision and is often called *lattice scattering*. The description is something of a misnomer since it is not the lattice that produces the scattering so much as its thermally induced vibrations. Scattering interactions between carriers and lattice vibrations become more probable the higher the temperature because of the larger amplitude of vibrations. Thus, we see qualitatively that the average time between collisions, or relaxation time, τ_r and hence the carrier mobility decreases with increasing temperature in materials in which lattice scattering is the dominant mechanism, such as relatively pure or structurally perfect crystals.

A further scattering mechanism is attributable to the presence of impurity atoms in the lattice, which may be ionized or otherwise, although the former are more important. Such atoms alter the local electrostatic potential and create the necessary aperiodicity in the field to cause *impurity scattering* of the electrons. The effectiveness of the deflection of an electron by an ionized impurity is greater the lower the velocity of the electron; hence impurity scattering tends to dominate in purer crystals at lower temperatures when thermal scattering is weak, as well as being important when the impurity concentration is high.

Other possible scattering mechanisms are due to vacancies, dislocations, and other lattice imperfections. It is also conceivable that conduction electrons could be scattered by holes and vice versa but the probability that these processes occur is slight.

Now let us try to estimate more quantitatively the effects that departures from periodicity have on the resistivity of a real solid. Again, it is convenient to revert to the dielectric disc-loaded coaxial line model of a solid discussed in section 5.22. For a uniform disc spacing, a, we saw that there was no attenuation in the line, i.e., all reflected waves cancel, unless $ka = n\pi$. If we now assume a small deviation from periodicity δ, such that $\delta \ll a$, it can be shown that the reflection coefficient will be proportional to δ and the back-scattered power to $\overline{\delta^2}$. Thus the fraction of power reflected, dP, in a length of line dx is given by

$$\frac{dP}{P} = K\overline{\delta^2}\, dx$$

where K is some constant. Integrating we have:

$$P(x) = P_0 e^{-K\overline{\delta^2}x} \tag{5.19}$$

where P_0 is the power at $x = 0$.

Applying this result to the analogous case of electron waves travelling in the periodic potential of a solid, then if the mean square departure from periodicity in potential is $\overline{\delta^2}$, it follows by comparison with eq. (5.19) that

$$\psi^2 = \psi_0^2\, e^{-K\overline{\delta^2}x} \tag{5.20}$$

In other words, electrons are scattered by the aperiodic potential and the probable electron density falls off with distance as $\exp\left(-K\overline{\delta^2}x\right)$. Notice that if $\overline{\delta^2} = 0$ there is no scattering. When δ is finite, however, the electron density falls to $1/e$ of its initial value in a mean free path, $\overline{l}$, and so

$$\overline{l} \propto 1/(K\overline{\delta^2}) \tag{5.21}$$

Since the principal scattering mechanism is due to thermal vibrations we shall consider the consequences of eq. (5.21) applied to this case. Ion cores in a realistic solid have a natural frequency of vibration about their equilibrium position; also, as one is displaced the position of its neighbour is affected and acoustic waves propagate. A simple mechanical analogy is that of a linear chain of masses, M, joined by springs of stiffness C. Each simple oscillator has kinetic energy $Mx^2/2$ and potential energy $Cx^2/2$. Now, the equipartition of energy condition requires that the *mean* energy in each energy state at any particular temperature, T, is $kT/2$. Hence

$$\frac{C\overline{x^2}}{2} = \frac{kT}{2} \tag{5.22}$$

and the mean square deviation from the equilibrium is proportional to T. Thus, for a practical solid:

$$\overline{\delta^2} \propto T$$

and from eq. (5.21)

$$\overline{l} \propto T^{-1}$$

It follows from (4.37) that the conductivity, σ, is proportional to $\overline{l}$ and hence

$$\sigma \propto T^{-1}$$

or the resistivity, ρ, is proportional to temperature. This result is in accordance with practice where

$$\rho = \rho_0[1 + \alpha_T\, T] \tag{5.23}$$

where α_T is the temperature coefficient of resistance. The residual resistivity term in the expression is due to lattice defects which are present even at very low temperatures. Such defects are particularly large in disordered alloys such as nichrome and their effect is to tend to swamp the increase in ρ due to lattice vibrations. Hence such alloys are useful where high resistance combined with a low temperature coefficient of resistance are required.

Now, the energy of the acoustic wave due to thermal vibrations of the lattice is quantized and can only change in units of hf. The quantum of acoustic energy is called a *phonon* (cf. photon of electromagnetic energy).

99

Hence, at very low temperatures, eq. (5.22) is no longer valid since kT becomes comparable to hf and a phonon description of the interaction must be used. This can account for the departure from linearity of the ρ-T curve of a practical solid at very low temperatures.

Although a phonon is actually an acoustic wave propagating through a solid, it is often convenient to think of the associated quantum of energy, the phonon, as a particle in the solid capable of interacting with other particles. Thus, the mechanism we have discussed can be considered as the collision between electrons and phonons and is indeed sometimes referred to as *electron-phonon collisional scattering.*

It is now evident that the classical collisions which have been postulated to account for resistive effects are realized in a solid by the interaction of electron waves with other waves due to lattice vibrations.

Problems

1   The E–k diagram for an energy band in a particular material is as shown.

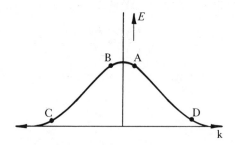

If an electric field is applied to the material in the negative k direction (force in the positive direction) find (a) the polarity of the effective masses of the four wavepackets made up of groups of states near A, B, C and D, (b) the direction of the velocity of each of the four wavepackets and (c) the direction of the acceleration of each. What are the physical consequences of these results?

    Ans. (a) −, −, +, + (b) −, +, +, − (c) −, −, +, +.

2   The conductivity of a metal having n free electrons per unit volume is given by equation (4.37) and the Fermi energy by equation (4.22). Consider a metal with a simple cubic lattice structure of side 0·2 nm and one free conduction electron per atom. Assuming that the mean free path for electron collisions with the lattice is 100 lattice constants, find the relaxation time for an electron with the Fermi energy.

    Ans. 2·2 x 10^{-14} s.

6. Semiconductors

6.1 Introduction

We have seen, in chapter 5, that the electrical properties of a solid are
characterized by its band structure. In particular, a semiconductor has two
bands of interest (neglecting the bound electrons, since these play no part in
any conduction process); these are the valence band and the conduction band,
which are separated by a forbidden energy gap, E_g, as depicted in Fig. 6.1. At

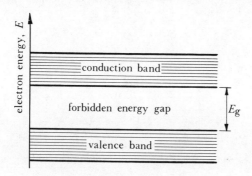

Fig. 6.1 Band structure of a semiconductor.

0 K the valence band is completely full and the conduction band is empty;
the semiconductor behaves as an insulator.

It is the possibility at higher temperatures of electrons being transferred
across the energy gap into the conduction band, leaving vacant levels in the
valence band, which gives the semiconductor its particular conducting properties. In the following section, we shall discuss the properties of semiconducting crystals which give rise to their distinguishing band composition.

6.2 The crystal structure of semiconductors

When atoms, similar or dissimilar, are brought together in close proximity to
each other, they may link together to form a stable solid; *bonds* exist between
adjacent atoms. There are several mechanisms for bonding but we shall only
concern ourselves with those pertinent to semiconductors. It has been shown

that there is a tendency for an atom to form closed outer shells. In order to satisfy this requirement, atoms in solids tend to lose or gain valence electrons, or share them with other neighbouring atoms. It is the manner in which the valence electrons are shared or interchanged which determines the nature of the bond between atoms.

In a semiconducting material the tendency for each atom to form closed outer shells is satisfied by means of a covalent bond; adjacent atoms share electrons which are located predominantly in the region between the atoms. As a simple example of the mechanism of this type of bonding let us first consider the hydrogen molecule. This is synthesized from two hydrogen atoms, each of which has a single electron in its vicinity. Both constituent atoms have unfilled shells, since there is a vacancy for one additional electron. As the two atoms are brought into close proximity, the orbitals of each unpaired electron overlap. Provided the electrons have opposite spins, they move together to form an electron pair bond. Electrons with identical spins cannot form bonds since this would violate the Pauli exclusion principle. The two electrons lie predominantly between and are shared by the atoms, in this way completing the outer shell of each, as shown in Fig. 6.2. The term *covalent*

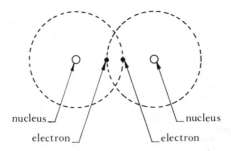

Fig. 6.2 Covalent bonding of a hydrogen molecule.

is used to describe this particular type of electron pair bond because neighbouring atoms share valence electrons to complete the bond.

The covalent bonding which takes place in semiconductors and which is typified in the hydrogen molecule can be derived in a more rigorous and quantitative manner by means of quantum mechanics. Such a theory is a little beyond our scope but its elements can be mentioned briefly. Because the hydrogen molecule is symmetrical, each electron has an identical wave function, which can be either symmetric or antisymmetric, as discussed in chapter 5. When Schrödinger's equation is solved for the case of electrons having opposite spins, the resulting symmetric wave functions of both electrons can be evaluated. They predict a relatively high value of $|\psi|^2$ midway between the nuclei; there is high probability that the binding electrons are located in this region and a charge density exists there.

The elements which form the basic materials used in semiconducting devices all form covalent bonds. Such covalent crystals are characterized by their hardness and brittleness. They are brittle because adjacent atoms must remain in accurate alignment, since the bond is strongly directional and is formed along a line joining the atoms. The hardness is a consequence of the great strength of the paired electron bonding.

The most important elemental semiconducting elements all appear in Group IV of the periodic table, as shown in Fig. 6.3. Silicon and germanium

Valency group	IIIA	IVA	VA	VIA	VIIA
	B 5 2p Boron	C 6 $2p^2$ Carbon			
	Al 13 3p Aluminium	Si 14 $3p^2$ Silicon	P 15 $3p^3$ Phosphorus	S 16 $3p^4$ Sulphur	
	Ga 31 4p Gallium	Ge 32 $4p^2$ Germanium	As 33 $4p^3$ Arsenic	Se 34 $4p^4$ Selenium	
	In 49 5p Indium	Sn 50 $5p^2$ Tin	Sb 51 $5p^3$ Antimony	Te 52 $5p^5$ Tellurium	I 53 $5p^5$ Iodine
			Bi 83 $6p^3$ Bismuth		

Key:

Chemical symbol		Atomic number
	Number of	
(Outer	electrons in	
subshell)	subshell	
Name of the element		

Fig. 6.3 Part of the periodic table of elements showing those elements of principal interest for application to semiconductor devices.

are of principal interest; the other elements only have semiconducting properties in unusual conditions. Elements in adjacent columns, such as boron, phosphorus, arsenic, antimony, bismuth, sulphur, selenium, tellurium, and iodine, also can possess some semiconducting properties to a greater or lesser degree. However, we will initially concern ourselves only with Group IV elements, C, Si, and Ge, since these materials have the most useful electrical properties. Their unifying characteristic is that they each have only four electrons in their outer s- and p-shells, while there are four vacancies in the

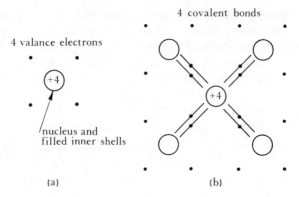

Fig. 6.4 Two-dimensional representation of (a) a tetravalent atom and (b) a crystalline solid formed from such atoms.

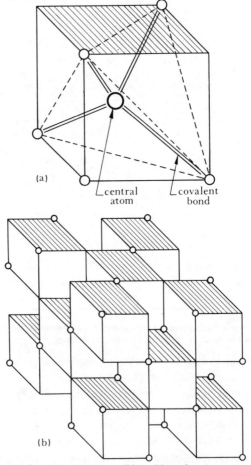

Fig. 6.5 (a) A unit cell of a tetravalent atom, (b) packing of such atoms to form a crystal with a diamond structure.

outer subshell, facts which can be ascertained from the periodic table, Table 2.1. Such elements are said to be *tetravalent*; we would expect them to have similar bonding mechanisms and chemical properties. Each constituent atom can be represented schematically by the simple model depicted in Fig. 6.4(a).

Because there is a tendency for the atoms to complete outer shells in the solid state, these materials crystallize into what is known as the *diamond structure*. Since each atom of the solid has four vacancies in its outer shell, covalent bonds exist between the atom and its four nearest neighbours; it shares one of its valence electrons with each of the four neighbours, thus effectively filling its outer shell. This situation is illustrated schematically in Fig. 6.4(b). In order that the four surrounding atoms shown in Fig. 6.4(b) may each in turn have four neighbouring adjacent atoms, the three-dimensional lattice is built up from a basic building block consisting of an atom surrounded by four others which occupy the corners of a rectangular tetrahedron, as shown in Fig. 6.5(a). In this diagram the tetrahedron is enclosed in an imaginary unit cube so that the packing of such unit cells in the crystalline solid can be illustrated a little more clearly. The diamond-structure crystal is built up from many such primitive cells in the manner shown in Fig. 6.5(b).

The three-dimensional model of the crystal structure is too cumbersome for most of our discussions; it may be replaced by the two-dimensional representation, shown in Fig. 6.6(a). Although the model is oversimplified and overemphasizes the role of the covalent bonding, it will be adequate for most purposes.

In the next section, conduction processes in elemental semiconductors will be discussed in terms of the model and compared with the band-structure description of conduction.

A further important group of semiconductors are the compounds formed from two elements, one in Group III of the periodic table and one in Group V, the so-called intermetallic III–V compounds. The most common examples of these compounds are gallium arsenide and indium antimonide. Since one constituent atom has a vacancy of three and the other five, the bonding in this solid is covalent in character, eight electrons being shared by two neighbouring atoms. Each atom is again surrounded by a tetrahedral arrangement of the other atomic type; the crystal structure is thus similar to the diamond structure of Fig. 6.5, with alternate Group III and Group V atoms. Although preparation of the intermetallic compounds to produce single crystals of sufficiently high quality is more difficult than for elemental semiconductors, they offer additional technical advantages which make this worth while. For instance, the range of semiconducting compounds offers a much wider selection of possible energy gaps than is available with elemental semiconductors and there is a corresponding flexibility in the value of mobility by the choice of a particular III-V compound. We shall see later how both these parameters contribute to influence the electrical properties of a semiconductor.

105

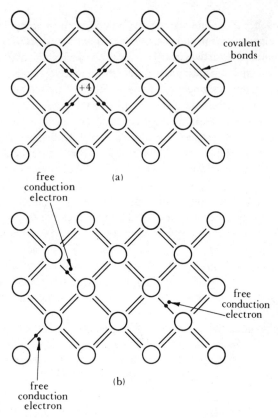

free
conduction
electron   (a)

covalent
bonds

free
conduction
electron

free   (b)
conduction
electron

**Fig. 6.6 A representation of a tetravalent semiconductor crystal (a) at low temperature
and (b) at room temperature.**

6.3 Conduction processes in semiconductors

We have seen that in the absence of thermal excitation or any external
stimulus the valence band of a semiconductor is filled to capacity and the
conduction band is completely empty. In terms of our crystal model, provided
the crystal is sufficiently cool and is shielded from, for example, extraneous
light sources, all valence electrons take part in covalent bonding and none
are free to move through the crystal. If conduction is to occur the valence
electrons as a consequence must move to higher energy levels, but this is
precluded at low temperatures since there are no available energy levels in the
valence band and the empty states in the conduction band can only be
reached if the valence electron is given energy in excess of the forbidden gap
energy, E_g. It is evident that the covalent bands can be broken since, for
example, it is possible to smash a diamond crystal, but this indicates that
energy is required to break the bond. The unifying feature of the band and
crystal representation of a semiconductor is that the minimum energy required
to break a covalent bond is equal to the gap energy, E_g.

106

The covalent bond can be ruptured in several ways, depending on the means whereby energy is imparted to the electrons in the bond. One way is to increase the temperature of the crystal above 0 K. Some of the energy of the resulting lattice vibrations is transferred to the valence electrons. Eventually, as the temperature is increased, sufficient energy is given to an electron in a bond to allow it to break free. This process can be pictured crudely as the shaking loose of electrons by thermal vibration of atoms of the crystal lattice. Fig. 6.6(b) illustrates this situation schematically.

A freed electron can move through the body of the material under the influence of applied fields until it encounters another broken bond, when it is drawn in to complete the bond, or *recombines*, and takes no further part in the conduction process. Thus, by increasing the temperature of a semiconductor above 0 K, its electrical characteristics are changed from those of an insulator to those of a conductor.

When a covalent bond is broken, releasing an electron, a net positive charge exists which is associated with the broken bond and which arises because of the loss of negative electronic charge from an originally neutral environment. This is the crystallographic manifestation of the hole, which was discussed in the previous chapter. It is possible for the positively charged vacancy, or hole, to move under the influence of an applied field, even though the atom whose bond was broken initially remains stationary. The sequence of events is illustrated in Fig. 6.7(a)-(d).

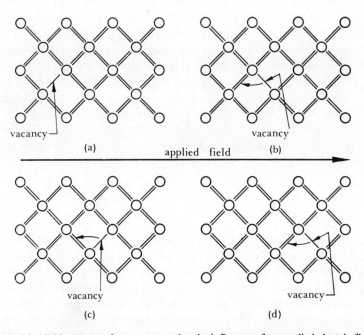

Fig. 6.7 (a)-(d) Movement of a vacancy under the influence of an applied electric field.

107

If the electron field is applied in the direction shown it is possible for one of the electrons in a neighbouring covalent bond to move to fill the vacancy, as in Fig. 6.6(b). This process is repeated in (c) and (d) and we see that motion of electrons in covalent bonds causes migration of the hole in the direction of the applied field. Thus, as we would expect from previous arguments the vacant site moves like a fictitious positively charged particle which has an effective mass, a charge of approximately the same magnitude as, but of opposite sign to, that of an electron, and all the characteristics of a real particle. The concept of a hole is valuable in that it is much simpler to discuss the motion of positive charged particles than that of bound electrons moving into vacancies.

Notice that for every bond broken one conduction electron is liberated and one hole created. The subsequent motion of the electron is independent of the hole motion and vice versa; both proceed until they recombine with particles of the opposite sign. It is the presence of two charge-carrier types in the semiconductor which causes the essential difference in conduction mechanism between semiconductors and metallic conductors. Because the conduction process described is inherently dependent on the structure of pure crystalline materials, such materials are called *intrinsic* semiconductors.

Attractive though the semiconductor model, typified by Figs. 6.6 and 6.7 is, both as a pedagogical device and as an easily visualized pictorial representation of the motion of charged carriers in semiconductors, it has serious limitations which should always be borne in mind. The limitations come about because of the uncertainties implicit in the uncertainty principle, discussed in chapter 1. Suppose, for instance, we estimate the mean thermal velocity of an electron in the semiconductor, v_{th}, by equating its mean kinetic energy, $\frac{1}{2}mv_{th}^2$ to $3kT/2$, by invoking the equipartition of energy law. At room temperature, this relation yields a mean thermal velocity of about 10^5 m/s. Now, for the sake of argument, let us assume that the instantaneous thermal velocity lies in the range of one half to one and one half the mean value. Thus the uncertainty in velocity, Δv, is 10^5 m/s. The corresponding uncertainty in momentum, Δp, is $m\Delta v$. The Heisenberg relationship then predicts that the uncertainty in particle location, Δx, is in this instance at least

$$\Delta x = \frac{h}{\Delta p} = \frac{6 \cdot 63 \cdot 10^{-34} \cdot 10^{10}}{9 \cdot 11 \cdot 10^{-31} \cdot 10^5} \approx 7 \text{nm}$$

Thus, even when the momentum of the electron is known only very approximately, the electron can still only be located to within a range of about 30 times the lattice constant, if this is assumed to be of the order of $0 \cdot 2$ nm. If the momentum is specified more accurately, then the uncertainty in location becomes even more pronounced. It is clear that the concept of an electron moving between adjacent bonds to effect hole movement can only be pictorial and has not real physical significance. Nevertheless, if the problem is treated in a

108

more rigorous quantum-mechanical way, as in chapter 5, the motion of a positively charged hole can in most instances correctly represent that of bound electrons.

A further point to emphasize is that whenever the dynamics of holes and electrons in solids is being considered in a classical way, the mass parameter to be used in their *effective mass, m_h^** or m_e^*, as discussed in chapter 5. We saw there that the effective mass of a particle in a solid is dependent on its position in a particular band, but often the mass can be considered constant in practice since electrons and holes are usually located near band edges. Further, the effective masses of holes and electrons in a particular solid are not usually identical.

6.4 Density of carriers in intrinsic semiconductors

Returning to the energy band representation of a semiconductor, we have seen that a broken covalent bond corresponds to an electron being raised in energy so as to occupy the conduction band, leaving a hole in the valence band, as shown in Fig. 6.8. Conduction, as well as being possible because of

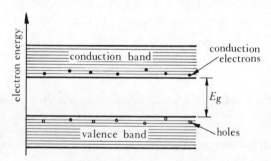

Fig. 6.8 Band structure of an intrinsic semiconductor, illustrating electron–hole pair generation.

electrons in the conduction band, can also occur as a result of the vacancies created in the valence band and both electrons and holes contribute to the overall conduction process as discussed in the previous chapter.

If the material is sufficiently pure, as is assumed for the intrinsic semiconductor, each broken bond generates an electron–hole pair and electrons and holes thus occur in equal numbers. Thus

$$n = p = n_i \tag{6.1}$$

where n is the number density of electrons, p the number density of holes, and n_i, the number density of charge carriers of either sign in an intrinsic semiconductor, is called the *intrinsic density*.

Whenever an electron–hole pair is created thermally, the state of excitation of the resulting particles is brief. For instance, the electron may undergo a transition which carries it to another energy state in the conduction band or it may revert to a vacant site in the valence band, i.e., it may *recombine* with a hole. Under thermal equilibrium conditions, the number of conduction electrons per unit volume, n, and the concentration of holes, p, is constant. How do these concentrations vary with the temperature? A simple argument is as follows:

At some particular absolute temperature, T, let the number of electrons in the conduction band be n and the number of holes in the valence band be p. Our initial simplifying assumptions are that the width of energy bands are small compared with the gap energy and that as a consequence all levels in each band can be considered as having the same energy. This situation is illustrated in Fig. 6.9, where we have, for convenience, taken an arbitrary

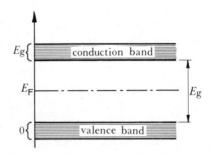

Fig. 6.9 Simplified band structure of an intrinsic semiconductor.

zero-energy reference level at the top of the valence band.

Now the number of electrons in the conduction band is

$$n = N . P(E_g)$$

where $P(E_g)$, the probability of an electron having energy E_g, is given by the Fermi–Dirac function, eq. (3.37), and N is the total number of electrons in both bands. Thus, in this case,

$$n = \frac{N}{1 + \exp\left[(E_g - E_F)/kT\right]} \tag{6.2}$$

where E_F is the Fermi level, as usual.

The probability of an electron being in the valence band with zero energy is again obtained from the Fermi–Dirac function. eq. (3.37), by putting $E = 0$, and the number of electrons in the valence band is thus

$$n_v = \frac{N}{1 + \exp\left[-E_F/kT\right]} \tag{6.3}$$

Now, the total number of electrons in the semiconductor, N, is the sum of those in the conduction band, n, and those in the valence band, n_v. Therefore, using (6.2) and (6.3),

$$N = \frac{N}{1 + \exp\left[(E_g - E_F)/kT\right]} + \frac{N}{1 + \exp\left[-E_F/kT\right]}$$

which can be simplified to give:

$$E_F = \frac{E_g}{2} \tag{6.4}$$

Thus, in the intrinsic semiconductor, the Fermi level lies midway between the conduction and valence bands. That this conclusion is physically plausible is best seen with the aid of Fig. 6.10. At 0 K all available energy levels are

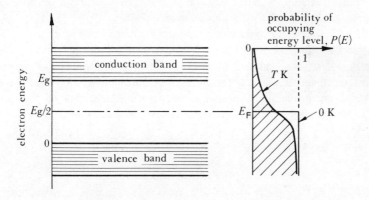

Fig. 6.10 Position of the Fermi level in an intrinsic semiconductor.

filled, up to E_F, and since energies in the forbidden gap are excluded, this indicates that the valence band is completely filled and the conduction band is empty, as we would expect. This fact only locates the Fermi level *somewhere* in the forbidden gap but it is the symmetry of the distribution function about E_F that ensures that E_F is located midway between the valence and conduction bands. Thus, if E_F is in the position shown in Fig. 6.10, the probability that an electron occupies an energy level in the conduction band, at energy $E_g/2$ above the Fermi level, is identical with the probability that an electron *does not* occupy a level in the valence band, at $E_g/2$ below the Fermi level, which is equal to the probability of there being a hole in the valence band. This is in accordance with the physical arguments that the number of electrons in the conduction band equals the number of holes in the valence band.

111

The number of conduction electrons at any given temperature, T, which also equals the number of holes in the intrinsic material, is given by eq. (6.2), which, using (6.4), becomes:

$$n = \frac{N}{1 + \exp[E_g/2kT]} \tag{6.5}$$

Now, typically, the gap energy in a semiconductor varies from a fraction of an electronvolt to several electronvolts. Thus, at room temperature, when kT is of order 0.025 eV, $E_g \gg kT$ and the exponential part of the denominator of (6.5) dominates. Then

$$n \approx Ne^{-E_g/2kT} \tag{6.6}$$

Thus, the number of conduction electrons, and hence the number of holes, in an intrinsic semiconductor decreases exponentially with increasing gap energy, which accounts for the lack of charge carriers in insulators with large gap energies. It will also be noted that the number of available charge carriers increases exponentially with increasing temperature.

The foregoing treatment is only very approximate since we have seen that all states in either the conduction or valence bands do not possess the same energy, as has been assumed. A more rigorous analysis must include additional terms which account for the density of available energy states in either band, as well as the probability function, as was discussed in chapter 4.

The number of conduction band electrons then becomes:

$$n = \int_{\substack{\text{conduction} \\ \text{band}}} S(E)P(E)\,dE \tag{6.7}$$

where $S(E)$ is the density of available states in the energy range between E and $E + dE$, and $P(E)$ is the probability that an electron can occupy a state of energy E.

We saw in chapter 4 that the density of a state function for free electrons in a metal is given by

$$S(E) = \frac{8\pi m^{\frac{3}{2}} \sqrt{2}}{h^3} E^{\frac{1}{2}} \text{ per unit volume} \tag{6.8}$$

Now, electrons in the conduction band are not free, but expression (6.8) can be used to describe the density of state of electrons in the periodic potential of the crystal lattice if we replace m by an effective mass m_e^*, as we have already discussed. At the same time, we shall again arbitrarily choose the origin of the energy axis to be at the top of the valence band. Under these conditions the density of state term becomes:

$$S(E) = \frac{8\pi(m_e^*)^{\frac{3}{2}} \sqrt{2}}{h^3} \cdot (E - E_g)^{\frac{1}{2}} = C(E - E_g)^{\frac{1}{2}} \tag{6.9}$$

112

where C for the moment is taken as constant.

The number density of conduction electrons using eqs. (6.7) and (6.9) is then given by

$$n = C \int_{E_g}^{\infty} \frac{(E - E_g)^{\frac{1}{2}} \, dE}{1 + \exp\left[(E - E_F)/kT\right]} \tag{6.10}$$

Notice that we have assumed that the upper limit in the integration becomes infinity so as to introduce some mathematical simplification. It does not significantly increase the value of the definite integral because of the very rapid increase of the exponential term in the Fermi factor with increasing energy, which makes contributions from the top of the conduction band relatively unimportant. We can simplify (6.10) by again ignoring 1 in the denominator in comparison with the exponential term, since, as we have seen in our approximate treatment, energies in the conduction band are many times kT above the Fermi level. Thus

$$n \simeq C \int_{E_g}^{\infty} (E - E_g)^{\frac{1}{2}} \exp\left[-(E - E_F)/kT\right] dE \tag{6.11}$$

This equation is best solved by making the substitution

$$x = (E - E_g)/kT$$

and evaluating the resulting definite integral using tables of standard integrals. Following this procedure and inserting the value of the constant C we obtain:

$$n = 2 \left(\frac{2\pi m_e^* kT}{h^2} \right)^{\frac{3}{2}} \exp\left[-(E_g - E_F)/kT\right] \tag{6.12}$$

The non-exponential term is only relatively slowly varying with temperature compared to the exponential term and it is convenient to consider it as a pseudo-constant, N_c, and write

$$n = N_c \exp\left[-(E_g - E_F)/kT\right] \tag{6.13}$$

Turning now to the density of holes in the valence band, p, this is computed by a development analogous to the previous one. The essential difference is that the Fermi factor used must now be the one pertinent to holes. This can be obtained by equating the probability of a hole occupying a given energy level to the probability that an electron *does not* occupy that level. Thus the Fermi factor for holes is given by

$$1 - P(E) = 1 - \frac{1}{1 + \exp\left[(E - E_F)/kT\right]} = \frac{\exp\left[-(E_F - E)/kT\right]}{1 + \exp\left[-(E_F - E)/kT\right]} \tag{6.14}$$

Again, we know from our earlier approximate analysis that the energy levels in the valence band lie many kT below the Fermi level; $(E_F - E) \gg kT$ and hence eq. (6.14) can be expressed approximately as

$$1 - P(E) \simeq \exp\left[-(E_F - E)/kT\right] \tag{6.15}$$

The density of available states in the valence band is again taken to be the same as that pertaining to free electrons, with the necessary effective mass and energy zero change, giving:

$$S(E) = \frac{8\pi(m_h^*)^{\frac{3}{2}}\sqrt{2}}{h^3}(-E)^{\frac{1}{2}} \tag{6.16}$$

The density of holes is then obtained by multiplying eqs. (6.15) and (6.16) together as before and integrating over all energies from $-\infty$ to 0. The lower limit of the integration is again chosen for mathematical convenience and is permissible because of the rapid decay of the exponential term of eq. (6.15) with decreasing energy. We then arrive at:

$$p = 2\left(\frac{2\pi m_h^* kT}{h^2}\right)^{\frac{3}{2}} \exp\left(-E_F/kT\right) \tag{6.17}$$

Again, it is usual to write the first term as a pseudo-constant with temperature, N_v; then

$$p = N_v \exp\left(-E_F/kT\right) \tag{6.18}$$

A most interesting and useful result can be obtained by forming the product of the number densities of holes and electrons, using eqs. (6.13) and (6.18). thus:

$$np = n_i^2 = N_c N_v \exp\left(-E_g/kT\right) \tag{6.19}$$

or, for the intrinsic material,

$$n_i = 2\left(\frac{2\pi kT}{h^2}\right)^{\frac{3}{2}} (m_e^* m_h^*)^{\frac{3}{4}} \exp(-E_g/2kT) \tag{6.20}$$

Notice that this expression agrees with the less quantitative one derived earlier in (6.6), since the temperature dependence is largely controlled by the rapidly varying exponential term. We see that the density of carriers in an intrinsic semiconductor is independent of the Fermi level and for a given material is constant at any given temperature. It is also most important to observe that, since the gap energy does not change with impurity concentration, and since eq. (6.19) does not contain E_F, this equation, although derived by considering intrinsic semiconduction, is equally valid for semiconductors containing impurities. We shall return to this point later.

We can calculate the position of the Fermi level in our improved model of the intrinsic semiconductor by equating the electron and hole concentrations, using eqs. (6.12) and (6.17). Then:

$$(m_e^*)^{\frac{3}{2}} \exp\left[-(E_g - E_F)/kT\right] = (m_h^*)^{\frac{3}{2}} \exp\left[-E_F/kT\right]$$

114

which is rearranged to give:

$$E_F = \frac{E_g}{2} - \tfrac{3}{4} kT \log\left(\frac{m_e^*}{m_h^*}\right) \tag{6.21}$$

Thus, if the effective masses of holes and electrons are identical, the Fermi level is again midway between valance and conduction band, as in our more approximate model. Otherwise, the Fermi level is temperature-dependent, and E_F increases slightly with temperature if, as is generally the case, $m_h^* > m_e^*$.

A final point to note before leaving this subject is that we have tacitly assumed throughout that the effective masses are constant, whereas we know them to be functions of position in an energy band. Since they are functions of energy they should be included under the integrals over the energy bands. However, this step leads to unnecessary mathematical complication and is usually ignored with only a small error, since, for example, the mass of the electron remains sensibly constant over the narrow lower portion of the conduction band which it usually occupies.

The mathematical derivation of the density of carrier in the intrinsic material via the Fermi and density of state functions is illustrated in Fig. 6.11, which may serve as additional clarification of the process.

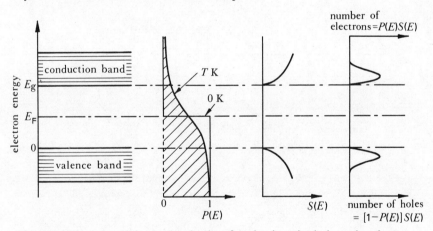

Fig. 6.11 Calculation of the number density of carriers in an intrinsic semiconductor.

6.5 Extrinsic or impurity semiconductors

Intrinsic semiconductors as such are comparatively rarely included in semiconductor devices but, because of their purity and predictable electrical characteristics, they often constitute the basic raw material which is modified during the manufacturing process by the addition of controlled amounts of impurity. We shall see that the number of available charge carriers, their type, and hence, the electrical conductivity of a semiconductor, are extremely sensitive to the concentration of certain types of impurity. It is the ability to alter the electrical characteristics of the material at will by the addition of impurities which makes the *extrinsic* semiconductor so important and interesting.

The most significant impurities which are introduced into the semiconductors we have discussed so far, notably silicon and germanium, are those elements which occur at either side of them in the periodic table, in Columns III and V. Deliberate addition of controlled quantities of these impurity elements is called *doping.* Usually, only minute quantities of such *dopants* are required, in the range one part in 10^{10} to one part in 10^3. Extrinsic or doped semiconductors are classified into two main categories, according to the type of charge carrier which predominates, n-type and p-type, which are discussed in the following sections.

6.5.1. n-type semiconductors. If controlled amounts of impurity elements from Column V of the periodic table, e.g., phosphorus, arsenic, antimony, are added to an intrinsic elemental semiconductor, the extrinsic material as a result is rich in negative conduction electrons and is said to be n-type. These dopants are all characterized by a valency of five, since they have five electrons in their outer shells. They can be represented diagrammatically as in Fig. 6.12(a).

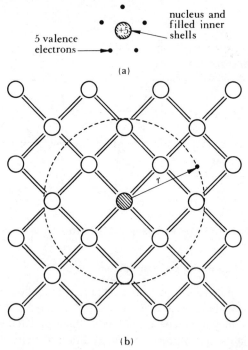

Fig. 6.12 (a) Representation of an n-type impurity atom and (b) substitution of an n-type impurity atom into a semiconductor crystal lattice.

116

When the intrinsic material is doped with one of the Column V dopants, say for example antimony, each antimony atom occupies a site usually occupied by a germanium or silicon atom, since, apart from the difference in number of valence electrons, both parent and impurity atoms are similar in dimensions and electronic structure. The substitutional nature of the dopant atoms has been verified, for example, by X-ray crystallography. The substituted atimony impurity atom, depicted in the two-dimensional model of Fig. 6.12(b), requires only four.of its five valence electrons to form covalent bonds with its neighbours and as a result, it has net positive charge. That the 'extra' electron is not so tightly bound as the other valence electrons can be seen by an extension of the Bohr theory for the hydrogen atom, given in chapter 1. It is reasonable to assume that the fifth electron rotating round the positively charged impurity atom behaves in a manner similar to that of the electron in the Bohr model. There are, however, two principal differences; firstly, the electron is influenced by the periodic potential of the crystal lattice and it is thus its effective mass, m^*, rather than its free mass, m, which is important; secondly, if we assume that the radius of the orbit is sufficient to embrace many crystal lattice points, as we shall verify later, the electron may be considered to be moving in a dielectric medium of relative permittivity ϵ_r.

In chapter 1 the ionization energy for the hydrogen atom was shown to be

$$E = -\frac{m_e\, e^4}{8\epsilon_0^2\, h^2} = -13 \cdot 6 \text{ eV}$$

By analogy, the binding energy of each extra electron in the doped semiconductor is then:

$$E_b = -\frac{13 \cdot 6}{\epsilon_r^2}\left(\frac{m_e^*}{m_e}\right) \text{ eV} \tag{6.22}$$

In order to test the validity of our assumption regarding the radius of the orbit, we again modify the expression for the radius in atomic hydrogen, obtained in chapter 1, so as to include the effective mass of the electron and the relative permittivity of the semiconductor, thus:

$$r_h = r_{\text{hydrogen}} = \frac{h^2\, \epsilon_0}{\pi\, e^2\, m_e} \approx 0 \cdot 05 \text{nm}$$

and, similarly,

$$r_n = r_{\substack{\text{n-type} \\ \text{semiconductor}}} = \frac{h^2\, \epsilon_r\, \epsilon_0}{\pi\, e^2\, m_e^*} = \epsilon_r\left(\frac{m_e}{m_e^*}\right) r_h \tag{6.23}$$

If we include characteristic values of $m_e^* = 0 \cdot 6\, m_e$ for the effective mass of conduction electrons in germanium and $\epsilon_r = 16$, then the radius in germanium is approximately 27 times that in hydrogen, or about 1·4 nm. This radius is sufficiently large to include many hundreds of lattice points within an orbit and our use of the relative permittivity of the bulk material is justified.

117

We can now substitute typical values in eq. (6.22) to estimate the binding energy of electrons in n-type semiconductors. For example, for germanium,

$$E_b = -\frac{13 \cdot 6 \cdot 0 \cdot 6}{16^2} = 0 \cdot 03 \text{ eV}$$

In practice, the experimentally determined values for the binding energies of P, As and Sb in germanium are almost identical and are about 0·01 eV, which gives additional support for our simple model.

Because the binding energies are so small, then, even at room temperatures, nearly all the impurity atoms lose an electron into the conduction band by thermal ionization. The additional electrons in the conduction band contribute to the conductivity in exactly the same way as those excited thermally from the valence band. The essential difference between this mechanism and the intrinsic process is that the ionized impurities remain as fixed positively charged centres in the lattice and no *holes* are produced. Thus, Group V impurities donate extra carrier electrons, without producing additional holes and are called *donors* or sometimes *n-type dopants*.

In the energy-band scheme, each donor atom gives rise to a new isolated donor level, E_D, just below the bottom of the conduction band. Thus, as a consequence of the introduction of n-type dopant, an additional set of highly localized electronic states, with discrete energies situated in the forbidden energy gap, is introduced. At 0 K all donor levels are filled but at room temperature and above they are empty, as shown in Fig. 6.13.

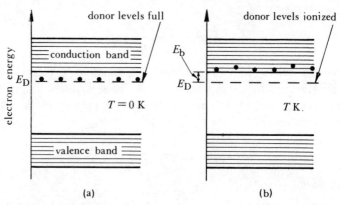

Fig. 6.13 **Band structure of an n-type semiconductor: (a) at 0 K and (b) at higher temperatures.**

Since at room temperature each impurity atom donates an additional charge carrier, even small concentrations of dopant substantially increase the carrier concentration and hence the conductivity. As a simple example, let us compute the electron density in intrinsic germanium and compare this with n-type germanium, doped with phosphorus. If we assume the gap energy

$E_g = 0.75$ eV, that $kT \approx 0.025$ at room temperature, and that $m_e^* = m_h^* = m$ for simplicity, eq. (6.20) predicts that $n_i = 10^{19}/m^3$. There are about 10^{28} atom/m^3 in germanium; hence if we assume that it is doped with Ph at the rate of one part in 10^6, then 10^{22} atom/m^3 of impurity are introduced into the intrinsic material. At room temperature each dopant atom is ionized and contributes one conduction electron; thus 10^{22} conduction electron/m^3 have been donated. We see that the introduction of impurity atoms at the rate of one part in a million has increased the carrier concentration and hence the conductivity a thousandfold!

6.5.2. p-type semiconductors. Semiconductors with a majority charge carrier concentration of holes are called p-type. They can be produced by adding impurities from Column III of the periodic table, e.g., boron, aluminium, gallium, or indium, to intrinsic silicon or germanium. These p-type impurities are characterized by the three valence electrons in their outer shell, Fig. 6.14(a).

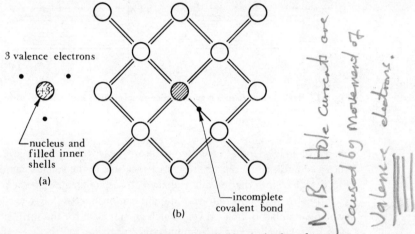

N.B Hole currents are caused by movement of valence electrons.

Fig. 6.14 (a) Representation of a p-type impurity atom and (b) substitution of a p-type impurity atom into a semiconductor crystal lattice.

Each impurity atom again adds substitutionally to the parent crystal lattice but this time there is one electron short for completing the four covalent bonds between it and the four neighbouring atoms, as shown in Fig. 6.14(b). The vacancy thus created by the impurity is not a hole, since it is bound to the atom, but at some temperature above 0 K an electron from a bond of a neighbouring parent atom can fill the vacant electron site, leaving a hole in the valence band for conduction. In accordance with our concept of the hole as a positively charged particle of effective mass, m_h^*, and since it may be considered to rotate at large radii round a fixed negative charge, we can again estimate the ionization energy in a way analogous to that used in the preceding section. The only difference to the result in eq. (6.22) is that the effective mass of a hole replaces that of an electron. Hence, the energy required by a valence electron for it to fill the vacancy created by an impurity atom and thus create a hole, E_A, is of similar magnitude to the ionization energy of a donor atom and is typically of order 0·01 eV.

Dopants from Column III are called *acceptors*, since they accept electrons to create holes for conduction. Such impurities create discrete acceptor levels just above the top of the valence band, separated from it by energy E_A, as shown in Fig. 6.15(a). Again, since E_A is small compared with the thermal

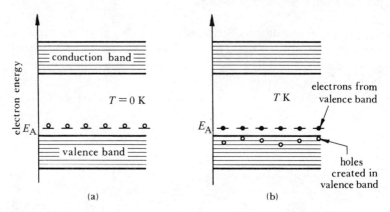

Fig. 6.15 Band structure of a p-type semiconductor: (a) at 0 K and (b) at higher temperatures.

energy of an electron at room temperature, nearly all acceptor levels are occupied and each acceptor atom creates a hole in the valence band, as in Fig. 6.15(b). Note that no additional electrons are created by the process but, as before, each acceptor atom of dopant can produce a charge carrier and the available number of holes is very much greater than for the intrinsic material, even for relatively moderate doping concentrations.

We have seen that in extrinsic semiconductors there are often more carriers of one type than of the other. It is convenient to designate those which predominate as *majority carriers* and the remainder as *minority carriers*. By using these terms it is often possible to discuss the general characteristics of doped semiconductors without specifying whether the material is n- or p-type.

6.6. Recombination and trapping processes

We have seen that recombination takes place in a semiconductor when an electron is permanently removed from the conduction band to recombine with a hole in the valence band. Although such a process is possible in InSb and GaAs, the probability for direct recombination is very slight in the elemental semiconductors Si and Ge, because momentum must be conserved and this

120

is rarely possible for the colliding free electron and hole. In these materials the conduction-band electron usually returns to the valence band only after several intermediate transitions. For instance, it may first drop to some localized state in the forbidden gap, whence, after some random time interval, it is translated to some empty state in the valence band; in other words, it recombines with a hole from the valence band at the localized level, which is called a recombination centre. The sequence of events is illustrated in Fig. 6.16(a).

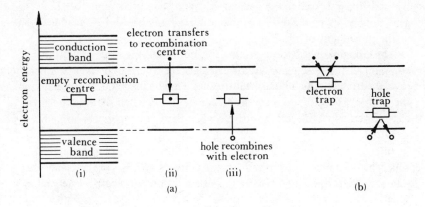

Fig. 6.16 (a) Sequence of events in the recombination process and (b) trapping in semiconductors.

Whereas recombination results in the permanent loss of a carrier, *trapping* describes the temporary removal of a carrier to a localized level, again usually located in the forbidden gap, whence it may eventually return to its original band. This process is shown diagrammatically in Fig. 6.16(b). If the trapping is fast, and it can be for as short a time as, say, 10^{-7} s, then little signal information is lost at relatively low frequencies, but 'slow' traps which can retain the carrier for many seconds completely modify electrical information being processed by a particular device.

Recombination and trapping centres thus occur at isolated energy levels in the forbidden gap. Such states are associated with some kind of imperfection in the crystal or its surface and are a consequence of lattice defects, especially dislocations, vacancies, or additional atoms in the lattice. Such imperfections can be avoided by modern high-quality crystal growth. Sometimes, however, impurities are added deliberately to create additional trapping centres. For example, gold is often added to Si to remove unwanted holes. Similarly, impurities producing 'slow' traps are introduced into some phosphorescent materials used for clock faces, for example, so that they luminesce long after excitation.

121

6.7. The density of carriers and the position of the Fermi level in extrinsic semiconductors

The distribution of electrons or holes in allowed energy states is dependent on the position of the Fermi level. If this can be determined for a particular semiconductor, the number of charge carriers of either type available for conduction at any particular temperature is readily determined.

In general, a semiconductor can be doped with both acceptor and donor impurities and in this case it is difficult to obtain an exact analytical expression for E_F, which usually has to be obtained by numerical computation. We will firstly consider the general case and then relax some of the generality so as to make the problem more tractable and to produce trends in the movement of the Fermi level.

The principle used to determine the Fermi level is not unique but is common to many semiconductor calculations. The Fermi level in a particular crystal automatically adjusts itself so that overall charge neutrality exists in the crystal. Therefore, if a condition can be found when the total negative charge is equal to the total positive charge, the Fermi energy is immediately specified.

In an extrinsic semiconductor, it is not only the holes and electrons which have charge, but ionized impurity atoms are also present and they, too, are charged, as we have seen. The condition for electrical neutrality is thus

$$p + N_d^+ = n + N_a^- \tag{6.24}$$

where N_d^+ is the number density of ionized donor atoms and N_a^- is the number density of ionized acceptor atoms, which is the number of acceptors that have received an electron from the valence band and have thus generated a hole.

If we consider the energy level structure shown in Fig. 6.17, the number of electrons and holes per unit volume are given by eqs. (6.13) and (6.18).

$$n = N_c \exp\left[-(E_g - E_F)/kT\right]$$
$$p = N_v \exp\left[-E_F/kT\right]$$

The concentration of ionized acceptors, N_a^- is equal to the total acceptor concentration, N_a, multiplied by the probability of finding an electron at the acceptor level, E_A, at some particular temperature T. Thus

$$N_a^- = \frac{N_a}{1 + \exp\left[(E_A - E_F)/kT\right]} \tag{6.25}$$

Similarly, N_d^+, the concentration of ionized donors, is equal to the total number density of donors times the probability of finding a hole at energy

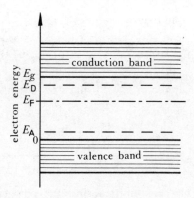

Fig. 6.17 Energy levels in an extrinsic semiconductor.

E_D, or, alternatively, times one minus the probability of finding an electron at that level. Thus

$$N_d^+ = N_d \left(1 - \frac{1}{1 + \exp[(E_D - E_F)/kT]} \right) = \frac{N_d}{1 + \exp[-(E_D - E_F)/kT]} \quad (6.26)$$

Substituting the expression for n, p, N_a^- and N_d^+ into the charge neutrality expression, eq. (6.29), gives:

$$N_v \exp[-E_F/kT] + \frac{N_d}{1 + \exp[-(E_D - E_F)/kT]} = N_c \exp[-(E_g - E_F)/kT]$$

$$+ \frac{N_a}{1 + \exp[(E_A - E_F)/kT]} \quad (6.27)$$

If the gap energy and the various doping concentrations and impurity levels are known, this equation can be used to determine the exact position of the Fermi level and hence the carrier concentrations in a particular crystal sample.

By considering the following special cases and using simplifying assumptions, it is possible to reduce the complexity of eq. (6.27) and to gain some insight into the approximate location of the Fermi level.

6.7.1.(a) n-type material. In this type of crystal the donor concentration is much greater than the acceptor concentration, or $N_d \gg N_a$. Also, since the electron density is much higher than its intrinsic value, the relationship $np = n_i^2$, which is always true as we have seen, indicates that the hole density is much lower than the intrinsic density, n_i, or $p \ll n$. Thus, the first and last terms of eq. (6.24) and (6.27) are negligibly small and

$$\frac{N_d}{1 + \exp[-(E_D - E_F)/kT]} = N_c \exp[-(E_g - E_F)/kT]$$

which can be rearranged to give:

$$\{\exp\left[-(E_D + E_g)/kT\right]\}\,e^{2E_F/kT} + \{\exp\left[-E_g/kT\right]\}\,e^{E_F/kT} - \frac{N_d}{N_c} = 0$$

This equation is quadratic in $e^{E_F/kT}$ and its solution is:

$$\exp\left[E_F/kT\right] = \frac{-1 + \left\{1 + \dfrac{4N_d}{N_c}\exp\left[(E_g - E_D)/kT\right]\right\}^{\frac{1}{2}}}{2\exp\left[-E_D/kT\right]} \tag{6.28}$$

The negative root has been omitted, since the exponential at the left-hand side of the equation can never be negative.

Equation (6.28) can usually be solved to obtain E_F at some particular temperature. Again, it is instructive to consider limiting cases to locate the Fermi level approximately in· these conditions.

6.7.1(b). n-type at low temperature, or with high doping concentration. In this case, the second term under the root sign of eq. (6.28) becomes much greater than unity and

$$\exp\left[E_F/kT\right] \simeq \frac{2\left(\dfrac{N_d}{N_c}\right)^{\frac{1}{2}}\exp\left[(E_g - E_D)/2kT\right]}{2\exp\left[-E_D/kT\right]} = \left(\frac{N_d}{N_c}\right)^{\frac{1}{2}}\exp\left[(E_g + E_D)/2kT\right]$$

and

$$E_F = \frac{E_g + E_D}{2} + \tfrac{1}{2}kT\log\left(\frac{N_d}{N_c}\right) \tag{6.29}$$

Thus, at 0 K the Fermi level lies midway between the donor level and the bottom of the conduction band. If this Fermi energy is substituted in eq. (6.13) we can obtain the number density of electrons in the semiconductor:

$$n = N_c\exp\left[-E_g/kT\right]\left(\frac{N_d}{N_c}\right)^{\frac{1}{2}}\exp\left[(E_g + E_D)/2kT\right]$$

$$= (N_c N_d)^{\frac{1}{2}}\exp\left[(E_D - E_g)/2kT\right] \propto N_d^{\frac{1}{2}} \tag{6.30}$$

6.7.1(c). n-type at higher temperature, or low doping concentration. If the concentration of impurity atoms is low, such that $N_d \ll N_c$, or if the temperature is high, provided it is not so high that the material becomes near-intrinsic, which would invalidate our earlier assumptions, then $kT \gg E_g - E_D$ and the second term under the root sign of eq. (6.28) is much

124

smaller than unity. Then, taking the first two terms of the binomial expression, this equation reduces to:

$$\exp\left(E_F/kT\right) = \frac{-1 + 1 + \dfrac{4N_d}{2N_c}\exp\left[(E_g - E_D)/kT\right]}{2\exp\left[-E_D/kT\right]}$$

or

$$E_F = E_g - kT \log\left(\frac{N_c}{N_d}\right) \tag{6.31}$$

Thus, the Fermi level falls as the temperature is increased. Again the density of majority carriers is given by eqs. (6.13) and (6.31), or

$$n = N_c \exp\left(-E_g/kT\right) \cdot \frac{N_d}{N_c} \exp\left(E_g/kT\right) = N_d \tag{6.32}$$

and in this case the majority carrier density is equal to the concentration of donor impurities.

We see from these extreme cases studied that for fairly high doping levels or low temperatures, the Fermi level remains in the vicinity of the donor level. However, if the donor concentration is small or the temperature high, the Fermi level falls until, when the number of thermally excited electrons is much greater than those donated by donors and the material is essentially intrinsic, it approaches the mid-gap position, E_{Fi}. This situation is illustrated diagrammatically in Fig. 6.18(a).

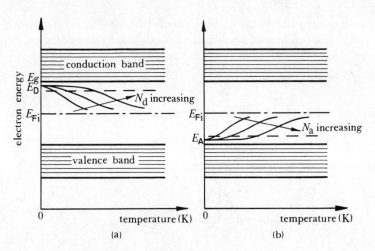

Fig. 6.18 Variation of Fermi level with impurity concentration and temperature for (a) n-type and (b) p-type semiconductors.

125

6.7.1(d). p-type material. By arguments similar to those used for n-type material, it can be shown that for a p-type semiconductor the Fermi level lies midway between the top of the valence band and the acceptor level, E_A, at 0 K. Again, as the temperature is raised above this level, all the acceptors are ionized, $p = N_a$, and the Fermi level increases. At much higher temperatures the material becomes intrinsic and the Fermi level eventually approaches E_{Fi}, as shown in Fig. 6.18(b).

It should be emphasized that eqs. (6.28) to (6.31) are only approximate. It is always best in a particular case when the doping concentrations are known for a material to evaluate E_F directly using eq. (6.37) and thus obtain the carrier concentration at a particular temperature.

6.8 Compensation doping

When both acceptor and donor impurities are added simultaneously to an intrinsic semiconductor, *compensation* takes place. Usually, all the added impurities are ionized at room temperature. Whether the material is n-type or p-type and also the concentration of the carriers depend on the degree of doping of each impurity type. Suppose, for example, that a silicon crystal contains 10^{22} donor impurities and 10^{21} acceptor impurities per cubic metre. It is clear that this crystal will be n-type since n-type impurities predominate. The free carriers supplied by the less concentrated dopant will recombine with an equal number of carriers of opposite type, supplied by the more concentrated dopant, leaving an excess of electrons or holes (in the above example electrons). Some of the donor states have been effectively cancelled by the acceptor states, a process known as *compensation.*

If we assume that all the impurities are ionized, it is thus the quantity $(N_d - N_a)$, which may be positive or negative, which largely determines the carrier concentrations. In this case, the condition for electrical neutrality is

$$n + N_a = p + N_d$$

Also, we make use of the relationship between n and p:

$$np = n_i^2$$

Substituting this in the previous equation gives

$$n^2 - (N_d - N_a)n - n_i^2 = 0$$

which is a quadratic equation in n with solution:

$$n = \frac{N_d - N_a}{2} + \frac{N_d - N_a}{2}\left[1 + \left(\frac{2n_i}{N_d - N_a}\right)^2\right]^{\frac{1}{2}} \qquad (6.33)$$

and likewise

$$p = -\frac{(N_d - N_a)}{2} + \frac{(N_d - N_a)}{2}\left[1 + \left(\frac{2n_i}{N_d - N_a}\right)^2\right]^{\frac{1}{2}} \quad (6.34)$$

The negative roots have been omitted so that n and p remain positive.

Equations (6.33) and (6.34) can be simplified in two extreme cases:

6.8.1. Extrinsic compensated material. In this case the intrinsic carrier density is low compared with the difference between the densities of donors and acceptors, or $n_i \ll |N_d - N_a|$. The equations then reduce to

$$\left.\begin{aligned} n &\simeq N_d - N_a \\ p &\simeq \frac{n_i^2}{N_d - N_a} \end{aligned}\right\} \text{ for } N_d > N_a$$

and

$$\left.\begin{aligned} p &\simeq N_a - N_d \\ n &\simeq \frac{n_i^2}{N_a - N_d} \end{aligned}\right\} \text{ for } N_a > N_d$$

In such materials the majority concentration is large, approximately equal to $|N_d - N_a|$, and is almost temperature-independent, whereas the minority concentration is small and varies rapidly with temperature.

6.8.2. Intrinsic compensated material. In this case the difference in donor and acceptor concentrations is small compared to the density of intrinsic carriers, or $n_i \gg |N_d - N_a|$, and, in contrast to the previous case, the Fermi level lies near the middle of the forbidden gap. Equations (6.33) and (6.34) then have the approximate forms:

$$n = n_i + \frac{N_d - N_a}{2}$$

and

$$p = n_i - \frac{N_d - N_a}{2}$$

Such materials are said to be *intrinsic* or *near-fully compensated*. This condition can also apply for the material in the previous case, at high temperatures, when the number of hole pairs generated in the intrinsic process can become large compared with $|N_d - N_a|$. The semiconductor is then said to be in the *intrinsic temperature range*.

6.9 Electrical conduction in semiconductors

Electrical conduction by electrons in the conduction band of a semiconductor has some similar characteristics to that for metals which was described

127

previously. The drift velocity of electrons in the presence of an applied field is again limited by scattering effects and is determined by an electron mobility, μ_e. The electron current density, by analogy with eq. (4.34), is then:

$$J_e = n e \mu_e \, \mathscr{E} \tag{6.35}$$

The expression for the mobility of free electrons, eq. (4.33), must be modified to account for the motion of electrons in the lattice of a semiconductor by replacing the free mass m by the effective mass of electrons m_e^* and including the appropriate relaxation time τ_{re}.

In a semiconductor, there is a further contribution to the total conduction current from holes which occur in the valence band. The drift velocity of holes can again be specified a hole mobility term, μ_h, which is given by eq. (4.33) provided the effective mass of holes in the semiconductor, m_h^*, and the relevant relaxation time, τ_{rh}, are included. The drift current density due to hole conduction is then

$$J_h = p e \mu_h \, \mathscr{E} \tag{6.36}$$

Although an applied electric field causes electrons and holes to flow in opposite directions, the direction of conventional current flow due to the motion of each carrier is in the same direction as the field. The total current density in a semiconductor is thus:

$$J = J_e + J_h = e(n\mu_e + p\mu_h) \, \mathscr{E} \tag{6.37}$$

and the electrical conductivity, σ, is given by

$$\sigma = e(n\mu_e + p\mu_h) \tag{6.38}$$

Since μ_e and μ_h are of the same order, typically about $0 \cdot 1 \ \mathrm{m^2/V\,s}$ at room temperature, eqs. (6.37) and (6.38) must in general be used when n and p are comparable, for example when the semiconductor is near-intrinsic. For doped materials at room temperature when one carrier predominates it is usually only necessary to include the term pertaining to the majority carrier. For example, for the n-type semiconductor, $n \gg p$ and

$$\sigma_n \simeq e n \mu_e \simeq e N_d \mu_e \tag{6.39}$$

Similarly, for p-type:

$$\sigma_p \simeq e p \mu_h \simeq e N_a \mu_h \tag{6.40}$$

6.9.1. Diffusion of charge carriers in semiconductors. It is also possible for current to flow in a semiconductor, even in the absence of fields, owing to a concentration gradient of carriers in the crystal. Such a diffusion current can flow as a result of non-uniform densities of either electrons or holes.

Let us first of all consider diffusion in a neutral gas. We will assume an arbitrarily shaped concentration gradient of neutral particles which varies only in the x-direction, as shown in Fig. 6.19(a). When the density increases as x

increases, as is assumed in the diagram, it is to be expected that diffusion of particles takes place in the negative x-direction, from the high-pressure to the low-pressure region.

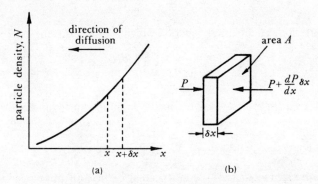

Fig. 6.19 Diffusion of particles when a density gradient exists.

We consider an elemental volume, of thickness δx and area in the y-z plane A. If $P(x)$ is the pressure at x the overall force on the elemental volume is

$$\left[P(x) - \left(P + \frac{dP}{dx}\delta x \right) \right] A = -\frac{dP}{dx}\delta x\, A$$

Thus, if there are N molecules/per unit volume at x, that is, $N\delta x A$ molecules in the volume considered, the force acting on each molecule is

$$F_D = -\frac{1}{N}\frac{dP}{dx} \tag{6.41}$$

This diffusion force acts in a way entirely analogous to that in which the force due to an electric field acts, to acclerate particles in the opposite direction to the concentration gradient; the flow of particles is again limited by collisions or, in the case of charged particle gradients in semiconductors, by scattering phenomena. The same arguments can be used to calculate the particle drift velocity as were used for calculating the mobility, but F_D replaces the force due to the electric field, $-e\mathscr{E}$. Thus, using eqs. (6.41) and (4.30), we see that the drift velocity of neutral particles is:

$$v_D = -\frac{\tau_r}{M}\cdot\frac{1}{N}\frac{dP}{dx} \tag{6.42}$$

where τ_r is again the mean time between collisions and M is the mass of a particle. Now, the pressure is related to particle density and temperature T by the relationship

$$P = NkT$$

129

so the expression for drift velocity can be rewritten:

$$v_{\mathrm{D}} = -\frac{\tau_r . kT}{M} \cdot \frac{1}{N} \cdot \frac{dN}{dx} \qquad (6.43)$$

This expression is a diffusion equation which is often written:

$$v_{\mathrm{D}} = -D \cdot \frac{1}{N} \frac{dN}{dx} \qquad (6.44)$$

where D is a *diffusion coefficient* which is in units of m^2/s and is given by

$$D = \frac{\tau_r kT}{M} \qquad (6.45)$$

The negative sign in eq. (6.44) confirms that particle diffusion occurs from the region of high concentration to the region of low concentration, as we presupposed.

Diffusion effects occur for any concentration gradient of particles; that the particles are charged does not affect the analysis. For example, for a density gradient of electrons in a semiconductor, the drift velocity is, from eq. (6.44)

$$v_{\mathrm{De}} = -D_e \frac{1}{n} \cdot \frac{dn}{dx}$$

which causes an electron diffusion current density, J_{De}, to flow where:

$$J_{\mathrm{De}} = -nev_{\mathrm{D}} = eD_e \frac{dn}{dx} \qquad (6.46)$$

Notice that this expression is positive since the electrons flowing in the direction opposite to the positive gradient of electron density correspond to a conventional current flow in the same direction as the positive gradient, as in Fig. 6.20(a).

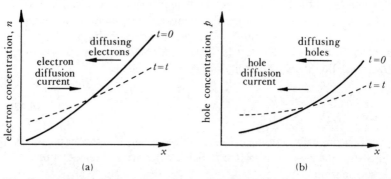

Fig. 6.20 Diffusion currents for (a) electrons and (b) holes, when a carrier concentration gradient exists.

130

Similarly, for a gradient of hole concentration in the x-direction in a semi-conductor, dp/dx, there is a resultant diffusion current density, J_{Dh}, given by

$$J_{Dh} = -eD_h\frac{dp}{dx} \qquad (6.47)$$

which flows in the opposite direction to the positive gradient, as in Fig. 6.20(b).

In eqs. (6.46) and (6.47), D_e and D_h are the diffusion coefficients for electrons and holes. Typical values, for germanium for example, are $D_e = 0 \cdot 0093 \text{ m}^2\text{s}^{-1}$ and $D_h = 0 \cdot 0044 \text{ m}^2\text{s}^{-1}$. The magnitude of the diffusion coefficient for either carrier is an indication of the ability of the carrier to move through the crystal; subsequently, it would not be surprising if it were related to the mobility of the carrier in some way. That there is a relationship between the two parameters can be seen by inserting the electron effective mass and relaxation time in eq. (6.45) to obtain expression for D_e and comparing this with eq. (4.33). It follows that:

$$D_e = \left(\frac{kT}{e}\right)\mu_e \qquad (6.48)$$

Using similar arguments, it can be verified that

$$D_h = \left(\frac{kT}{e}\right)\mu_h \qquad (6.49)$$

Thus, at any given temperature the diffusion coefficients and the mobility of carriers in a given material are not independent of each other, since

$$\frac{D_e}{\mu_e} = \frac{D_h}{\mu_h} = \frac{kT}{e} \qquad (6.50)$$

This equation is known as *Einstein's relation*.

6.9.2. Total current flow in a semiconductor. In the two previous sections we have seen that current flow in a semiconductor is due to motion of the charged carriers under the influence of applied fields or concentration gradients. It is quite possible to have these two effects occurring simultaneously and the net current flow is then the sum of drift and diffusion currents. Using eqs. (6.37), (6.46), and (6.47) we obtain the following general expressions for the total electron and hole currents:

$$J_e = ne\mu_e\mathscr{E} + eD_e\nabla n \qquad (6.51)$$

and

$$J_h = peu_h\mathscr{E} - eD_h\nabla p \qquad (6.52)$$

131

These flow relations have been generalized by allowing the electric field and the density gradients to be in any arbitrary direction.

An important effect which may be seen from these equations is that by suitable choice of $\mathscr{E}$-field the tendency for current to flow due to concentration gradients can be balanced out and the net current reduced to zero. For example, if we consider holes only, eq. (6.52) shows that if

$$\mathscr{E} = \frac{D_h \, \nabla p}{p \mu_h}$$

then the hole current becomes zero. This compensation of diffusion and drift currents to produce zero net current is vital for understanding transistor and diode action, which will be discussed later.

6.10 The continuity equation

The continuity equation as applied to semiconductors describes how the carrier density in a given elemental volume of the crystal varies with time. The variation in density is attributable to two basic causes, the rate of generation or annihilation of carriers within the element and drift of carriers into or out of the element. The problem can be simplified somewhat by first treating the two effects separately. We shall concern ourselves with the continuity equation for *minority* carriers since it is the density of these that changes most significantly in most practical cases of interest when carriers are injected into or created in a semiconductor.

6.10.1. No electron or hole current flow. To be more specific, let us consider a p-type semiconductor and derive the continuity equation for the minority electrons, firstly with no applied field and no concentration gradients, hence no current flow. In general terms, it is obvious that in this case, within an elemental volume of the semiconductor, the rate of change of electron density is equal to their rate of generation minus the rate at which they recombine with holes. Thus,

$$\frac{dn}{dt} = G - R \tag{6.53}$$

where n is the minority electron concentration at any time t, and G and R are the generation and the recombination rates for the minority carriers.

The generation rate, G, is a function of temperature only since charge carriers are produced only by thermal excitation in the absence of current flow. Hence, at a constant temperature, $G(T)$ is constant. On the other hand, the recombination rate will be proportional to the product of the local densities of holes and electrons, both of which may vary with time, or

$$R = rnp \tag{6.54}$$

where r, the constant of proportionality, is the *recombination coefficient.*

In equilibrium, $d/dt = 0$ and the generation and recombination rates will be equal. Thus, we let n_0 and p_0 be the equilibrium densities of minority and majority carriers; eqs. (6.53) and (6.54) give

$$0 = G(T) - rn_0 p_0$$

or

$$G(T) = rn_0 p_0 = rn_i^2 \tag{6.55}$$

Now, let us assume that at $t = 0$, δn additional electrons are injected into the material so that the electron density becomes

$$n = n_0 + \delta n \tag{6.56}$$

The hole concentration must change sympathetically so as to maintain charge neutrality; the density of holes is then

$$p = p_0 + \delta p \tag{6.57}$$

and the concentration of electrons and holes injected into the volume must be equal, $\delta n = \delta p$. Under these circumstances, the time rate of change of minority carrier concentration is given by eq. (6.53), which with eqs. (6.54), (6.56), and (6.57) gives:

$$\left.\frac{dn}{dt}\right|_{J=0} = \left.\frac{d(\delta n)}{dt}\right|_{J=0} = G(T) - r(n_0 + \delta n)(p_0 + \delta p)$$

We can eliminate the generation term by assuming constant temperature throughout the process and using eq. (6.55); then:

$$\left.\frac{d(\delta n)}{dt}\right|_{J=0} = -rn_0\,\delta p - rp_0\,\delta n - r\,\delta n\,\delta p$$

Ignoring second-order quantities, and remembering that in a p-type material $p_0 \gg n_0$, this equation reduces to

$$\left.\frac{d(\delta n)}{dt}\right|_{J=0} = -rp_0\,\delta n = -\frac{\delta n}{\tau_{Le}} \tag{6.58}$$

Where τ_{Le} is the *lifetime* of the electrons. The physical meaning of τ_{Le} can be made clearer by integrating eq. (6.58) to give

$$\delta n(t) = \delta n|_{t=0}\, e^{-t/\tau_{Le}} \tag{6.59}$$

Thus, after a sudden change in electrons density, $\delta n|_{t=0}$, the carrier density decays exponentially back to its equilibrium value by recombination, in a time comparable to τ_{Le}, as illustrated in Fig. 6.21(a). Thus, τ_{Le} is the average time that the electrons behave as free charge carriers before recombining or being lost by other mechanisms.

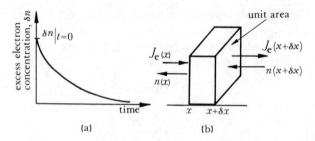

Fig. 6.21 (a) Decay of an excess electron concentration with time, due to recombination (b) current and electron flow into and out of an elemental volume.

Equation (6.58) is the continuity equation for minority electrons in the absence of current flow. A similar equation can be derived in an exactly analogous manner for the change in excess hole density with time in an n-type semiconductor, viz:

$$\frac{d}{dt}(\delta p) = -\frac{\delta p}{\tau_{Lh}} \tag{6.60}$$

where τ_{Lh} is now the lifetime of minority holes.

6.10.2. Continuity equation with current flow. Let us now consider the situation when electrons are being continuously injected into the volume of p-type material under consideration, when an electron current flows. For the sake of simplicity, let us assume initially that the electron current, J_e, flows in the positive x-direction and consider an elemental volume of semiconductor at some position x, of thickness δx and of unit area perpendicular to the direction of current flow, as shown in Fig. 6.21(b). Current flows in the direction shown as a result of electron flow in the negative x-direction.

The current density and electron concentration are related via eq. (4.28). Hence, the number of electrons entering the volume at $(x + \delta x)$ is

$$n_{x+\delta x} = \frac{J_e(x + \delta x)}{ev_D}$$

and the number leaving at x is

$$n_x = \frac{J_e(x)}{ev_D}$$

Thus, the net increase in the number of electrons in the volume element is

$$n_{x+\delta x} - n_x = \delta n = \frac{1}{ev_D}[J_e(x + \delta x) - J_e(x)]$$

$$= \frac{1}{ev_D}\left[J_e(x) + \frac{\partial J_e}{\partial x}\cdot \delta x - J_e(x)\right] = \frac{1}{ev_D}\cdot\frac{\partial J_e}{\partial x}\cdot \delta x$$

134

Now, $v_D = \partial x / \partial t$ and, in the limit, the equation reduces to:

$$\frac{\partial}{\partial t}(\delta n)\bigg|_{\substack{\text{current} \\ \text{flow}}} = -\frac{1}{e}\frac{\partial J_e}{\partial x} \qquad (6.61)$$

This is the continuity equation for minority electrons when current is flowing.

If we now allow recombination to take place inside the elemental volume, then the total rate of charge of excess minority electron, δn, due to both drift currents and recombination, is given by eqs. (6.58) and (6.61):

$$\frac{\partial}{\partial t}(\delta n)\bigg|_{\text{total}} = -\frac{\delta n}{\tau_{Le}} + \frac{1}{e}\frac{\partial J_e}{\partial x} \qquad (6.62)$$

There is, of course, a similar equation for the time-dependence of the excess hole concentration in an n-type semiconductor. Now, the electron current density J_e is in general due to both drift in an externally applied field and diffusion. In the one-dimensional case, we have seen that

$$J_{ex} = ne\mu_e\,\mathcal{E}_x + eD_e\frac{\partial n}{\partial x}$$

We substitute this expression in eq. (6.62), remembering that $n = n_0 + \delta n$ and that n_0 is not a function of x, to give:

$$\frac{\partial}{\partial t}(\delta n) = -\frac{\delta n}{\tau_{Le}} + \mu_e\,\mathcal{E}_x\cdot\frac{\partial}{\partial x}(\delta n) + D_e\frac{\partial^2}{\partial x^2}(\delta n) \qquad (6.63)$$

This is the one-dimensional continuity equation for excess minority electrons. The continuity equation for excess minority holes is derived in exactly the same way to give

$$\frac{\partial}{\partial t}(\delta p) = -\frac{\delta p}{\tau_{Lh}} - \mu_h\cdot\mathcal{E}_x\frac{\partial}{\partial x}(\delta p) + D_h\cdot\frac{\partial^2}{\partial x^2}(\delta p) \qquad (6.64)$$

The continuity equations enable us to calculate the excess density of electron or holes in time and space. These, together with eqs. (6.51) and (6.52) giving the electron and hole current densities, are the basic equations for describing the behaviour of many semiconductor devices, as we shall see.

6.11 Semiconductor measurements

6.11.1. Hall effect measurements. If a current is passed through a semi-conductor and a magnetic field, B, is applied at right angles to the direction of current flow, an electric field is induced in a direction mutually perpendicular to B and the direction of current flow. This phenomenon is known as the Hall effect. A Hall measurement experimentally confirms the validity of the concept that it is possible for two independent types of charge carrier,

135

electrons and holes, to exist in a semiconductor. We shall also see that a measurement of the Hall coefficient determines not only the sign of the charge of the carriers but also their density. If the conductivity is measured simultaneously by, say, the method to be described in Section 6.11.2, this yields the mobility and the two experiments can thus provide experimental information which is vital for evaluating the subsequent performance of devices made from the material.

Let us, for simplicity, consider a bar of p-type material, as shown in Fig. 6.22 and assume the carriers to be positive holes, of charge e, only. We will

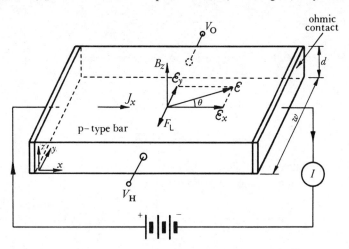

Fig. 6.22 Hall effect in a p-type semiconductor.

assume that a current density J_x is produced in the bar by application of an electric field E_x and that a magnetic field of flux density B_z is applied in the z-direction. Since the holes are flowing with some drift velocity v_{Dx} under the influence of the applied field, they experience a Lorentz force:

$$F_L = ev \times B$$

of magnitude

$$|F_L| = ev_{Dx} B_z \tag{6.65}$$

and directed in the negative y-direction. This force tends to drive holes towards the front face of the block (see the figure); there is an excess of holes there and a deficiency of holes at the back face. Since there can be no net flow in the y-direction, the movement of holes to front and back creates an electric field in the positive y-direction, $\mathscr{E}_y$. This produces a force on the holes which exactly compensates for the Lorentz force field and prevents transverse current flowing. Hence, in equilibrium:

$$e\mathscr{E}_y = F_L = ev_{Dx} B_z \tag{6.66}$$

136

Also, the current density J_x is given by

$$J_x \simeq pev_{\mathrm{D}x}$$

which can be substituted in (6.66) to give

$$\mathscr{E}_y = \frac{J_x B_z}{pe} \tag{6.67}$$

Thus, if voltage probes are attached to front and back faces, assumed separated by a distance w, a voltage

$$V_{\mathrm{H}} = \mathscr{E}_y w$$

may be measured.

The Hall coefficient, R_{H}, defined from eq. (6.67), is

$$R_{\mathrm{H}} = \frac{\mathscr{E}_y}{J_x B_z} = \frac{1}{pe}$$

Alternatively, if the current through the bar of thickness d is I:

$$R_{\mathrm{H}} = \frac{V_{\mathrm{H}}}{wIB_z} \cdot wd = \frac{V_{\mathrm{H}}d}{IB_z} = \frac{1}{pe} \tag{6.68}$$

It will be easily verified that for n-type material where the current is carried by majority electrons, the polarity of the Hall voltage, V_{H}, is reversed and

$$R_{\mathrm{He}} = -\frac{1}{ne} \tag{6.69}$$

We see that the measurement of current and the magnitude and sign of the Hall voltage for any given magnetic flux density gives the sign of the charge carriers, that is, it shows whether the doped semiconductor is n- or p-type, together with the density of the majority carriers.

It will be noticed that the net electric field in the semiconductor, which is the vector sum of $\mathscr{E}_x$ and $\mathscr{E}_y$ is not directed along the axis but is at some angle θ to it. From Fig. 6.22 it will be seen that θ, called the *Hall angle,* is given by

$$\tan \theta = \frac{\mathscr{E}_y}{\mathscr{E}_x} \tag{6.70}$$

which, using eq. (6.67) and remembering that $J_x = \sigma \mathscr{E}_x$, gives

$$\tan \theta = \frac{J_x B_z}{pe} \cdot \frac{\sigma}{J_x} = \mu_{\mathrm{h}} B_z \tag{6.71}$$

or alternatively

$$\mu_{\mathrm{h}} = R_{\mathrm{H}} \sigma \tag{6.72}$$

137

Thus, provided the assumptions made in this simple model are correct, a simultaneous measurement of R_H and σ can lead to an experimental value for the carrier drift mobility.

We have tacitly assumed that all the carriers move with an average drift velocity, v_D, and hence have the same collision time. If the problem is treated on a more rigorous statistical basis, it can be shown that, if the principal scattering mechanism is thermal scattering, then an additional numerical factor is introduced into the expression for the Hall coefficient and

$$R_H = \frac{3\pi}{8} \cdot \frac{1}{pe} \tag{6.73}$$

If other types of scattering predominate, the numerical factor has a different value. We see that, in this case, eq. (6.70) becomes

$$\tan \theta = \frac{3\pi}{8} \cdot \mu_h B_z = \mu_H B_z \tag{6.74}$$

where μ_H is known as the *Hall mobility*. It is related to the drift velocity via eq. (6.74)

$$\mu_H = \frac{\tan \theta}{B_z} = \frac{3\pi}{8} \mu_h \tag{6.75}$$

and is equal to the product of Hall coefficient and conductivity:

$$\mu_H = R_H \sigma \tag{6.76}$$

We have further assumed that the conduction process is by means of one type of carrier only. In some semiconductors, for example, in intrinsic or nearly fully compensated material, the assumption is not valid and the Hall coefficient must be modified to account for the presence of two types of charge carrier, as follows.

Both types of carrier will drift under the influence of the applied field $\mathcal{E}_x$ with drift velocities:

$$v_{Dh} = \mu_h \mathcal{E}_x \quad \text{in the positive } x\text{-direction}$$

and
$$v_{De} = \mu_e \mathcal{E}_x \quad \text{in the negative } x\text{-direction}$$

using the same coordinate system as in Fig. 6.22. As a consequence, the holes and electrons each experience a Lorentz force given by

$$F_h = e(v_{Dh} \times B) = -ev_{Dh} B_z$$

and
$$F_e = e(v_{De} \times B) = -ev_{De} B_z$$

Both deflecting forces are in the same direction, deflecting electrons and holes to the front face, as before. The carriers recombine at the surface and the net charge there produces an electron field in the y-direction, $\mathcal{E}_y$. In equilibrium,

138

the current due to the deflected electrons and holes must be exactly cancelled out by current flowing in the opposite direction due to the Hall field. If the transverse velocities of the deflected carriers are v_{yh} and v_{ye}, the current in the transverse direction due to deflection of electrons and holes by the magnetic field is $(epv_{yh} - env_{ye})$ and, therefore, in equilibrium:

$$\sigma \mathscr{E}_y = e(pv_{yh} - nv_{ye}) \tag{6.77}$$

Expressions for the transverse velocities can be obtained from the Hall angle equations, (6.70) and (6.71), which give:

$$v_{yh} = \mu_h(\mathscr{E}_x \tan \theta) = \mu_h(\mathscr{E}_x \mu_h B_z)$$

and, similarly,

$$v_{ye} = \mu_e^2 \mathscr{E}_x B_z$$

These are substituted in eq. (6.77) to give:

$$\sigma \mathscr{E}_y = e(p\mu_h^2 - n\mu_e^2) \mathscr{E}_x B_z \tag{6.78}$$

The generalized version of Ohm's law is used to eliminate $\mathscr{E}_x$ from this equation, which can then be rearranged to give the Hall coefficient:

$$R_H = \frac{\mathscr{E}_y}{J_x B_z} = \frac{e(p\mu_h^2 - n\mu_e^2)}{\sigma^2}$$

Finally, we include the general expression for the conductivity, given in eq. (6.38), to give:

$$R_H = \frac{(p\mu_h^2 - n\mu_e^2)}{e(p\mu_h + n\mu_e)^2} \tag{6.79}$$

Again, a more rigorous treatment, which does not assume that the time between scattering events is the same for all carriers, results in the introduction of an additional numerical factor in the Hall coefficient expression. For example, if lattice scattering is the principle loss mechanism

$$R_H = \frac{3\pi}{8} \frac{p\mu_h^2 - n\mu_e^2}{e(p\mu_h + n\mu_e)^2} \tag{6.80}$$

Comparison of this expression with eqs. (6.68) and (6.69) shows that the Hall coefficient, and hence the Hall voltage, are generally smaller for near-intrinsic materials than for the more highly doped extrinsic materials. Notice, too, that measurement of the Hall coefficient of the intrinsic material does not lead immediately to values for the carrier concentrations, as it does in the extrinsic material.

6.11.2. Four-point probe method for conductivity measurements. In principle, the conductivity of a semiconductor may be found by measuring the current drawn when a voltage is applied between two contacts formed at the ends of

139

a bar of the material. In practice, such a measurement is not straightforward because of the difficulty of making uniform ohmic contacts to the sample. Further, it is not always convenient to produce a specimen of known dimensions for a conductivity measurement. The four-point probe method eliminates the difficulties referred to; it is used to measure, non-destructively and accurately, the conductivity of ingots or slices, both thick and thin, of semiconductor crystals.

The probe head basically employs four spring-loaded, equispaced needles which make contact with a plane lapped surface on the specimen, as shown in Fig. 6.23. A stabilized current is passed through the outer pair of probes, A

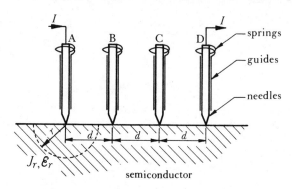

Fig. 6.23 Four-point conductivity measurement.

and D, and the voltage, V, between the other two, B and C, is measured by, say, a digital voltmeter which draws negligible current.

Let us firstly consider the sample dimensions to be large compared with the probe spacing, d. We can treat the source current at A and the sink at D independently, using the principle of superposition to find their combined effect later. Thus, the current density, J_r, at radius r from A, due to the current I entering at A is

$$J_r = \frac{I}{2\pi r^2}$$

since current only flows in the bottom half-plane. We then use Ohm's law to find the corresponding electric field at r, $\mathscr{E}_r$

$$\mathscr{E}_r = \frac{J}{\sigma} = \frac{I}{2\pi\sigma r^2}$$

where σ is the conductivity of the material.

By definition, the floating potential at some radius a is then:

$$V_a = -\int_{-\infty}^{a} \mathscr{E}_r \, dr = -\frac{I}{2\pi\sigma} \int_{-\infty}^{a} \frac{1}{r^2} \, dr = \frac{I}{2\pi\sigma a} \tag{6.81}$$

140

The potential difference between probes B and C due to the current source at A is then:

$$V_{B-C} = \frac{I}{2\pi\sigma d} - \frac{I}{2\pi\sigma(2d)} = \frac{I}{4\pi\sigma d} \tag{6.82}$$

If, now, we consider the current leaving at D separately, there exists a potential difference between B and C which, because of symmetry, is the same as that due to the current source above, given in eq. (6.82). By superposition, the total voltage measured between B and C is thus twice that for current source or sink alone or:

$$V = \frac{I}{2\pi\sigma d}$$

from which the conductivity is obtained:

$$\sigma = \frac{1}{2\pi d} \cdot \frac{I}{V} \tag{6.83}$$

This equation is valid only for materials whose dimensions are large compared with the probe spacing, d. If this is not the case, for example, when measurements are made on thin slices or small dice of material, then a correction factor, F, is introduced and the conductivity is given by:

$$\sigma = \sigma_0 F$$

where σ_0 is the uncorrected value of σ, found using eq. (6.83). Factor F is a function of slice thickness, breadth, and width, normalized to the probe spacing; the reader is referred to the more specialized literature for the derivation and tabulation of values of F for various slice geometries.*

6.11.3. Measurement of minority carrier lifetime and mobility. It is possible to measure the drift mobility, μ, and the lifetime of minority carriers, τ_L, by a simple technique, the basic arrangement of which is as shown in Fig. 6.24. A bar of semiconducting crystal, length l, has ohmic contacts formed at each end and a voltage V is applied between them. Two small pn junctions distance d apart are formed on one face of the bar as shown, by locally diffusing p-type impurity into the bar. We shall see later that if a voltage is applied at A such that the p-type material is biased positively with respect to the n-type material, minority holes can be injected into the bar at that point. These excess minority carriers drift to the other junction under the influence of the electric field due to the applied voltage, V. If the junction at B is biased in the reverse direction to that at A, any excess of holes at B will be collected, as explained below.

* L. B. Valdes, 'Resistivity measurements on Ge for transistors', *Proc. I.R.E.,* **42**, 420 (1954)

Pulses of voltage are applied at A in a direction such that minority carriers are injected during the pulse. The voltage across resistor R connected to B is displayed on an oscilloscope which thus monitors the collected current as a function of time. The time of flight of the minority carriers between injection

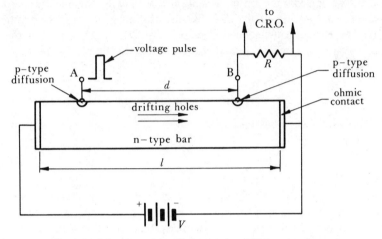

Fig. 6.24 Minority carrier lifetime and mobility measurement.

at A and extraction at B, t_0, can be measured if both sets of pulses are displayed simultaneously on the oscilloscope. There will be some attenuation and spreading of the received pulse at B due to recombination and diffusion of the carriers as they traverse the bar.

The drift velocity of minority carriers is then found using:

$$v_D = \frac{d}{t_0}$$

and hence the drift mobility can be found from:

$$\mu E = \frac{\mu V}{l} = \frac{d}{t_0}$$

or

$$\mu = \frac{ld}{t_0 V} \tag{6.84}$$

The same experimental arrangement can be used to estimate the lifetime of the minority carriers, τ_L. If the excess hole density at A is δp_0 at $t = 0$, when the voltage pulse is applied there, we know that the hole density will decay back to its equilibrium value exponentially with time, with a time constant τ_{Lh}, and from eq. (6.59):

$$\delta p = \delta p_0 \, e^{-t/\tau_{\text{Lh}}}$$

Since the time of flight of holes is t_0, the excess minority carrier density collected at B is:

$$\delta p = \delta p_0 \, e^{-t_0/\tau_{\text{Lh}}} \tag{6.85}$$

Now, if we assume the height of the received pulse is proportional to the excess hole density at the collector, then, varying the transit time, t_0, by changing the voltage, V, and plotting the pulse height and transit time semilogarithmically allow the lifetime τ_{Lh} to be estimated. It should be noted that the lifetime measured is influenced principally by recombination at the surface of the bar and may thus not be the same as the lifetime in bulk material.

It is also theoretically possible to estimate the diffusion constant for holes, D_{h}, by noticing the dispersion of arrival time of the excess carriers as the time of flight is varied, but in practice such a measurement does not yield accurate results.

6.12 Photoconductivity

We shall concern ourselves in this section only with the interaction of radiation, such as light, with bulk semiconductors, deferring discussion of the effects of incident light on junction devices until later.

As a consequence of the relatively small number of carriers created thermally by the electron–hole pair generation process, an intrinsic semiconductor has a low conductivity at all temperatures when $kT < E_{\text{g}}$. The pair generation rate at a particular temperature can be enhanced, however, by illuminating the semiconductor with radiation. If the radiant energy is of such a wavelength that the photon energy, hf, is greater than the gap energy, E_{g}, then each absorbed photon releases sufficient energy for an electron–hole pair to be produced. For this direct process to occur:

$$hf \geqslant E_{\text{g}}$$

or, in terms of wavelength, λ,

$$\lambda \leqslant hc/E_{\text{g}} \tag{6.86}$$

For example, for germanium with a gap energy 0·66 eV, $\lambda \leqslant 1900$ nm. At wavelengths larger than this, the photon energy transferred to the lattice is not sufficient to generate carriers. Thus, provided the above wavelength criterion is satisfied, radiation incident on a semiconductor surface can create additional carriers and the conductivity can be substantially increased over that of the sample in the dark.

If we let g be the number of photons absorbed per second per unit volume, this will equal the generation rate of carrier pairs in the semiconductors. We know that in an intrinsic material, the number of carriers of each type is equal to the intrinsic density, n_i. Thus, since the recombination rate will be proportional to the concentration of each carrier type, the rate of carrier production can be written

$$\frac{dn}{dt} = \frac{dp}{dt} = g - rnp = g - rn_i^2 \tag{6.87}$$

where r is the recombination coefficient, as usual. If n_{i0} is the density when steady state has been achieved, i.e., when $d/dt = 0$,

$$n_{i0} = \left(\frac{g}{r}\right)^{\frac{1}{2}} \tag{6.88}$$

Now, the conductivity of the intrinsic material is

$$\sigma = n_{i0}(\mu_e + \mu_h)e$$

Thus, the current density in the illuminated semiconductor when an electric field $\mathscr{E}$ is applied to it is

$$J = \sigma \mathscr{E} = \left(\frac{g}{r}\right)^{\frac{1}{2}} (\mu_e + \mu_h) e\mathscr{E} \tag{6.89}$$

We see from this equation that, in this case, the photocurrent is proportional to the square root of the intensity of the incident radiation.

So far, we have assumed that each absorbed photon generates an electron-hole pair, causing a single electron to flow in the external circuit. This direct process is relatively rare and occurs only in pure crystals with large applied fields and low light intensities. Other processes are much more probable and can yield greater external currents. For example, consider the following possible sequence of events. An incident photon produces a carrier pair as before, but only the electron is swept into the external circuit by the applied field, the generated hole being trapped. The trapped-hole density, p_t, will then vary with time as:

$$\frac{dp_t}{dt} = -\frac{p_t}{\tau_{Lth}} + g \tag{6.90}$$

where τ_{Lth} is the lifetime of a trapped hole. The trapped holes create a positive space-charge $p_t e$ in the semiconductor and an equal density of mobile electrons flows in from the external circuit to maintain charge neutrality. The injected electrons cause the material to be conducting while the holes remain trapped and the conductivity is given by

$$\sigma = en\mu_e = ep_t\mu_e \tag{6.91}$$

The ability of a semiconductor to detect radiation, its *photosensitivity*, is measured in terms of its *photoconductive gain*, G, which is defined as the

144

ratio of the photocurrent to the rate of generation of electron–hole charges by the incident light; if we consider a crystal of cross-section A, length l, and carrying a photocurrent I,

$$G = \frac{I}{eg(Al)} = \frac{J}{egl}$$

We then express the current density, J, in terms of the applied electric field, $\mathcal{E}$, and the conductivity given in eq. (6.91) to obtain:

$$G = \frac{\sigma\mathcal{E}}{egl} = \frac{(ep_t\,\mu_e)\mathcal{E}}{egl} = \frac{p_t\,\mu_e\,\mathcal{E}}{gl}$$

Now, the steady-state density of trapped holes is given by eq. (6.90). Hence

$$G = \tau_{Lth}\left(\frac{\mu_e\,\mathcal{E}}{l}\right)$$

Further, the bracketed term is the reciprocal of the transit time of electrons along the length of the crystal, T, say. Therefore

$$G = \frac{\tau_{Lth}}{T} \tag{6.92}$$

We see from this expression that the photosensitivity increases with increasing lifetime but since the speed at which the photoconductor can respond to a light stimulus is also a function of τ_{Lth}, if τ_{Lth} is made large to increase the photoconductive gain, this can lead to a sluggish response.

While photoconduction occurs in single-crystal semiconductors, some of the most successful light-sensing devices employ polycrystalline materials, for example cadmium sulphide, selenides, and oxides, whose high defect density is a source of trapping states, which as we have seen can often be most beneficial.

We have seen that for intrinsic materials the wavelengths of the incident radiation must be below some maximum value, λ_{max}, for photoconduction to occur. In many common semiconductor materials, detection of far infra-red radiation, with wavelengths of tens of microns, is precluded since the gap energies are such that λ_{max} is less than the infra-red wavelength; the materials are transparent. However, it is possible to dope the intrinsic material with deep-lying impurities, for example, copper in germanium, to produce success-ful infra-red detectors. If such a material is held at low temperatures, all the impurity levels remain occupied but free carriers can be excited if infra-red phonons whose energies correspond to the energy depth of the impurity level are absorbed by the crystal.

Problems

1   Find the fraction of the electrons in the valence band of intrinsic germanium which can be thermally promoted across the forbidden energy gap of 0·72 eV into the conduction band at (a) 30 K, (b) 300 K (c) the melting point, 937°C.

    Ans. 10^{-60}, 10^{-6}, $10^{-1.5}$

2   Estimate the fraction of electrons in the conduction band at room temperature of (a) Germanium (E_g = 0·72 eV) (b) Silicon (E_g = 1·10 eV) and (c) Diamond (E_g = 5·6 eV). What is the significance of these results?

    Ans. 10^{-6}, $10^{-9.3}$, 10^{-47}.

3   The resistivity of intrinsic silicon at 270°C is 3000 ohm-m. Calculate the intrinsic carrier density. Assume μ_e = 0·17 and μ_h = 0·035 m^2/V. s

    Ans. 1·1 × 10^{16} m^{-3}.

4   Compare the drift velocity of an electron moving in a field of 10 kVm^{-1} in intrinsic germanium with that of one that has moved through a distance of 10 mm in this field in a vacuum. Assume μ_e = 0·39 m^2/V. s

    Ans. 3·9 × 10^3 m/s, 5·93 × 10^6 m/s.

5   Given that the mobilities in germanium vary with temperature as follows: $\mu_e \propto T^{-1.6}$ and $\mu_h \propto T^{-2.3}$, show that the conductivity of intrinsic germanium as a function of temperature is of the form

$$\sigma = C_1 \exp\left(\frac{-3900}{T}\right)\left[C_2\left(\frac{290}{T}\right)^{0.1} + C_3\left(\frac{290}{T}\right)^{0.8}\right]$$

where the C's are constants to be found and μ_e = 0·38 m^2/V. s, μ_h = 0·18 m^2/V . s and E_g = 0·67 eV are assumed. Hence estimate the conductivity of germanium at its melting point, 958°C.

6   Measurements of the conductivity of germanium have shown that in the intrinsic range, the conductivity varies with temperature as exp (−4350/T). Use this information to estimate the energy gap width in germanium.

    Ans. 0·67 eV.

7   Show that a semiconductor has a minimum conductivity at a given temperature when

$$n = n_i \sqrt{\frac{\mu_h}{\mu_e}} \quad \text{and} \quad p = n_i \sqrt{\frac{\mu_e}{\mu_h}}.$$

Find the intrinsic and minimum conductivities for germanium at a temperature such that $n_i = 2 \cdot 5 \times 10^{19}$ m^{-3}, $\mu_e = 0 \cdot 38$ m^2/V . s, $\mu_h = 0 \cdot 19$ m^2/V . s. For what values of n and p (other than $n = p = n_i$) does this crystal have a conductivity equal to the intrinsic conductivity?

     Ans. $2 \cdot 28$ S/m, $2 \cdot 15$ S/m, $1 \cdot 25 \times 10^{19}$, 5×10^{19} m^{-3}.

8   A current density of 10^3 A/m^2 flows through an n-type germanium crystal which has resistivity $0 \cdot 05$ ohm-m. Calculate the time taken for electrons in the material to travel 50 μm.

     Ans. $2 \cdot 5$ μs.

9   Intrinsic silicon has a resistivity of 2000 ohm-m at R.T. and the density of conduction electrons is $1 \cdot 4 \times 10^{16}$ m^{-3}. Calculate the resistivities of samples containing acceptor concentrations of 10^{21} and 10^{23} m^{-3}. Assume that μ_h remains as for intrinsic silicon and that $\mu_h = 0 \cdot 25 \, \mu_e$.

     Ans. $0 \cdot 135$ amd $0 \cdot 001$ 35 ohm-m.

10   A rod of p-type germanium 6 mm long, 1 mm wide and $0 \cdot 5$ mm thick has an electrical resistance of 120 ohms. What is the impurity concentration? Assume $\mu_h = 0 \cdot 19$, $\mu_e = 0 \cdot 39$ m^2/V . s and $n_i = 2 \cdot 5 \times 10^{19}$ m^{-3}. What proportion of the conductivity is due to electrons in the conduction band?

     Ans. $3 \cdot 29 \times 10^{21}$ m^{-3}, $8 \cdot 4 \times 10^3$.

11   A 10 mm x 10 mm x 10 mm cube of silicon at room temperature has 10^{19} atom/m^3 of gallium (p-type) impurities and $1 \cdot 5 \times 10^{19}$ atom/m^3 of arsenic (n-type) impurities in the material. Determine the resistance of the bar between any two opposite faces. Assume $n_i = 1 \cdot 5 \times 10^{16}$ m^{-3}, $\mu_e = 0 \cdot 12$ m^2/V . s, $\mu_h = 0 \cdot 05$ m^2/V . s.

     Ans. $1 \cdot 04$ kΩ.

12   A sample of germanium is doped to the extent of 10^{20} donor atom/m^3 and 7×10^{19} acceptor atom/m^3. At the temperature of the sample the resistivity of intrinsic germanium is $0 \cdot 6$ ohm-m. If the applied electric field is 200 V/m find the total conduction current density. Assume $\mu_e = 0 \cdot 38$ and $\mu_h = 0 \cdot 18$ m^2/V.s.

     Ans. 524 A/m^2.

13   Show that for a two-carrier semiconductor the Hall coefficient is given by

$$R_{\mathrm{H}} = \frac{1}{e} \cdot \frac{p\mu_h^2 - n\mu_e^2}{(p\mu_h + n\mu_e)^2}$$

What is the basic difficulty in applying this result to determine the properties of a two-carrier semiconductor?

14   The resistivity of a doped silicon crystal is $9 \cdot 27 \times 10^{-3}$ ohm-m and the Hall coefficient is $3 \cdot 84 \times 10^{-4}$ m^3 C^{-1}. Assuming that conduction is by a single type of charge carrier, calculate the density and mobility of the carrier.

   Ans. $1 \cdot 6 \times 10^{22}$ m^{-3}, $0 \cdot 0414$ $m^2/V \cdot s$.

15   A rectangular, n-type germanium bar has a thickness of 2 mm. A current of 10 mA passes along the bar and a field of $0 \cdot 1$ Tesla is applied perpendicular to the current flow. The Hall voltage developed is $1 \cdot 0$ mV. Calculate the Hall constant and the electron density in the semiconductor. Find the Hall angle, assuming a mobility of $0 \cdot 36$ $m^2/V \cdot s$ for the carriers.

   Ans. 2×10^{-3} m^3/C, 3×10^{21} m^{-3}, $2 \cdot 1°$.

16   A bar of n-type germanium 10 mm x 1 mm x 1 mm is mounted in a magnetic field of $0 \cdot 2$ Tesla. The electron density in the bar is 7×10^{21} m^{-3}. If one millivolt is applied across the long ends of the bar, determine the current through the bar, the Hall coefficient and the voltage between Hall electrodes placed across the short dimensions of the bar. Assume $\mu_e = 0 \cdot 39$ $m^2/V \cdot s$.

   Ans. $43 \cdot 6$ μA, $8 \cdot 9 \times 10^{-4}$ m^3/C, $0 \cdot 78$ μV.

7. The dielectric properties of insulators

7.1 Introduction

So far, we have been largely concerned with the properties of charge carriers in conducting materials. However, there are many other materials in which all valence electrons are permanently attached to parent atoms and are not available for conduction. Such materials have *dielectric* properties and behave as insulators. Their band structure is typically as shown in Fig. 5.14(b). The forbidden gap energy, E_g, is sufficiently large to prohibit the excitation of electrons from the normally full valence band into the empty conduction band and so conduction is not possible in ideal materials. Of course, it is possible for dielectric materials to contain impurities but the impurity levels are usually sufficiently removed from band edges to preclude extrinsic conduction of the type which occurs in doped semiconductors.

In spite of being poor conductors of electricity, or perhaps because of it, dielectrics are most interesting and useful electrical engineering materials. They find extensive application in insulators and capacitors and their properties can predetermine the electrical performance and quality of such devices.

It is usual to describe the properties of a dielectric phenomenologically by modifying the electrostatic equation pertaining to a vacuum by a factor, the relative permittivity, so as to account for the insertion of a dielectric medium. Our object is to develop a microscopic theory based on the interaction of particles of atomic size in order to understand the basic mechanisms responsible for the peculiar properties of particular dielectrics and which can be used to predict their electrical performance on a macroscopic scale.

7.2 Polarization

In pure dielectric materials, although valence electrons remain in the vicinity of parent atoms they can be displaced from their equilibrium position by the application of an external field. The relative displacement of valence electrons and positive nucleus causes elementary electric dipoles to be induced in the

149

material, a process known as *polarization*, which can account for the electrical properties of the bulk material.

When an electric field $\mathcal{E}$ is impressed on a dielectric, an *electric flux density*, D, occurs in the material which is related to the field by the defining equation:

$$D = \epsilon\mathcal{E} = \epsilon_r \epsilon_0 \mathcal{E} \qquad (7.1)$$

where ϵ_0 is the permittivity of free space and ϵ_r is the relative permittivity of the material. It is found convenient to define a *polarization vector*, P, to account for the additional flux density contribution due to the presence of the dielectric, as follows:

$$D = \epsilon_0 \mathcal{E} + P \qquad (7.2)$$

Equations (7.1) and (7.2) can be rearranged to yield the following relationship between the polarization vector and the relative permittivity:

$$P = \epsilon_0(\epsilon_r - 1) E \qquad (7.3)$$

This new equation can serve as a link between a molecular treatment of dielectrics, which gives rise to the polarization term, and a macroscopic approach in which the bulk material is characterized by its relative permittivity.

Let us consider a parallel plate capacitor with charge density on its plates, ρ C/m^2. By Gauss's law the electric flux density between the plates, D, is equal to the charge density and the polarization in the dielectric, P, using eqs. (7.1) and (7.2) is then

$$P = (1 - 1/\epsilon_r)\rho \qquad (7.4)$$

Note that when $P = 0$, $\epsilon_r = 1$, which corresponds to the case of an air-filled capacitor.

If any initially air-filled capacitor has a dielectric material, relative permittivity ϵ_r, introduced so as to completly fill the space between its plates while at the same time maintaining the charge on the plates constant, it is an experimental fact that the capacitor voltage is reduced by a factor $1/\epsilon_r$, or the capacitance of the system is increased by a factor ϵ_r, as shown in Figs. 7.1(a) and (b). Since voltage is the line integral of electric field, the field in the capacitor is reduced in the same proportion or

$$\mathcal{E}_{\text{(dielectric)}} = \mathcal{E}_{\text{(air)}}/\epsilon_r$$

In order to bring about such a change in electric field, the net charge enclosed inside a Gaussian surface such as that shown in Fig. 7.1(c) must be reduced correspondingly. This can occur only if charge exists on the surface of the dielectric of opposite polarity to that on the plates. It follows that the net charge density must be reduced to ρ/ϵ_r, which happens when a charge density of $-\rho(1 - 1/\epsilon_r)$ is induced on the surface of the dielectric. Thus, the dielectric, on being placed in the capacitor, acquires a negative surface charge density $-\rho(1 - 1/\epsilon_r)$ on the face nearest the positive capacitor plate and a

150

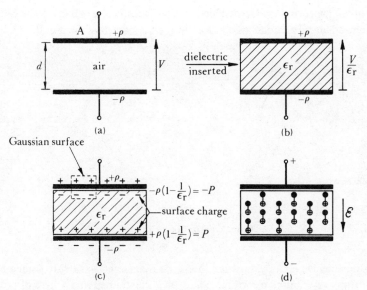

 appears here as the figure above.

Fig. 7.1 (a) and (b) Introduction of a dielectric into a plane capacitor, (c) induced surface charge, (d) dipole model showing uncompensated charges at surfaces.

positive charge density $\rho(1 - 1/\epsilon_r)$ on its face nearest the negative plate, as shown in Fig. 7.1(c).

The occurrence of surface charge at each face of the dielectric can be visualized as being due to the alignment of electrostatic dipoles, which are in some way induced in the material, with the electric field, as shown in Fig. 7.1(d). The charges associated with each dipole then cancel inside the body of the material but not at the surfaces, as shown. Now, by definition, the *dipole moment*, m, resulting from two equal charges of opposite polarity, $\pm Q$, separated by a distance x is Qx. It follows that the dielectric inserted into the air-filled capacitor acquires a dipole moment, given by

$$m = \rho(1 - 1/\epsilon_r)\, Ad \tag{7.5}$$

where A is the area of the capacitor plates and d their separation. The expression for the polarization, P, given in eq. (7.4) can now be introduced to show that

$$m = PAd \tag{7.6}$$

Since the volume of the dielectric is Ad, the equation leads to an alternative definition of the polarization, P, as being the induced dipole moment per unit volume of dielectric.

7.3 Microscopic models of polarization processes

7.3.1. Electronic polarization.
Why should the application of an electric field produce a dipole moment in materials with no free electrons? The

151

possible mechanism can be deduced by consideration of the much over-simplified classical model of an atom in such a material shown in Fig. 7.2(a).

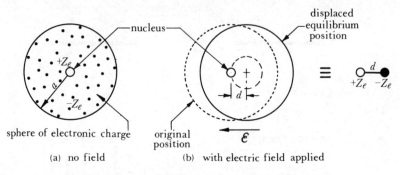

Fig. 7.2 Electronic polarization in a simple atomic model.

The nucleus which has a positive charge Ze is assumed to be surrounded by a uniformly distributed electronic charge $-Ze$, contained in a sphere of radius a. When a field is applied the nucleus and electrons experience oppositely directed forces and the electron orbitals are distorted in such a way that the centre of gravity of the negative charge no longer coincides with the nucleus, as shown in Fig. 7.2(b). Such a neutral configuration is equivalent to an electric dipole, as shown.

To calculate the induced dipole moment in the atomic model it is firstly assumed that only the electron cloud is displaced by the field. In equilibrium, the force on the electrons due to the field, $-Ze\mathcal{E}$, is exactly balanced by the coulomb force due to the separation of positive and negative charges. Under these conditions, let the centre of gravity of the electron cloud move distance d, as shown in Fig. 7.2(b). If the sphere of charge is sub-divided into two regions, one a sphere of radius d and the other the remaining volume, it is a consequence of Gauss's law that the nucleus only experiences a field due to the charge contained in the former. Now, the charge in this inner sphere is equal to $(-Ze)\, d^3/a^3$ and, by Gauss's law, the field due to this charge at radius d, i.e., at the nucleus, is

$$\mathcal{E}_{\text{induced}} = -\frac{Zed^3}{4\pi d^2 \,\epsilon_0\, a^3} = -\frac{Zed}{4\pi\epsilon_0\, a^3}$$

In equilibrium, this coulomb field at the nucleus must be equal in magnitude to the applied field, $\mathcal{E}$. Hence:

$$\mathcal{E} = \frac{Zed}{4\pi\epsilon_0\, a^3}$$

$$Zed = (4\pi\epsilon_0\, a^3)\,\mathcal{E} \tag{7.7}$$

152

Further, a separation d between the charge on the nucleus Ze, and the electronic charge, $-Ze$, which is assumed concentrated at the centre of gravity of negative charge, is equivalent to an induced dipole moment Zed in the atom. Equation (7.7) shows that the induced dipole moment, m_i say, is proportional to the field, for small displacements at least, or

$$m_i = Zed = \alpha_e \mathscr{E} \tag{7.8}$$

The constant of proportionality, α_e, is the *electronic polarizability* which is defined, using eq. (7.8), as the induced dipole moment *per atom* per unit of electric field. Comparing eqs. (7.7) and (7.8) it can be seen that the simple model predicts a value for the polarizability as

$$\alpha_e = 4\pi\epsilon_0\, a^3 \tag{7.9}$$

The assumption that the electronic charge density is constant to some radius a and then drops to zero is not in accord with the quantum description of an atom, as discussed in chapter 2. A more realistic charge distribution might be, for example, as shown in Fig. 2.4, where the charge density falls off exponentially with radius. A quantum-mechanical treatment would therefore indicate larger polarizabilities than those obtained from the classical model since the outermost electronic charge at large radii is weakly bound to the nucleus and is more influenced by an applied field. Nevertheless, eq. (7.9) is found to give the right order of magnitude for the polarizability, particularly for rare gases. Also, the dependence of α_e on a^3, or the volume of the atom, has been experimentally verified to be approximately correct. So as to get a feel for the quantities involved, let us assume that $a = 0\cdot1$ nm, $\mathscr{E} = 10^4$ V/m, and $Z = 10$. Equation (7.9) then indicates that $\alpha_e \simeq 10^{-40}$ MKS units and eq. (7.8) then gives $d \simeq 10^{-9}$ nm, which is indeed a very small fraction of the atomic radius!

7.3.2. Ionic polarization. When atoms form molecules electronic polarization is still possible but there may be additional polarization due to a relative displacement of the atomic components of the molecule in the presence of an electric field. Consider, for simplicity, a sodium chloride molecule; it is composed of Na^+ ions bound to Cl^- ions and their inner atomic distance is a, say. It is evident that such molecules have a built-in permanent dipole moment, equal to ae, which exists even before the field is applied. Such materials are said to be *polar*. Not all molecules are polar since an essential requirement is that the centres of gravity of negative and positive charge in the molecule should not.coincide and this is not true for all materials, for example in an oxygen molecule. We can estimate the permanent dipole moment of the NaCl molecule by assuming an interatomic separation of $0\cdot1$ nm; the dipole moment is then of order 10^{-29} C m.

When a field is applied to the molecule, the sodium and chlorine atoms are displaced in opposite directions until ionic binding forces stop the process, thus increasing the dipole moment. Again it is found that this induced dipole moment is proportional to the applied field and an *ionic polarizability*, α_i, is introduced to account for the increase, giving:

$$m_{\text{induced}} = \alpha_i \mathscr{E} \qquad (7.10)$$

Of course, the individual ions experience electronic polarization in addition. For most materials, the ionic polarizability is less than the electronic and typically $\alpha_i \approx 0.1 \, \alpha_e$.

7.3.3. Orientation polarization.

This type of polarization only occurs in polar substances. The permanent molecular dipoles in such materials can rotate about their axis of symmetry to align with an applied field which exerts a torque in them. This additional polarization effect is accounted for by an *orientational polarizability* term, α_0.

With electronic and ionic polarization processes, the force due to the externally applied field is balanced by elastic binding forces, but for orientation polarization no such forces exist. In thermal equilibrium with no field applied the permanent dipoles contribute no net polarization since they are randomly oriented. When a field is applied dipole alignment is largely offset by thermal agitation. However, since it is observed that orientational polarization is of the same order as the other forms of polarization, it is only necessary for one molecular dipole in 10^5 to be completely aligned with the field to account for the effect. Whereas the orientated polarizability, α_0, is temperature dependent, since the higher the temperature the greater is the thermal agitation and the lower is α_0, the distorting polarizability factors, α_e and α_i, are functions of molecular structure and are largely independent of temperature.

7.4 The relationship between polarizability and permittivity

It is important to establish the relationship between the polarizability of a dielectric and its relative permittivity, since the former is a function of its atomic structure while the latter determines the electrical properties of the bulk material.

In general, the molecules in a dielectric have contributions to their overall polarization from electronic, ionic, and orientational polarization, provided they are polar molecules, and the total polarizability is the sum of the individual factors, or

$$\alpha = \alpha_e + \alpha_i + \alpha_0 \qquad (7.11)$$

The dielectric is composed of many such molecules, N per unit volume, and if each experiences a field, $\mathscr{E}_{\text{int}}$, then, by the definition of polarizability, the overall polarization of the material, P, is given by

$$P = N\alpha \mathscr{E}_{\text{int}} \qquad (7.12)$$

154

Here, $\mathscr{E}_{int}$ is the net field acting on individual molecular dipoles. In dense materials such as liquids and solids, $\mathscr{E}_{int}$ is not equal to the applied field, since P is large and the total field experienced by a molecule has contributions from both the applied field and the fields due to the polarization of atoms in its neighbourhood.

In order to discuss the problem more quantitatively, consider a one-dimensional chain of atoms, each of polarizability α_e and spaced a apart, as shown in Fig. 7.3. An external electric field $\mathscr{E}$ is applied parallel to the chain,

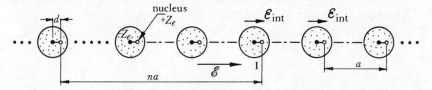

Fig. 7.3 One-dimensional model of a dielectric.

as shown, and we shall find the net internal field, $\mathscr{E}_{int}$, experienced by one of the atoms, I, say. The field at I due to the dipole induced in an atom situated distance na away is:

$$\mathscr{E}_n = \frac{Ze}{4\pi\epsilon_0}\left(\frac{1}{(na)^2} - \frac{1}{(na+d)^2}\right)$$

Since $d \ll a$ this can be simplified to give

$$\mathscr{E}_n \simeq \frac{2\,Zed}{4\pi\epsilon_0\,(na)^3} = \frac{2m_i}{4\pi\epsilon_0(na)^3} \tag{7.13}$$

where the induced dipole moment per atom, m_i, has been introduced. Now, the induced dipole moment can be expressed in terms of the polarizability and the field experienced by the atom, i.e.,

$$m_i = \alpha_e \mathscr{E}_{int} \tag{7.14}$$

Hence, the field experienced by atom I due to the atom distance na away is

$$\mathscr{E}_n = \frac{2\alpha_e \mathscr{E}_{int}}{4\pi\epsilon_0(na)^3} \tag{7.15}$$

Now, the net field at I, $\mathscr{E}_{int}$, is equal to the applied field, $\mathscr{E}$, plus contributions similar to that expressed in eq. (7.14) from all atoms in the chain, and remembering that there are atoms to the left and to the right of I in the infinite chain we have:

$$\mathscr{E}_{int} = \mathscr{E} + \frac{2\alpha_e \mathscr{E}_{int}}{4\pi\epsilon_0}\left\{2\sum_{n=1}^{\infty}\frac{1}{(na)^3}\right\}$$

Summing the series and rearranging gives

$$\mathcal{E}_{\text{int}} = \frac{\mathcal{E}}{1 - \dfrac{1 \cdot 2\alpha_e}{\pi\epsilon_0 a^3}} \tag{7.16}$$

It will be seen that the combined effect of the induced dipoles of neighbouring atoms is to produce a net field at an atom which is bigger than the applied field; and the greater the polarizability α_e or the smaller the interatomic spacing, a, the greater is the internal field.

Referring to eq. (7.15) again and incorporating eq. (7.13) gives, for the special case of the one-dimensional model

$$\mathcal{E}_{\text{int}} = \mathcal{E} + \frac{1}{\epsilon_0} \cdot \frac{1 \cdot 2}{\pi} \cdot \frac{m_i}{a^3} \tag{7.17}$$

In a more general three-dimensional solid, while the internal field is more difficult to evaluate, the general expression for $\mathcal{E}_{\text{int}}$ is similar in form to eq. (7.17); the number density of atoms, N, replaces a^{-3} and since Nm_i is equal to the polarization, P, the general expression becomes:

$$\mathcal{E}_{\text{int}} = \mathcal{E} + \frac{\gamma P}{\epsilon_0} \tag{7.18}$$

Here the value of the dimensionless constant γ, called the *internal field constant,* is dependent on the internal arrangement of atoms in the material. It is usually of order unity; for example, for the one-dimensional model it equals $1 \cdot 2/\pi$. For the special cases of either solids with cubic atomic structure, or media in which the atoms or molecules are in complete disorder, $\gamma = \frac{1}{3}$ and the internal field is then:

$$\mathcal{E}_{\text{int}} = \mathcal{E} + \frac{P}{3\epsilon_0} \tag{7.19}$$

This is the so called *Lorentz field,* named after its originator.

Now, the polarization P can be written either in terms of the internal field and the polarizability, or in terms of the permittivity of the bulk material and the applied field, as in eq. (7.3), to give

$$P = N\alpha\mathcal{E}_{\text{int}} = \epsilon_0(\epsilon_r - 1)\mathcal{E} \tag{7.20}$$

Substituting these two expressions into eq. (7.18) gives the required relationship between the permittivity and the polarizability, as follows:

$$\frac{\epsilon_r - 1}{1 + \gamma(\epsilon_r - 1)} = \frac{N\alpha}{\epsilon_0} \tag{7.21}$$

156

For the special case of materials in which the internal field is the Lorentz field, $\gamma = \frac{1}{3}$ and eq. (7.21) becomes:

$$\frac{\epsilon_r - 1}{\epsilon_r + 2} = \frac{N\alpha}{3\epsilon_0} \tag{7.22}$$

This is the *Clausius Mosotti* equation which is strictly valid only for high degrees of crystal symmetry or complete molecular disorder.

Equations (7.21) and, in special cases, (7.22) are applicable to dense materials such as solids, liquids, and high-pressure gases; measurement of the relative permittivity can then determine the polarizability. For low-pressure gases where molecules are sufficiently far apart that the field due to their induced dipole moment is not experienced by neighbouring molecules, $\mathscr{E}_{int} = \mathscr{E}$. Substituting this condition into eq. (7.20) leads to the much simpler expression for the relative permittivity

$$\epsilon_r = 1 + N\alpha/\epsilon_0 \tag{7.23}$$

As an example of the orders of magnitude of the quantities involved, consider a hypothetical material in which the atoms are assumed spherical of radius a and stacked as shown in Fig. 7.4. The number density of atoms is

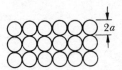

Fig. 7.4 Hypothetical solid used for the estimation of ϵ_r.

then $N = \frac{1}{8}a^3$. If the material is non-polar, its polarizability will be given approximately by eq. (7.9); eq. (7.22) then gives:

$$\frac{\epsilon_r - 1}{\epsilon_r + 2} = \frac{1}{8a^3} \cdot \frac{4\pi\epsilon_0 a^3}{3\epsilon_0} = \frac{\pi}{6}$$

which yields a value of 4·3 for the relative permittivity. For comparison, the simpler expression of eq. (7.23) which neglects the interaction of the closely packed induced dipoles gives $\epsilon_r = 2\cdot6$, which indicates that eq. (7.23) is only applicable to low-pressure gases when $\epsilon_r \simeq 1$.

7.5 Relative permittivity of polar materials

The expression for the relative permittivity given in eq. (7.21) is not applicable to polar materials since, as we have discussed, partial alignment of permanent dipoles within such materials with this field can cause additional polarization.

Let us consider a polar dielectric containing permanent elementary dipoles of moment m_p. If one of the dipoles makes an angle θ with an applied field, $\mathscr{E}$, it suffers a torque $m_p \mathscr{E} \sin \theta$ which tends to align it with the field. Thus

157

an unaligned dipole has a greater energy than an aligned one and it is readily shown that it possesses energy $-m_p \mathcal{E} \cos \theta$. In the absence of thermal motion all dipoles would move to line up in the same direction as an applied field, but this motion is opposed by thermal agitation energy at some temperature T, which tends to redistribute the dipoles randomly so that on average there is only a net partial alignment. Now, it was seen in chapter 3 that in an interacting system in thermal equilibrium, the number of system components in a given potential energy range centred around energy E is proportional to the size of the range and to a Bolzmann factor, $\exp(-E/kT)$. We apply this maxim by considering a sphere in the dielectric which contains N permanent dipoles per unit volume, the applied field being in the x-direction, as shown in Fig. 7.5(a). Since the number of dipoles, dN_θ, whose orientation lies within an

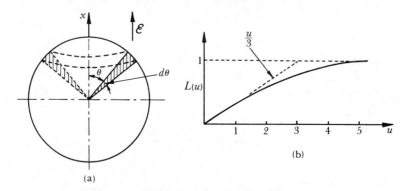

Fig. 7.5 (a) The geometry used to calculate the average dipole moment of a polar material, (b) the Langevin function $L(a)$.

angle between θ and $\theta + d\theta$ to the field, is then proportional to the size of the range or the solid angle $2\pi \sin \theta \, d\theta$ shown and, since each will have potential energy $-m_p \mathcal{E} \cos \theta$, corresponding to a Bolzmann factor $\exp(m_p \mathcal{E} \cos \theta / kT)$, then

$$dN_\theta \propto 2\pi \sin \theta \, d\theta . \exp(m_p \mathcal{E} \cos \theta / kT) \qquad (7.24)$$

Since each of these dipoles is oriented at an angle θ to the field, its contribution to the polarization is the component in the direction of $\mathcal{E}$, $m_p \cos \theta$. The mean dipole moment, $\overline{m}_p$, at some temperature T is the sum of all such contributions divided by the number of dipoles, or, from (7.24):

$$\overline{m}_p = \frac{\int_0^\pi dN_\theta \, m_p \cos \theta}{\int_0^\pi dN_\theta} = \frac{m_p \int_0^\pi \exp(u \cos\theta) \sin\theta \, \cos\theta \, d\theta}{\int_0^\pi \exp(u \cos \theta) \sin \theta \, d\theta} \qquad (7.25)$$

where

$$u = m_p \mathcal{E} / kT \qquad (7.26)$$

158

The integration is solved by making the substitution

$$t = u\cos\theta$$

which leads to the result:

$$\overline{m}_p = m_p\left[\coth(m_p\mathscr{E}/kT) - \frac{kT}{m_p\mathscr{E}}\right] \qquad (7.27)$$

This equation is known as the *Langevin equation* after the man who first derived it for magnetic dipoles. The *Langevin function*, $L(u) = \coth u - 1/u$ has the shape shown in Fig. 7.5(b). For large values of u, for example for large fields or low temperatures, there is a saturation effect; $\overline{m}_p$ approaches m_p and all the dipoles are aligned. However, we have seen that m_p is typically of order 10^{-29} and so, even for extremely high electric field strengths, u as defined by eq. (7.26) is very much less than unity at ordinary temperatures. Under these conditions, the Langevin function can be expanded to give:

$$L(u) = \frac{1 + \dfrac{u^2}{2!} + \dfrac{u^4}{4!}}{u + \dfrac{u^3}{3!} + \dfrac{u^5}{5!}} \cdots - \frac{1}{u} \simeq \frac{u}{3}$$

if $u \ll 1$ and high-order terms are neglected. Hence, usually

$$\overline{m}_p \simeq \frac{m_p^2}{3}\cdot\frac{\mathscr{E}}{kT} \qquad (7.28)$$

We can use this expression to find the orientational polarizability, α_0 since this by definition is the induced dipole moment per atom per unit of electric field. Hence

$$\alpha_0 = \frac{\overline{m}_p}{\mathscr{E}} = \frac{m_p^2}{3kT} \qquad (7.29)$$

In a material which can experience all forms of polarization, this value of α_0 can be substituted into eq. (7.11) to give the overall polarizability

$$\alpha = \alpha_e + \alpha_i + \frac{m_p^2}{3kT} \qquad (7.30)$$

Equation (7.22) can be modified using this expression so as to be applicable to polar materials in which the dipoles are free to rotate and yields:

$$\frac{\epsilon_r - 1}{\epsilon_r + 2} = \frac{N}{3\epsilon_0}\left(\alpha_e + \alpha_i + \frac{m_p^2}{3kT}\right) \qquad (7.31)$$

159

7.6 Properties of dielectrics in time-dependent fields

It is most important that the properties of dielectrics subjected to alternating fields be understood since it is precisely these conditions that are most often encountered in engineering applications. Of particular interest are the loss of energy in a real dielectric and the variation of permittivity with frequency. It will become apparent that the permittivity must be a complex quantity, the imaginary part being a measure of the loss.

7.6.1. Complex permittivity of lossy dielectrics.
Consider for simplicity a parallel-plate capacitor, capacitance C, area of plates A, separation d, filled with the dielectric and having a sinusoidal voltage V_{rms} of angular frequency ω applied. If the dielectric were perfect, a root mean square current, I_q, would flow which is in quadrature with the applied voltage, as shown in Fig. 7.6.

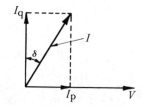

Fig. 7.6 Phasor diagram for a lossy capacitor.

For all practically realizable dielectric fillings there will be some small loss in the capacitor and a resistive current, I_p, will flow, as shown on the phasor diagram. The resultant circuit current, I, of magnitude $(I_q^2 + I_p^2)^{\frac{1}{2}}$, lags behind the quadrature component by an angle δ, where

$$\tan \delta = I_p/I_q \qquad (7.32)$$

The tangent of the *loss angle*, δ, is known as the *loss tangent*. Both are a measure of the lossiness of a particular dielectric and for a perfect dielectric $\tan \delta = \delta = 0$ since $I_p = 0$.

For a perfect dielectric, relative permittivity ϵ_r', filling the capacitor the current is given by:

$$I_q = \omega C V = \frac{\omega \epsilon_0 \, \epsilon_r' A V}{d} \qquad (7.33)$$

However, for a lossy dielectric filling, the total current flowing is

$$I = I_p + j|I_q| = j|I_q|\,(1 - jI_p/|I_q|)$$

or, using eqs. (7.32) and (7.33):

$$I = \frac{j\omega A V \epsilon_0 \, \epsilon_r'}{d}(1 - j \tan \delta) \qquad (7.34)$$

Comparing eqs. (7.33) and (7.34) we see that the behaviour of the lossy dielectric can be accounted for by introducing a complex relative permittivity, ϵ_{rc}, given by

$$\epsilon_{rc} = \epsilon_r'(1 - j \tan \delta) \tag{7.35}$$

It is customary and convenient to write the magnitude of the imaginary part of this expression as ϵ_r'', giving:

$$\epsilon_{rc} = \epsilon_r' - j\epsilon_r'' \tag{7.36}$$

where

$$\tan \delta = \epsilon_r''/\epsilon_r' \tag{7.37}$$

It is clear that the lossy dielectric can be treated by assigning to it a complex permittivity, the imaginary part of which is related to its loss tangent by eq. (7.37). It should be noted that this definition does not indicate anything about the type of loss mechanism present in the dielectric.

The energy stored in a dielectric can be deduced from the simple capacitor example. Since the energy stored in the capacitor is

$$\tfrac{1}{2}CV^2 = \frac{1}{2}\frac{\epsilon_0 \epsilon_r' A}{d} V^2$$

it follows that the mean energy stored per unit volume of dielectric is

$$\text{energy stored/unit volume} = \tfrac{1}{2}\epsilon_0 \epsilon_r' \mathscr{E}^2 \tag{7.38}$$

where $\mathscr{E}$ is the root mean square electric field strength.

Similarly, the power dissipated in the lossy capacitor is

$$VI_p = VI_q \tan \delta = V\left(\frac{\omega\epsilon_0 \epsilon_r' AV}{d}\right)\frac{\epsilon_r''}{\epsilon_r'}$$

using eqs. (7.33) and (7.37). Hence, the power dissipated in the dielectric is given by:

$$\text{power dissipated per unit volume} = \omega\epsilon_0 \epsilon_r'' \mathscr{E}^2 \tag{7.39}$$

It is apparent that if the complex permittivity of a dielectric is specified at any frequency, its complete electrical performance at that frequency can readily be deduced.

7.6.2. Variations of permittivity with frequency.

The frequency dependence of the complex permittivity will be discussed on an atomic scale in terms of the various polarization processes in the dielectric. The possible variations of both components of the complex permittivity of a polar dielectric with frequency are shown schematically in Fig. 7.7. In region (a) all types of polarization are possible and the material is characterized by a polarizability $(\alpha_e + \alpha_i + \alpha_o)$. In region (b) at some frequency ω_1, usually in the radio-frequency or microwave band, permanent dipoles are no longer able to align with the field because of their inertia; the real part of the permittivity falls

161

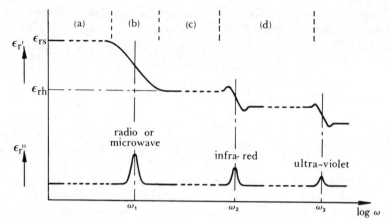

Fig. 7.7 Variation of the components of the complex permittivity of a lossy dielectric with frequency.

to a value corresponding to a polarizability $(\alpha_e + \alpha_i)$ and there is absorption of power typified by a corresponding resonance in the ϵ_r'' curve. Only electronic and ionic polarization are present in region (c). Above some frequency ω_2, typically in the infra-red region, the system inertia prohibits ionic polarization; ϵ_r' falls again to a value corresponding to a polarizability α_e only in region (d) and resonance absorption occurs again. For even higher frequencies, usually in the ultra-violet region, the electronic contribution to the polarization ceases, $\alpha_e = \alpha = 0$, and the relative permittivity approaches unity at frequencies above ω_3. The various regions of interest in the permittivity spectrum will now be discussed in more detail.

The frequency dependence of the electronic polarizability α_e and hence ϵ_{rc} in region (d) and above is best explained by use of the simple atomic model described in section 7.2.1. If an electron in this model is displaced a distance x from its equilibrium position, it experiences a restoring force, F, due to the field induced, $e\mathscr{E}$, and eq. (7.7) then gives

$$F = \frac{Ze^2}{4\pi\epsilon_0\, a^3}\, x$$

which shows that the restoring force is proportional to the electronic displacement, x. The one-dimensional equation of motion for the electrons is then

$$m\frac{d^2 x}{dt^2} + \frac{Ze^2}{4\pi\epsilon_0\, a^3}\, x = 0$$

or

$$\frac{d^2 x}{dt^2} + \omega_3{}^2 x = 0 \qquad (7.40)$$

162

This is, of course, an equation of simple harmonic motion and ω_3 is the natural resonance frequency at which electrons vibrate about their equilibrium position, where

$$\omega_3 = \sqrt{\frac{Ze^2}{4\pi\epsilon_0 a^3 m}} \qquad (7.41)$$

The reader may verify by substituting $Z = 1$ and $a = 0.1$ nm that ω_3 is typically 10^{16} rad/s, which is in the ultra-violet part of the spectrum. When the field varies at a frequency below ω_3, the electron cloud follows the field variations and the material exhibits an electronic polarizability, α_e. However, when the frequency of the driving field reaches ω_3 a resonance absorption occurs which corresponds to emission of radiation by the accelerating electrons; this can be accounted for by an additional damping term in the equation of motion which is proportional to dx/dt. For driving field frequencies greater than ω_3, electrons fail to follow the excursions of the field and α_e falls to zero.

The frequency dependence of ϵ_{rc} around ω_2 can be explained in terms of the natural resonance of ionic dipoles in a way analogous to the electronic resonance described above. When one component of the ionic dipole is displaced relative to the other, it again experiences a restoring force proportional to the displacement and executes simple harmonic motion at frequency ω_2. The masses involved are molecular and are of order $10^4\ m$, so the resonance frequency corresponding to that given in eq. (7.41) is lowered by a factor of order $1/100$, to around 10^{14} rad/s, which is in the infra-red part of the spectrum. When the frequency of an applied field exceeds the resonance at $\omega = \omega_2$, ionic dipoles can no longer follow electric field charges alteration and α_i falls to zero.

The frequency dependence of orientation polarization, illustrated in regions (a) to (c) of Fig. 7.7, is of greatest engineering interest since the mechanism can produce dielectric losses over a possible range from d.c. to several GHz. The real part of the relative permittivity varies from a maximum value of ϵ_{rs} to a minimum of ϵ_{rh} over this range, as shown. ϵ_{rs} is the static relative permittivity for d.c. or slowly varying fields; it corresponds to a polarization, P_s, which is a function of the total polarization, including α_o. The high-frequency permittivity, ϵ_{rh}, corresponds to region (c) and is associated with a polarization P_h, which corresponds to electronic and ionic polarizability only.

Now, suppose an electric field, $\mathscr{E}$, is applied at $t = 0$, in a time which is much less than the time taken for dipoles to orient themselves but not so short that electronic or ionic resonances occur, as shown in Fig. 7.8(a). At $t = 0$, the polarization can only be due to distortion polarizability and from eq. (7.3) is given by

$$P_h = \epsilon_0(\epsilon_{rh} - 1)\mathscr{E} \qquad (7.42)$$

163

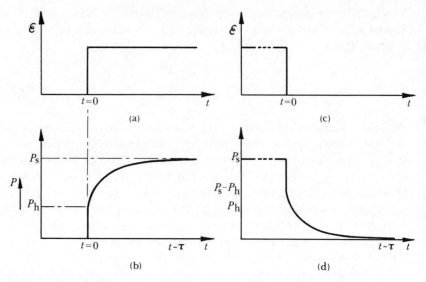

Fig. 7.8 Effect of sudden changes of electric field on the polarization of a polar dielectric.

as shown in Fig. 7.8(b). After some time of order τ, say, which is sufficiently long for those permanent dipoles which are partially to align with field to do so, the polarization becomes

$$P_s = \epsilon_0(\epsilon_{rs} - 1)\mathscr{E} \qquad (7.43)$$

Next, suppose that the field $\mathscr{E}$ has been present for much longer than τ and is suddenly switched off, at some new time origin $t = 0$, as shown in Fig. 7.8(c). The static polarizability, P_s, is suddenly reduced to $P_s - P_h$ by removal of distortion polarization. The remaining polarization subsequently decays away or *relaxes* to zero, again in a time comparable to τ, when the dipoles are randomly oriented. Time τ is called the *relaxation time* and the process is referred to as *dipolar relaxation.* It seems reasonable to assume that the growing and decaying parts of the $P(t)$ curves are exponential and can thus be represented by:

$$P = P_h + (P_s - P_h)(1 - e^{-t/\tau}) \text{ for } \mathscr{E} \text{ applied at } t = 0 \qquad (7.44)$$

and

$$P = (P_s - P_h)e^{-t/\tau} \text{ for } \mathscr{E} \text{ removed at } t = 0 \qquad (7.45)$$

We are particularly interested in the response of the circuit to alternating rather than step-function fields. This problem can be discussed in terms of the electric circuit analogy of the relaxation process shown in Fig. 7.9(a). Suppose

164

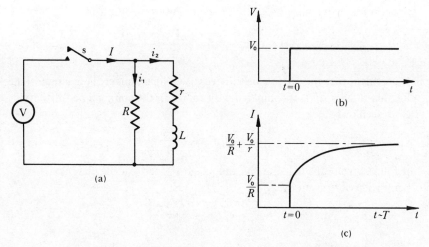

Fig. 7.9 Response of the analogous electric circuit to a sudden application of voltage.

that the voltage source to the circuit is initially a battery, V_0. After switch s is closed, at $t = 0$, the total current supplied, I, is shown as a function of time in Fig. 7.9(c) and is given by

$$I = \frac{V_0}{R} + \frac{V_0}{r}(1 - e^{-t/T}) \tag{7.46}$$

where T is the time constant of the r-L branch. Notice that eqs. (7.44) and (7.46) are of the same form and the circuit responds to the applied voltage in a way entirely analogous to the response of the dielectric to the electric field; time constant T measures the approximate time for the current to rise to its maximum value just as τ in the dielectric is the approximate time for dipoles to reach their equilibrium position.

Now, if a sinusoidal voltage, V_{rms}, of angular frequency ω is applied to the electric circuit analogue, the total current flowing, I_{rms}, is obviously

$$I = \frac{V}{R} + \frac{V}{(r + j\omega L)} = \frac{V}{R} + \frac{V}{r(1 + j\omega T)} \tag{7.47}$$

Now, since it has been shown that the electric circuit has a behaviour analogous to that of a dielectric, the result in eq. (7.47), together with a comparison of eqs. (7.44) and (7.46), can be used to show that the response of a dielectric to a sinusoidally impressed field, of angular frequency ω, is such as to produce a polarization given by:

$$P = P_h + \frac{P_s - P_h}{1 + j\omega\tau} \tag{7.48}$$

165

Substituting from eqs. (7.42) and (7.43) modifies the result to:

$$P = \epsilon_0(\epsilon_{rh} - 1)\mathscr{E} + \frac{\epsilon_0(\epsilon_{rs} - \epsilon_{rh})\mathscr{E}}{1 + j\omega\tau} \tag{7.49}$$

It is evident that the relative permittivity is complex under these circumstances. Further, if eq. (7.49) is compared with eq. (7.3), the complex permittivity ϵ_{rc} is seen to be:

$$\epsilon_{rc} = \epsilon_r' - j\epsilon_r'' = \epsilon_{rh} + \frac{\epsilon_{rs} - \epsilon_{rh}}{1 + j\omega\tau}$$

It follows from this that the real and imaginary parts of the complex permittivity are given by:

$$\epsilon_r' = \epsilon_{rh} + \frac{\epsilon_{rs} - \epsilon_{rh}}{1 + \omega^2\tau^2} \tag{7.50}$$

and

$$\epsilon_r'' = \frac{\omega\tau(\epsilon_{rs} - \epsilon_{rh})}{1 + \omega^2\tau^2} \tag{7.51}$$

The loss tangent for the material can then be deduced, using eq. (7.37), and is

$$\tan\delta = \frac{\omega\tau(\epsilon_{rs} - \epsilon_{rh})}{\epsilon_{rs} + \omega^2\tau^2\epsilon_{rh}} \tag{7.52}$$

Equations (7.50) to (7.52) are the *Debye equations* which give the frequency dependence of the complex permittivity of a polar dielectric. The components of relative permittivity are plotted in Fig. 7.10. It is left as an exercise to

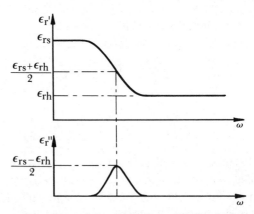

Fig. 7.10 Frequency dependence of the complex permittivity of a polar dielectric.

show that maximum dielectric losses occur at a frequency such that $\omega\tau = 1$ and that the values of ϵ_r' and ϵ_r'' at the frequency are as indicated in the figure.

Problems

1   The relative permittivity of argon at $0°C$ and 1 atmosphere is $1·000\,435$. Find (a) the polarizability of an argon atom and (b) the approximate radius of an argon atom.

    Ans. $1·4 \times 10^{-40}$, $0·11$ nm.

2   A solid contains 5×10^{28} identical atoms per m^3, each with a polarizability of 2×10^{-40} F/m^2. Assuming a Lorentz internal field find (a) the ratio of internal to applied field and (b) the relative permittivity of the material.

    Ans. $1·6$, $2·81$.

3   Show that for gases at low pressure the Clausius–Mosotti equation reduces to:

$$N\alpha /\epsilon_0 \simeq \epsilon_r - 1$$

    The Claussius–Mosotti equation also applies to the optical frequency range. If the refractive index of a medium with respect to free space, η, is defined as the ratio of the velocity of a plane wave in free space to that in the medium, show that the equation becomes

$$\frac{N\alpha}{3\epsilon_0} = \frac{\eta^2 - 1}{\eta^2 + 2}$$

4   If it is assumed that the dielectric constant of a liquid is determined essentially by orientational polarization and that the internal field constant is zero, show that its relative permittivity is given by

$$\epsilon_r \simeq 1 + \frac{Nm_p^{\,2}}{3\epsilon_0 kT} - \frac{NE^2 m_p^{\,4}}{45\epsilon_0 k^3 T^3}$$

where m_p is the dipole moment of an elementary dipole in the liquid.

5   The equivalent circuit of a practical parallel-plate capacitor may be represented by a parallel combination of a pure capacitance C and a resistance R. If the relative permittivity of the dielectric filling is $\epsilon_{rc} = \epsilon_r' - j\epsilon_r''$, find the value of the elements C and R in terms of the permittivity, the area of the plates A and their separation d. Hence show that the power dissipated per unit volume of the capacitor is $\omega\epsilon_0\epsilon_r''\mathscr{E}^2$ where $\mathscr{E}$ is the r.m.s. electric field strength (i.e. equation 7.39).

    Ans. $d/(\omega\epsilon_0\epsilon_r''A)$, $\epsilon_0\epsilon_r'A/d$.

167

6.   Show that a parallel plate capacitor which is completely filled with two parallel layers of material, one layer with relative permittivity ϵ_r, zero conductivity and thickness t, the other with relative permittivity which can be neglected, a finite conductivity σ and thickness bt, behaves as if the space between the capacitor plates were filled with a homogeneous dielectric of relative permittivity ϵ_r^* given by

$$\epsilon_r^* = \frac{\epsilon_r(1+b)}{1+j\omega\epsilon_r\,\epsilon_0\,b/\sigma}$$

(Hint: equation (7.39) will be required.)

7   A certain dielectric, when subjected to an alternating field of frequency $f_1 = 4GHz$, has a measured real part of the complex permittivity of $2\cdot57$. The tangent of the loss angle is measured to be $0\cdot0032$. Determine (a) the imaginary part of the relative permittivity and (b) the power dissipated in the dielectric per unit volume if a field of $\mathscr{E} = 100 \cos 2\pi f_1 t$ V/m is applied.

Ans. $0\cdot0082, 9\cdot1$ W/m^3.

8   Given that the frequency dependent part of the oriental polarizability of a certain dielectric can be written

$$\alpha_0/(1+\omega\tau)$$

Where τ is the dipolar relaxation time and ω is the angular frequency of the applied field show that the loss tangent is given by

$$\tan\delta = \frac{\omega\tau(\epsilon_{rs}-\epsilon_{rh})}{\epsilon_{rs}+\epsilon_{rh}\,\omega^2\,\tau^2}$$

where ϵ_{rs} and ϵ_{rh} are the static and high frequency relative permittivities. Hence show that the imaginary part of the complex relative permittivity reaches a maximum at some frequency ω_m, given by $\omega_m\tau = 1$, and find this maximum value.

Ans. $\frac{1}{2}(\epsilon_{rs}-\epsilon_{rh})$.

8. Gaseous and solid-state plasmas

8.1 Introduction

A survey of all matter in the universe would indicate that the gaseous state, consisting of fully or partially ionized gases, predominates. The term *plasma* is used to denote the ionized state and for the moment we will regard a plasma simply as being a conglomeration of mobile electrons and ions contained in a region of space, with the possible addition of a background of neutral atoms. It is not necessary for both sets of charged particles to be mobile; for example, in a solid-state plasma the positive ions are located at lattice points and are relatively stationary. It is also possible to have a liquid plasma; for example, table salt in water is a plasma of mobile positive sodium ions and negative chlorine ions. The gaseous plasma is sometimes called the 'fourth state of matter'. This is because each step from a solid to a liquid to a gas to a plasma involves an increasing number of degrees of freedom. In gaseous plasmas, charge or current are additional parameters which neutral gases do not possess.

One of the basic properties of a plasma is that it is basically electrically neutral. If it were not neutral, large macroscopic coulomb forces would be set up to expell ions or electrons to restore neutrality. Thus, except near its boundaries, a plasma is characterized by

$$\left| \frac{n - n_i}{n} \right| \ll 1 \tag{8.1}$$

where n is the number density of electrons and n_i is the number density of ions. If there are N neutral atoms per unit volume in the plasma, the degree of ionization is given by

$$\frac{n_i}{N} \simeq \frac{n}{N} \tag{8.2}$$

A further characterizing feature of a plasma is its *temperature, T*. These three properties, number density, percentage ionization, and temperature, will serve initially in classifying the various types of plasma. Further properties will emerge on closer study but those mentioned will suffice for the moment. The chart of Fig. 8.1 compares these properties for some natural and man-made plasmas.

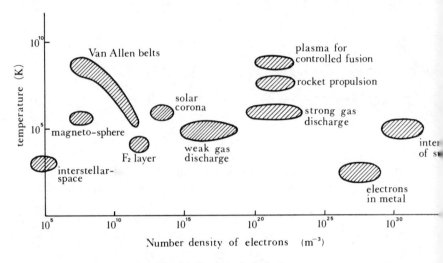

Fig. 8.1 Some typical plasmas.

Early work on plasmas was concerned with high-density, weakly ionized plasmas where particle motion is governed by collision processes. Recently it has become possible to produce in the laboratory very highly ionized plasmas for possible fusion devices, in which collisions play a minor role. On the other hand, much interest has been recently aroused in the study of plasma effects in solids where collision processes once again dominate. How can such a wide range of plasmas be studied? If the plasma is considered to be an equivalent, source-free, dielectric medium it is possible to use a unified treatment for all plasmas. Before going on to elaborate on this possibility, however, there are some basic properties of plasmas and waves which it will be fruitful to discuss.

8.2 Some important plasma parameters

8.2.1. Plasma oscillations.
Since plasma has a tendency to be macroscopically neutral, it tends to return to a neutral equilibrium state after a local perturbation is introduced in the form of an excess of positive or negative charge. The electric field produced by an excess of electrons say, causes the cloud to spread as shown in Fig. 8.2(a). The electrons acquire kinetic energy, pass through an equilibrium position, and leave a deficiency of electrons in the cross-hatched region, and a restoring electric field is established to pull them back; electrons thus oscillate about an equilibrium position.

The frequency of oscillation can be calculated by considering the plane slice through a plasma shown in Fig. 8.2(b). The ions are assumed stationary

170

because of their relatively large mass. If the electrons are assumed to move to the right *en masse* a distance x from their equilibrium position, as shown in Fig. 8.2(c), an electric field, $\mathscr{E}$, is created which can be obtained by applying

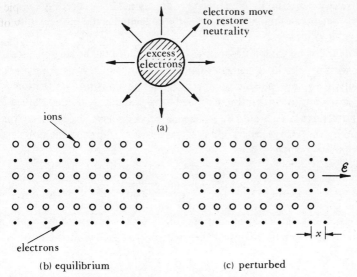

Fig. 8.2 **(a) An illustration of the mechanism of plasma oscillations; (b) and (c) a one-dimensional model.**

Gauss's law to the excess charge in the region of thickness x and cross-section A, which gives:

$$\mathscr{E}A = \frac{neAx}{\epsilon_0} \quad \text{or} \quad \mathscr{E} = \frac{nex}{\epsilon_0} \tag{8.3}$$

Since each electron in the cloud is thus subjected to a restoring force of $-e\mathscr{E}$, their equation of motion becomes:

$$\frac{d^2 x}{dt^2} = -\frac{ne^2}{m\epsilon_0} x \tag{8.4}$$

which is the equation of simple harmonic motion at an angular frequency ω_p given by

$$\omega_p{}^2 = \frac{ne^2}{\epsilon_0 m} \tag{8.5}$$

The quantity f_p which equals $\omega_p/2\pi$ is termed the *electron plasma frequency*. An *ion plasma frequency* f_{pi} is defined similarly but the concept is only useful at frequencies low enough for the electrons to have their equilibrium distribution of velocity and position at all times. The expression for f_{pi} for singly charged positive ions is obtained by dividing eq. (8.5) by $(1840Z)^{\frac{1}{2}}$. For mercury this number is ≈ 600 and for protons it is ≈ 40, so in general $f_{pi} \ll f_p$.

171

8.2.2. Debye length. In order to establish a more precise definition of a plasma, a more quantitative meaning to terms such as 'charge density' and 'charge neutrality' must be sought. A plasma may be considered to be electrically neutral only on a macroscopic scale. Microscopically, electric field gradients in the immediate vicinity of each charged particle inhibit local neutrality.

The following simple argument will give an idea of the sort of distance over which the field of a single particle is significant. Consider a plasma of density $n = n_i$ and in plane symmetry for simplicity. Consider the ions stationary but, owing to fluctuations brought about by a temperature T, the electrons are separated by a distance x. As we have already seen, the field set up by this charge separation is as given by eq. (8.3) and the potential distribution is then

$$V(x) = \int E dx = \frac{nex^2}{2\epsilon_0}$$

There occurs a particular separation, called the *Debye length*, l_D, when all the mean random kinetic energy of the electrons has been converted into potential energy and

$$\tfrac{1}{2}kT = eV(x) = \frac{ne^2 l_D^2}{2\epsilon_0}$$

or

$$l_D = \sqrt{\frac{\epsilon_0 kT}{ne^2}} \qquad (8.6)$$

l_D is thus a measure of the charge separation due to thermal motion that can be expected in a plasma of temperature T. It follows that it is also an indication of the scale of charge non-uniformity. One definition of a plasma, first suggested by Langmuir, is that an ionized gas can be considered to have plasma properties if l_D is much less than the size of the gas sample. For typical laboratory gaseous plasmas l_D is of the order of microns and this condition is satisfied.

The Debye length will now be interpreted in a slightly different way so as to gain further insight into its physical significance . Consider a neutral plasma $n = n_i$ into which a charge Q is placed. The plasma electrons will move freely but the ions because of their mass can be assumed fixed, after the introduction of the test charge. If the test charge is located at $r = 0$ and the potential at distance r from it is $V(r)$, the concentration of electrons in this field of force can be predicted from Boltzmann's law:

$$n_e = n e^{-(-eV)/kT} \simeq \left(1 + \frac{eV}{kT}\right) \qquad (8.7)$$

if it is assumed, as is usually the case for a realistic plasma, that $eV \ll kT$.

The particles must obey Poisson's equation and, assuming spherical symmetry, we can write

$$\nabla^2 V = \frac{1}{r^2} \frac{\partial}{\partial r}\left(r^2 \frac{\partial V}{\partial r}\right) = \frac{-e(n - n_e)}{\epsilon_0}$$

which, using eqs. (8.7) and (8.6)

$$\simeq -\frac{ne^2}{\epsilon_0} \frac{V}{kT} = -\frac{V}{l_D^2}$$

The solution of this equation, by integration, is

$$V = \frac{C}{r} \exp\left(-\frac{r}{l_D}\right) \tag{8.8}$$

where C is some constant to be found.

Now, very near to the charge introduced, Q, the potential will be the same as the potential of the charge in free space i.e., $V = Q/(4\pi\epsilon_0 r)$, for very small r. This equation can thus be combined with (8.8) to give the constant C and hence the potential due to charge Q in a neutral plasma:

$$V(r) = \frac{Q}{4\pi\epsilon_0 r} \exp\left(-\frac{r}{l_D}\right) \tag{8.8a}$$

The physical implication of this equation is that the presence of the plasma electrons and ions causes the electric field of an introduced charge to fall off much more rapidly than if it were in free space. Of course, the argument and eq. (8.8) still apply if instead of a test charge we consider the field of an existing charge in the plasma. Thus for $r \ll l_D$ the exponential term goes to unity and the field of a single charge in the plasma is hardly affected by the plasma, but for $r \gg l_D$ the potential is reduced exponentially and is largely obscured after distances of the order of l_D. The coulomb field associated with a single particle in a plasma is said to be *shielded* at a distance comparable to l_D by the presence of surrounding positive and negative particles.

One of the outstanding characteristics of a plasma is its ability to maintain internal charge neutrality. We have seen that this can only be so if l_D is small compared with the physical size of the plasma. Thus a plasma can be defined as a collection of approximately equal number of mobile positive and negative charges for which $l_D \ll L$, where L is some characteristic length of the plasma. In this case there is room in the plasma for shielding to occur and charge neutrality can be maintained.

8.2.3. Cyclotron frequency and Lamor radius. An electron moving in a magnetic field, B, experiences a Lorenz force perpendicular to its direction of motion and the magnetic field. If the field is uniform the force produces a uniform acceleration at right angles to the path of the electron; it consequently moves at a constant speed in a circular orbit, as shown in Fig. 8.3. The

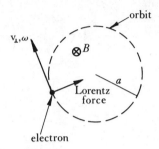

Fig. 8.3 Cyclotron motion of an electron in a magnetic field.

magnetic force on the electron provides the necessary inward acceleration for motion in a circle at a constant radius a, given by:

$$F = v_\perp eB = \frac{mv_\perp{}^2}{a} = ma \cdot \omega^2$$

where ω is the angular velocity of the electron and $v_\perp$ is the component of the particle's velocity perpendicular to B. This gives the radius of the orbit

$$a = \frac{mv_\perp}{eB} \qquad (8.9)$$

a is the *Lamor radius* and for electrons is approximately $5 \cdot 10^{-12} \, v_\perp/B \, m$. For example, an electron with energy of a few volts in a field of a few millitesla has a Lamor radius of the order of 1 mm. For ions, eq. (8.9) must be multiplied by a factor of $1840Z$, where Z is the atomic number. For example, mercury ions have $Z = 200$ so the right-hand side goes up by a factor of $1840 \cdot 200$. But for ions of the same temperature as the electron in the previous example, the velocity is down by $1/\sqrt{1840Z}$, and the Lamor radius is consequently 1 mm x $\sqrt{1840 \cdot 200} \approx 300$ mm.

The rate of angular rotation of the particles, ω_c, is independent of their speed and is given for electrons by

$$\omega_c = \frac{v_\perp}{a} = \frac{eB}{m} \qquad (8.10)$$

and the quantity $\omega_c/2\pi$ is known as the electron *cyclotron frequency*, f_c. For fields of $\approx 0 \cdot 1$ T, the electron cyclotron frequency lies in the microwave band, $f_c \approx 3$ GHz, whereas even for protons, because of the much higher masses involved, the ions' cyclotron frequency is only of the order of 1 MHz. For mercury this frequency is reduced to a few kHz.

Notice that we have only discussed motion of particles with a component of velocity perpendicular to the magnetic field, $v_\perp$. Any motion due to a component of velocity parallel to the field $v_{\parallel}$ will be unaffected by the field since the force is zero. The resultant particle trajectories will be helical about the field lines, the radius of the spiral being inversely proportional to B, from eq. (8.9). Notice also that electrons spiral in a clockwise or right-hand direction looking along a line of force, while positive ions spiral in an anti-clockwise or left-hand direction.

8.3 Wave propagation in plasmas

8.3.1. Infinite cold plasma. We shall examine the way in which a plasma can affect an electromagnetic wave propagating through it. For simplicity, we first consider an infinite plasma with no boundaries, in which collisions are negligible and the only motion of charged particles is a one-dimensional move-ment of electrons. Ions in the plasma are considered stationary by virtue of their much larger mass and create a neutral background to the electronic motion. We further assume that there are no static fields applied and there is no steady charge particle drift.

Under these conditions the equation of motion of electrons in the presence of an electric field in the wave $\mathscr{E}'$, which is assumed to have a time dependence $\exp(j\omega t)$, is

$$\frac{dv'}{dt} = \frac{\partial v'}{\partial t} + \frac{\partial v'}{\partial x} \cdot \frac{\partial x}{\partial t} = -\frac{e\mathscr{E}'}{m} \tag{8.11}$$

where v' is the electron velocity and the primes denote a.c. quantities. For small amplitude oscillations the second term of the equation can be neglected, which gives:

$$j\omega v' = -e\mathscr{E}'/m \tag{8.12}$$

The a.c. electron convection current density, J_c', is given by:

$$J_c' = -n_0 ev' \tag{8.13}$$

where n_0 is the electron concentration and the subscript zero denotes a steady-state value.

Eliminating v' from (8.12) and (8.13) gives:

$$J_c' = \frac{n_0 e^2}{m} \cdot \frac{\mathscr{E}'}{j\omega}$$

which using the definition for the electron plasma frequency, ω_p, given by eq. (8.5) becomes:

$$J_c' = \frac{\epsilon_0 \omega_0^2}{j\omega} \cdot \mathscr{E}' \tag{8.14}$$

175

Equation (8.14) implies that the electron currents lag the applied field of the wave by 90°; thus there is no energy dissipated in the plasma, which is to be expected since there are no collisions.

In addition to the convection current flowing, there will be a displacement current, J'_d, which would flow even in the absence of plasma, which is

$$J'_d = \frac{\partial D'}{\partial t} = \epsilon_0 \frac{\partial \mathscr{E}'}{\partial t} = j\omega\epsilon_0 \mathscr{E}' \tag{8.15}$$

Hence the total current flowing, J', is

$$J' = J'_c + J'_d = j\omega\epsilon_0(1 - \omega_p^2/\omega^2)\mathscr{E}' \tag{8.16}$$

Now, if the wave were travelling in a lossless dielectric medium of relative permittivity ϵ_r, the only current flowing would be a displacement current and

$$J = J_d = j\omega\epsilon_0 \, \epsilon_r \, \mathscr{E}' \tag{8.17}$$

Comparing eqs. (8.16) and (8.17) we arrive at the most interesting and important conclusion that when a wave is propagated through a plasma, the effect of conduction currents due to electron motion in the plasma can be accounted for by assigning an effective relative permittivity, ϵ_{rp}, to the plasma, which is given by

$$\epsilon_{rp} = 1 - \omega_p^2/\omega^2 \tag{8.18}$$

Wave propagation in the plasma can then be treated as if it were occurring in an equivalent dielectric with no free charge carriers and having a relative permittivity ϵ_{rp}.

For example, the phase velocity of a plane wave in the plasma is

$$v_{ph} = \frac{\omega}{\beta} = \frac{1}{\sqrt{\epsilon_0 \, \epsilon_{rp} \, \mu_0}} = \frac{c}{\sqrt{\epsilon_{rp}}} = \frac{c}{\sqrt{1 - \omega_p^2/\omega^2}} \tag{8.19}$$

The ω–β diagram which characterizes the waves can be deduced from this equation and is as shown in Fig. 8.4. Notice that the phase velocity is a

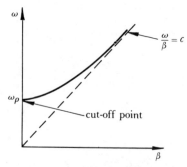

Fig. 8.4 The ω–β diagram for plane waves of wavelength $2\pi/\beta$ in an infinite, cold plasma.

176

function of frequency; the medium is *dispersive*. Further, below a critical frequency corresponding to $\omega = \omega_p$, no propagation of plane waves through the plasma is possible.

8.3.2. Effect of collisions.

Next we shall study how the effective relative permittivity is affected when a relatively small number of collisions is allowed in the plasma. It is convenient to define a *collision frequency*, ν, which is the reciprocal of the mean time between collisions. If $\nu = \nu_m$, the *collision frequency for momentum transfer*, then the electron to a first approximation is assumed to lose its entire momentum after each collision. Hence the rate of charge of momentum of the electrons due to collision is $m\nu\nu$ /s and, as a consequence of Newton's second law, this represents a force which is a viscous frictional force exerted on the moving electrons by the rest of the plasma. The equation of motion of electrons then becomes

$$\frac{dv'}{dt} + \nu_m v' = -\frac{e\mathscr{E}'}{m}$$

which if the usual time dependence is assumed gives:

$$v' = -\frac{e\mathscr{E}'}{(\nu + j\omega)m} \qquad (8.20)$$

Following the same procedure as before, this velocity is used to find the electron convection current which by adding a displacement component leads to an effective plasma relative permittivity of

$$\epsilon_{rp} = 1 - \frac{\omega_p^2}{\omega(\omega - j\nu)} \qquad (8.21)$$

In this case the effective relative permittivity is complex which, as was discussed in the previous chapter, corresponds to a loss mechanism which causes attenuation of a wave passing through the plasma.

8.3.3. Waves on drifting plasmas.

Let us consider the properties of waves which can propagate in plasmas which move bodily with some drift velocity, v_0. For simplicity, collisions and temperature effects will be ignored. All quantities will have an alternating and a time-independent component owing to the field of the wave and the d.c. applied fields necessary to produce the drift. If d.c. quantities are denoted by a subscript o and a.c. quantities by a prime, the total electron convection current can be written:

$$J_o + \vec{J}' = (\rho_o + \rho')(v_0 + v') \qquad (8.22)$$

where $\rho = -ne$ is the charge density. Since the d.c. component of current, J_o, is equal to $\rho_o v_o$, this can be subtracted from both sides of eq. (8.22) to give:

$$J' = \rho_o v' - v_o \rho' \qquad (8.23)$$

The second-order term, $\rho'v'$, has been neglected since it will be negligible for small signals.

The charge density ρ' and the current density J' are related by the continuity equation, which since J_o and ρ_o do not change with position or time becomes:

$$\frac{\partial J'}{\partial z} + \frac{\partial \rho'}{\partial t} = 0 \qquad (8.24)$$

If the wave parameters are assumed to vary with time and position as

$$\exp j(\omega t - \beta x)$$

where the phase constant $\beta = 2\pi/\lambda$, eq. (8.24) reduces to:

$$\beta J' = \omega \rho'$$

This relationship is substituted in eq. (8.23) to give:

$$J' = \frac{\rho_0 \, v'}{1 - \beta v_0/\omega}$$

We next use the same technique as previously and add a displacement current, comparing the sum with the displacement current of an equivalent dielectric. The effective relative permittivity of the plasma is then found to be:

$$\epsilon_{rp} = 1 + \frac{\rho_0 \, v'}{j\omega\epsilon_0(1 - \beta v_0/\omega)\,\mathscr{E}'} \qquad (8.25)$$

Finally, we require a relationship between v' and $\mathscr{E}'$ which can be obtained from the equation of motion of electrons:

$$\frac{dv}{dt} = \frac{\partial v'}{\partial t} + \frac{\partial v'}{\partial x} \cdot \frac{\partial x}{\partial t} = -\frac{e\mathscr{E}'}{m}$$

$$j(\omega - \beta v_0)\, v' = -e\mathscr{E}'/m \qquad (8.26)$$

This expression is substituted into eq. (8.25) to give

$$\epsilon_{rp} = 1 - \frac{\omega_p^2}{(\omega - \beta v_0)^2} \qquad (8.27)$$

Thus the drifting plasma can be treated as a stationary dielectric with relative permittivity given by eq. (8.27). Comparing this equation with (8.18) it can be seen that the drifting plasma behaves in the same way as a stationary plasma but the effective frequency of the wave is changed from ω to $(\omega - \beta v_0)$.

8.3.4. Waves in other plasma systems. The concept of treating a plasma as an equivalent dielectric medium with no free charge carriers and an effective

178

relative permittivity ϵ_{rp} can be extended to many of the plasma systems. For example, it is straightforward to account for ionic movement in a cold plasma by including an ion plasma frequency term, which leads to

$$\epsilon_{rp} = \left(1 - \frac{\omega_{pe}{}^2 + \omega_{pi}{}^2}{\omega^2}\right)$$

When a static magnetic field is applied to a plasma the electrons, we have seen, can spiral only in one direction round the field. As a result the plasma has anisotropic properties which can be described in terms of an equivalent permittivity which is now a tensor quantity. Many different wave types are possible in this situation which can all be specified by the tensor permittivity, but a detailed treatment would be out of place here.

Further types of plasma which can be treated by the general technique of finding their equivalent permittivity are those which occur in the solid state, for example a drifting electron–hole semiconductor plasma. In such plasmas collision effects are no longer negligible but dominate the conduction process. Again, the reader is referred to the literature for further details of this rather specialized topic.

Problems

1   Show that the phase velocity and the group velocity of plane electromagnetic waves propagating in a collisionless plasma when no static magnetic field is present are given by

$$v_{ph} = c[1 - \omega_{pe}{}^2/\omega^2]^{-\frac{1}{2}} \quad \text{and} \quad v_g = c[1 - \omega_{pe}{}^2/\omega^2]^{\frac{1}{2}}$$

2   Find an expression for the phase velocity of plane waves in a cold plasma with a collision frequency v. Hence for $v \ll \omega \ll \omega_p$ show that the skin depth δ or the distance in which the wave damps out to 37% of its initial value is given by

$$\delta \simeq \frac{c}{\omega_p}\left(1 - \frac{3v^2}{8\omega^2} + \frac{\omega^2}{2\omega_p{}^2} \cdots\right)$$

Also show that when $\omega > \omega_p$ and $\omega \gg v$ the skin depth expression becomes

$$\delta \simeq \frac{c}{\omega_p}\left(\frac{2\omega^2}{v\omega_p}\right)\left(1 - \frac{\omega_p{}^2}{\omega^2}\right)^{\frac{1}{2}}$$

What is the physical significance of the two expressions?

3   Show that the attenuation constant for plane waves propagating in a gaseous plasma with no static magnetic field but with collisions is given by

$$\alpha = 8 \cdot 686 \frac{\nu \omega_{pe}^2}{2c(\omega^2 + \nu^2)} \text{ db/m}$$

provided $(\omega^2 + \nu^2) \gg \omega_{pe}^2$

A space vehicle generates a plasma re-entry sheath 1 m thick which is characterized by a collision frequency $\nu = 10^{11}$ s^{-1} and an electron density of 5×10^{19} m^{-3}. What transmitter frequency is required to transmit waves through the plasma sheath with a minimum voltage attenuation of 20 db?

   Ans. 540 GHz.

4   Show that the effective permittivity of a k-component drifting, cold, collisionless plasma is given by

$$\epsilon_{eff} = \epsilon_0 \left(1 - \sum \frac{\omega_{pk}^2}{(\omega - \beta v_{ok})^2} \right)$$

Hence consider the special case of an electron beam, velocity v_0 and plasma frequency ω_{pb}, transversing a stationary plasma, whose plasma frequency is ω_{pp} and show that the propagation constant of waves on such a system is

$$\beta = \frac{\omega}{v_0} \pm \frac{\omega_{pb}}{v_0(1 - \omega_{pp}^2/\omega^2)^{\frac{1}{2}}}$$

What does this equation predict will happen physically for frequencies such that $\omega \leqslant \omega_{pp}$?

9. Junction diodes

9.1 Introduction

A perfectly uniform semiconductor crystal has limited device possibilities.
For instance, it may be incorporated in photocells, temperature-sensitive
resistors, and some bulk-effect high-frequency generators, which will be
discussed later. Apart from these specialized applications, the most useful
and interesting devices make use of semiconductors in which the type of
impurity changes within the single-crystal material; for example, it may be
p-type in one section and n-type elsewhere.

A pn *junction* may be formed from a single-crystal intrinsic semiconductor
by doping part of it with acceptor impurities and the remainder with donors.
We will establish that such junctions can form the basis of very efficient
rectifiers. Further, and more important since many other solid-state devices
contain several such junctions, if the mechanism of current flow in a simple
single pn junction is understood, this will lead to a clearer conception of the
operation of the more elaborate structures.

9.2 The pn junction in equilibrium with no applied voltage

A junction between p-type and n-type material may be fabricated in a
variety of ways, as we shall see later. The precise distance over which the
change from p- to n-type semiconductor occurs varies with fabrication
technique, but an essential feature of all junctions is that the change in
impurity concentration takes place in a very short length, typically much less
than one micron. If the junction extends over a longer distance, then the
characteristic behaviour to be described does not occur; the material then
acts as an inhomogeneous conductor containing two carrier types which vary
in concentration from point to point.

For the sake of mathematical simplicity, an *abrupt* pn junction in which
there occurs a sudden step change in impurity type at the junction plane will
usually be discussed. Although this model is adequate for describing junctions
fabricated in certain ways, for example, junction in alloyed and some
epitaxial diodes (see section 9.13), it is not universally applicable to all
junctions. For instance, a diffused junction may be *graded*, in which case the

donor and acceptor concentrations are functions of distance across the junction. Then the acceptor density, N_a, gradually decreases and the donor density, N_d, gradually increases as the junction is approached from the p-side until, when the junction is reached, $N_a = N_d$; thereafter, N_d becomes much larger and N_a decreases to zero. Such junctions are obviously more difficult to analyse than the abrupt junction, even if they are assumed *linear graded* and the net doping concentration, $(N_a - N_d)$, is assumed to be a linear function at distance through the junction. Fortunately, however, many of the results obtainable for abrupt junctions also apply to graded junctions. Whenever this does not apply, for example when estimating junction capacitance, attention will be drawn to the fact.

It is not necessary for the abrupt junction to be symmetrical, indeed it is usually desirable, as we shall discover, that the doping concentrations at either side of the junction are dissimilar. Let us assume that the acceptor concentration, N_a, is somewhat greater than the donor concentration, N_d. Typical doping concentrations in germanium might be one acceptor per 10^7 germanium atoms, giving a conductivity in the p-region, σ_p, of order 10^4 S/m, the corresponding values in the n-region being, say, $1 : 10^5$ and $\sigma_n \approx 100$ S/m. The majority and minority carrier densities in the extrinsic regions will then be as depicted in Fig. 9.1(a).

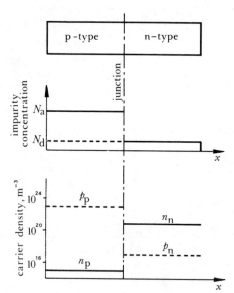

Fig. 9.1 (a) Impurity concentration and carrier density variations in an abrupt pn junction.

It will be noticed that a one-demensional model of the pn junction has been adopted, in which current is only allowed to flow in the x-direction, perpendicular to the junction. Whereas this model is not strictly correct, since in more realistic geometries the current flow is three-dimensional, as we shall see, it is not difficult to imagine a slice through a practically realizable junction which behaves in a very similar way to the model which we have assumed.

The carrier density concentrations, p_p, n_p, n_n, and p_n, depicted in Fig. 9.1(a) apply only at relatively large distances from the junction. At the junction these densities are modified since there is a tendency for holes to diffuse into the n-type material and for electrons to diffuse into the p-type material because of the severe concentration gradients appearing there. Thus, although the impurity concentration has been assumed to have an abrupt, step change, the carrier densities cannot change so abruptly but vary instead over a small distance either side of the junction, shown to an unrealistically large scale as d_1-d_2 in Fig. 9.1(b).

Even after the initial diffusion of majority carriers as described, large concentration gradients still exist but further diffusion is prevented in equilibrium by an electric field being set up in the junction region by the following mechanism. The majority holes diffusing out of the p-region leave behind negatively charged acceptor atoms bound to the lattice, thus exposing negative space charge in a previously neutral region. Similarly, electrons diffusing from the n-region expose positive ionized donor atoms and a double space-charge layer builds up at the junction, as shown in Fig. 9.1(c) and (d). It will be noticed that the space charge layers are of opposite sign to the majority carriers diffusing into them, which tends to reduce the diffusion rate; in other words the double space-charge layer causes an electric field to be set up across the junction directed from n- to p-regions, which is in such a direction as to inhibit diffusion of majority electrons and holes, as shown in Fig. 9.1(c) and (e). Thus, diffusion continues until the built-in electric field is great enough to inhibit the process; no current flows across the junction and the system is in equilibrium.

The double layer of charge, d_1-d_2, is known variously as the *space-charge layer*, for obvious reasons, the *depletion layer*, so called since this region is deplete of its usual complement of majority carriers, or the *barrier layer*, since the electric field across it is an electrical barrier which prevents diffusion currents flowing. The depletion layer is, typically, of order one micron thick.

As a consequence of the induced electric field across the depletion layer, an electrostatic potential difference is established between p- and n-regions, which is called the *contact* or *diffusion* potential, V_0, as shown in Fig. 9.1(f). The magnitude of the contact potential varies with doping levels and temperature, as we shall see, but it is typically of order one volt. An expression for the contact potential can be obtained by finding the electric field at the junction from the continuity equation and integrating across the depletion layer, as follows:

Consider, for example, the continuity equation for holes in the depletion layer, eq. (6.64). If we assume that the junction is in equilibrium, $\partial/\partial t = 0$, and if recombination in the depletion layer is ignored because of its extreme

183

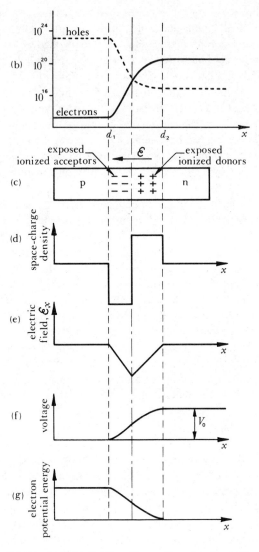

Fig. 9.1 (b)−(g) Depletion layer in a pn junction in equilibrium.

thinness, the first term on the right-hand side of the equation is zero and on integration eq. (6.64) reduces to:

$$\mathscr{E}_x = \frac{D_h}{\mu_h} \frac{1}{(\delta p)} \frac{d}{dx}(\delta p) \tag{9.1}$$

The diffusion forces are exactly balanced by electrostatic forces, as described. Using the Einstein relationship, eq. (6.50), the equation for $\mathscr{E}_x$ becomes:

$$\mathscr{E}_x = \frac{kT}{e} \frac{1}{(\delta p)} \frac{d}{dx}(\delta p) \tag{9.2}$$

Equation (9.2) is rearranged and integrated across the depletion layer to give:

$$-e \int_{d_1}^{d_2} \mathscr{E}_x\, dx = -kT \int_{p_\mathrm{p}}^{p_\mathrm{n}} \frac{d(\delta p)}{\delta p}$$

or

$$eV_{d_1-d_2} = eV_0 = -kT \log_e (p_\mathrm{n}/p_\mathrm{p})$$

which gives

$$p_\mathrm{p} = p_\mathrm{n} \exp\left(\frac{eV_0}{kT}\right) \tag{9.3}$$

Thus, if the concentration of holes at either side of the junction is known, the contact potential, V_0, can be calculated at any given temperature, T.

By considering the continuity equation for electrons in the depletion layer, we arrive at a similar expression for the electron concentrations in equilibrium, viz:

$$n_\mathrm{n} = n_\mathrm{p} \exp\left(\frac{eV_0}{kT}\right) \tag{9.4}$$

Let us now consider how the pn junction can be represented using the band structure concept of a semiconductor. Firstly, it will be necessary to discuss what is meant by equilibrium in the context of a junction between two semiconductor types. In classical electrostatics, two bodies which are in equilibrium have the same electrostatic potential. However, in semiconductors or metals, considered on an atomic scale, electronic equilibrium occurs only between two bodies in contact when there is no net current flow between them. This does not necessarily imply that they must each have the same electrostatic potential; on the contrary the condition for equilibrium in such a case is that the Fermi level, E_F, in each material must be at the same energy level.

This statement can be verified by considering the simple case of two metals, A and B, in contact. The metals can be represented by the box model described in Chapter 4. The work functions of the metals, ϕ_A and ϕ_B, correspond to the minimum height of the potential energy barrier at the respective metal surface. The situation (a) before the metals come into contact, (b) immediately on contact, and (c) a short while after contact, is shown diagrammatically in Fig. 9.2(a)–(c). Immediately on contact, electrons spill over from the material

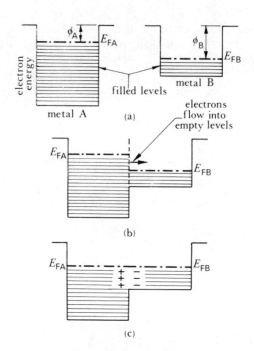

Fig. 9.2 Energy level diagrams of two metals in contact, (a) before contact, (b) immediately contact is made, and (c) in equilibrium.

with the highest Fermi level, A, to occupy empty levels in the other material. Thus, metal B becomes charged negatively and A positively. This charging process changes the potential of B relative to A and all electron energy levels in metal A, including E_{FA}, are lowered while those in B are raised. This process continues until the Fermi levels are aligned, as in Fig. 9.1(c), whereupon no further electron current flows. It is thus the Fermi level, rather than the electrostatic potential, which remains constant across the boundary between the two metals in contact.

The constancy of the Fermi level across a junction is quite general and applied equally well to semiconductors in equilibrium. Let us first of all consider two separate n- and p-type doped crystals of the same material, as depicted in Fig. 9.3(a), which are brought together to form a pn junction, as in Fig. 9.3(b). It should be realized that this process is not physically possible since the pn junction is usually formed in single-crystal material, but it will be instructive to develop the argument assuming for the moment that it is. Immediately contact is made, electron current flows as electrons transfer from the n-type material into empty levels in the conduction band of the p-type material, as in Fig. 9.3(b), and similarly holes transfer from the valence band of the p-type into that of the n-type material. The process stops only when the Fermi level is continuous through both materials, at which stage no net current flows across the junction and equilibrium is

186

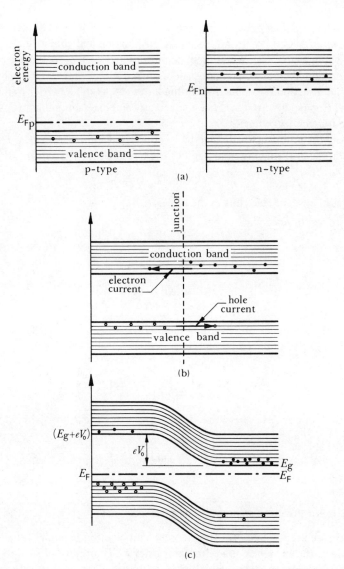

Fig. 9.3 Hypothetical contact between p- and n-type semiconductors. Band structure: (a) before contact, (b) immediately after contact, and (c) in equilibrium.

attained. Since the Fermi level in each material is fixed relative to its respective band structure, alignment of the Fermi levels is only achieved if all energy levels in one region move relative to those in the other; in other words, if each side of the junction takes up a different electrostatic potential. Thus, holes diffusing from the p-type region leave it negatively charged, raising all energy levels, and similarly electrons migrating in the opposite direction cause all levels in the n-type material to be lowered until, when the difference of potential existing between the two sections is equal to the contact potential, V_0, the Fermi level is continuous across the junction and equilibrium is establishe as shown in Fig. 9.3(c). When these conditions prevail, a potential hill prevents electron flow from n- to p-regions and a similar barrier prevents hole flow in the opposite direction (n.b., the 'hill' in the latter case is still a barrier to holes even though sloping downwards, since the energy band diagrams are conventionally drawn for electron energies).

Using the notation for the energy levels as shown in Fig. 9.3(c), the number of electrons in the conduction band of the n-region, n_n, is (from eq. (6.13)):

$$n_n = N_c \exp[-(E_g - E_F)/kT] \qquad (9.5)$$

and the number of electrons in the p-region, n_p, is

$$n_p = N_c \exp[-\overline{(E_g + eV_0 - E_F)}/kT] \qquad (9.6)$$

Dividing the two equations, we obtain:

$$\frac{n_n}{n_p} = \exp\left[\frac{eV_0}{kT}\right] \qquad (9.7)$$

which agrees with the expression obtained previously, eq. (9.4). The contact potential can be obtained by rearrangement and, using eq. (6.19), is:

$$V_0 = \frac{kT}{e}\log_e\left(\frac{n_n}{n_p}\right) = \frac{kT}{e}\log_e\left(\frac{n_n p_p}{n_i^2}\right)$$

Also, if all impurities are assumed ionized, $n_n \approx N_d$ and $p_p \approx N_a$ or:

$$V_0 \simeq \frac{kT}{e}\log_e\left(\frac{N_d N_a}{n_i^2}\right) \qquad (9.8)$$

9.3 Current flow in a pn junction with forward bias

We have seen that no current flows across a pn junction in equilibrium because of the existence of a potential barrier which prevents diffusion of majority carriers across the depletion layer. In order for current to flow, equilibrium must be disturbed in such a way as to reduce the height of the potential barrier. This can be accomplished by externally biasing the junction with a voltage, V, such that the positive terminal of the voltage source is connected to the p-region, as shown in Fig. 9.4. The junction is then said to be *forward-biased*. Now, the bulk materials at either side of the depletion layer have high conductivity because of their doping concentrations, whereas the depletion layer has a much lower conductivity, as a consequence of its lack of current carriers. As a result, the applied voltage is dropped almost entirely across the depletion layer, lowering the effective voltage across the depletion layer to $(V_0 - V)$. Thus, the potential barrier is lowered and current flows across the junction because drift and diffusion currents are no longer balanced, as for the junction in equilibrium.

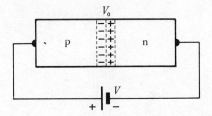

Fig. 9.4 A pn junction with forward bias voltage.

How is this situation described in terms of the band picture of a pn junction? In order to answer this question we must first digress slightly to discuss the effect of an applied field on the band structure of a uniform semiconductor, as shown in Fig. 9.5(a). The complete band structure tilts, as shown in Fig. 9.5(b).

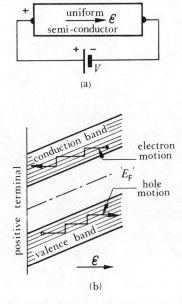

Fig. 9.5 Band structure of a uniform semiconductor with an applied electric field.

Electrons moving in the field acquire kinetic energy, moving horizontally in the diagram to higher energy levels in the conduction band, only to return to nearer the band edge after a scattering event. Similarly, holes, on acquiring energy for the field, move to lower levels in the valence band (since the band diagram is drawn for electron energies), again returning to nearer the top of the band after each collision.

189

When forward bias is applied to a pn junction, equilibrium is disturbed, and, at the instant V is applied, the energy bands tilt as described and as illustrated in Fig. 9.6(a). Majority carriers are now able to surmount the lowered potential

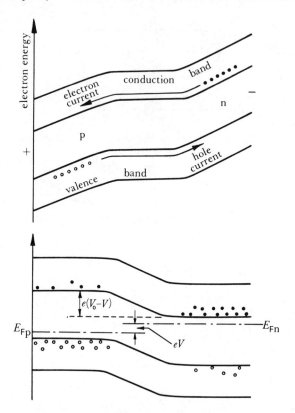

Fig. 9.6 Band structure of a pn junction with forward-bias voltage, (a) immediately on applying the bias and (b) in the steady state.

barriers and diffuse across the junctions; large currents can flow. Carriers then flow in from the external circuit to restore near-equilibrium conditions in the material far from the junction; almost all the applied voltage appears across the junction and the steady-state situation depicted in Fig. 9.6(b) exists. Notice that as soon as equilibrium is disturbed by the application of an external voltage the Fermi level is no longer continuous across the junction.

The reduction of barrier height by the applied bias thus causes holes to be injected from the p- to the n-region and electrons from the n- to the p-region and current flows round the external circuit in the conventional direction. The majority carriers become minority carriers immediately they are injected and their densities at the edge of the depletion layer, n_{po} and p_{no}, fall rapidly with distance from the junction because of recombination until, eventually, the minority carrier densities equal the equilibrium values, n_p and p_n. This situation is illustrated in Figs. 9.7(a) and (b). The majority carrier densities

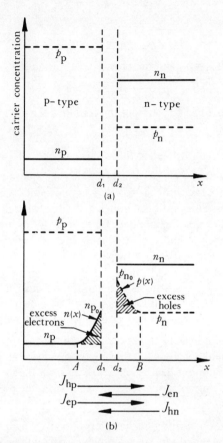

Fig. 9.7 Carrier concentrations and currents flowing in a pn junction: (a) with zero bias and (b) with forward bias applied.

are unaffected by the application of bias provided the forward bias voltage is not too large; each region acts as a reservoir of majority carriers which is hardly perturbed by the injection of a relatively small fraction of carriers across the depletion layer.

The diffusion forces at the junction must still be almost exactly balanced by the electric field corresponding to the reduced potential barrier, since only a very slight unbalance of these forces causes large currents to flow. We shall therefore assume that the equilibrium state of the depletion layer is not seriously disturbed when forward current flows and that to a first approximation the electric field at the junction is again given by eq. (9.2). Integrating

191

across the depletion layer, as before, and remembering that the barrier voltage is $(V_0 - V)$ for the forward-biased junction, gives:

$$e(V_0 - V) = -kT \log_e(p_{no}/p_p)$$

or

$$p_{no} = p_p \exp[e(V - V_0)/kT] \qquad (9.9)$$

But, when $V = 0$, $p_{no} = p_n$ and therefore eq. (9.9) simplifies to:

$$p_{no} = p_n \exp[eV/kT] \qquad (9.10)$$

Similar reasoning applied to electrons injected into the p-region from the n-region gives:

$$n_{po} = n_p \exp(eV/kT) \qquad (9.11)$$

Thus, the minority carrier densities just outside the depletion layer, p_{no} and n_{po}, are seen to increase exponentially with applied voltage as a result of the injection of carriers. This result can be substantiated using Boltzmann statistics; this implies that the number of electrons, for example, having sufficient energy to surmount the potential barrier at the junction is proportional to $\exp(-e\overline{V_0 - V})/kT)$, which equals (const.) . $\exp(eV/kT)$, which agrees with our findings.

Let us now consider in a little more detail the various currents flowing across the junction when forward bias is applied, as shown in Fig. 9.7(b). Four components of the total current flow across the junction, namely:

(a) A hole-current density, J_{hp}, flowing from the p-region.
(b) A hole-current density, J_{hn}, flowing from the n-region.
(c) An electron-current density, J_{en}, flowing from the n-region.
(d) An electron-current density, J_{ep}, flowing from the p-region.

The relatively small currents J_{hn} and J_{ep} are due to thermally generated minority carriers in the n- and p-regions, respectively, which fall down the potential hills at the junctions. Since all such carriers will be swept across the junction in this way, the associated current densities are largely independent of the bias voltage and are limited only by the thermal generation rate.

On the other hand, the larger currents J_{hp} and J_{en} are a result of the diffusion of majority carriers across the reduced potential barrier at the junction. These currents will be proportional to the number of majority carriers injected, p_{no} and n_{po}, and hence to $\exp(eV/kT)$. The constant of proportionality can be found by remembering that in equilibrium, when $V = 0$, the electron and hole currents at the junction must exactly balance so that there is no net junction current, or:

$$J_{hp} = J_{hn}$$

and

$$J_{en} = J_{ep}$$

192

Hence, when bias is applied the electron and hole currents are related by the expression

$$J_{hp} = J_{hn} \exp(eV/kT)$$

and

$$J_{en} = J_{ep} \exp(eV/kT)$$

The net hole current across the junction is thus:

$$J_h = J_{hp} - J_{hn} = J_{hn}[\exp(eV/kT) - 1]$$

and, similarly the net electron current is:

$$J_e = J_{en} - J_{ep} = J_{ep}[\exp(eV/kT) - 1]$$

Thus, the total junction current, J, which is the sum of hole and electron currents, is:

$$J = J_h + J_e = [J_{hn} + J_{ep}][\exp(eV/kT) - 1]$$

or

$$J = J_0[\exp(eV/kT) - 1] \tag{9.12}$$

where, J_0, the sum of the current densities carried by minority carriers across the junction, is called the *saturation current density*, for reasons which will become clearer later. We have, by these simple considerations, arrived at the so-called *diode or rectifier equation* which, as we shall discuss in more detail later, describes the electrical behaviour of a junction diode.

It is convenient to derive eq. (9.12) more rigorously, firstly to provide a quantitative expression for the evaluation of the constant J_0 and second as an example of an analytical technique which we will be able to apply to more complicated structures later. We commence by considering how the minority carrier densities just outside the depletion regions vary as a function of distance. Consider, for example, the continuity eq. (6.64) for minority holes injected into the n-region at $x = d_2$. The term on the left-hand side of the continuity equation is zero in the steady state and the term containing $\mathscr{E}$ is also zero, since we assume that there is no voltage drop and hence no electric field outside the depletion region. With these assumptions:

$$\frac{d^2(\delta p)}{dx^2} = \frac{\delta p}{\tau_{Lh} D_h} = \frac{\delta p}{L_h^2} \tag{9.13}$$

where we have defined:

$$L_h = (\tau_{Lh} D_h)^{\frac{1}{2}} \tag{9.14}$$

which has the dimensions of length.

The general solution of eq. (9.13) is of the form

$$\delta p = C_1 e^{-x/L_h} + C_2 e^{+x/L_h} \tag{9.15}$$

193

where C_1 and C_2 are constants. However, since δp, the excess minority hole concentration, falls to zero at large distances away from the junction because of recombination, constant C_2 must be zero. Now the excess concentration, δp, is equal to the difference between the local hole density, $p(x)$, and the equilibrium hole density, p_n; thus eq. (9.15) becomes:

$$p(x) = C_1 e^{-x/L_h} + p_n \qquad (9.16)$$

Finally, if for convenience we take the origin of x at d_2, when $x = 0$, $p(x) = p_{n0}$, which on substituting gives:

$$p(x) = (p_{n0} - p_n) e^{-x/L_h} + p_n \qquad (9.17)$$

This is the equation for the minority hole density in region d_2-B in Fig. 9.7(b) as a function of x, the distance from the edge of the depletion layer, d_2. We see that $p(x)$ falls off exponentially to the equilibrium value p_n with distance, x, the distance d_2-B being of order L_h, the *diffusion length for minority holes*, which is typically of order 1 mm.

A similar expression can be derived for minority electrons injected into the p-region, the corresponding diffusion length for electrons, L_e, again being about 1 mm.

Now, we have already argued that there is negligible electric field outside the depletion region, so any hole current flowing in the region d_2-B can only be due to diffusion of holes because of their gradient of density. Thus the hole current is given by eq. (6.47) which on substituting for dp/dx using eq. (9.17) gives:

$$J_h = -e D_h \left[-\frac{1}{L_h} (p_{n0} - p_n) e^{-x/L_h} \right] \qquad (9.18)$$

We see that the minority hole current decreases exponentially away from the junction because of recombination. However, electrons flow into the region from the end-contact of the n-type material to replace those lost by recombination and hence maintain charge neutrality. This electron current is itself x-dependent and just compensates for the decrease in hole current, thus ensuring that the total current at any point remains constant and independent of position, which is itself a consequence of Kirchhoff's law. It follows that the net current flowing in the n-region due to injected holes is equal to the hole current at the edge of the depletion layer, at $x = 0$, which from eq. (9.18) is:

$$J_h \bigg|_{d_2} = \frac{e D_h}{L_h} (p_{n0} - p_n)$$

or, substituting for p_{n0} from eq. (9.10):

$$J_h \bigg|_{d_2} = \frac{e D_h}{L_h} p_n (\exp eV/kT - 1) \qquad (9.19)$$

This type of analysis may be repeated for electrons injected into the p-region, to obtain an expression for the electron current at the boundary between depletion layer and p-region, d_1, given by:

$$J_e \bigg|_{d_1} = \frac{e D_e n_p}{L_e} (\exp eV/kT - 1) \tag{9.20}$$

Again, on moving further into the p-region, the total current density stays constant at the value given by eq. (9.20), although an increasing proportion of current is carried by holes which flow into the area to replace those lost by recombination with the injected electrons.

The total forward current density at the junction is the sum of hole and electron currents, or from eq. (9.19) and (9.20):

$$J = J_h + J_e = e \left(\frac{D_h p_n}{L_h} + \frac{D_e n_p}{L_e} \right) [\exp (eV/kT - 1)] \tag{9.21}$$

Comparing this equation with eq. (9.12), we see that the saturation current density is given by:

$$J_0 = e \left(\frac{D_h p_n}{L_h} + \frac{D_e n_p}{L_e} \right) \tag{9.22}$$

where the diffusion lengths are defined by eq. (9.14). It is sometimes more convenient to rewrite the expression for J_0, remembering that:

$$p_p n_p = n_i^2 = p_n n_n$$

or, for operation at such a temperature that all impurities are ionized,

$$p_n = n_i^2/N_d \quad \text{and} \quad n_p = n_i^2/N_a$$

and then

$$J_0 = e n_i^2 \left(\frac{D_h}{L_h N_d} + \frac{D_e}{L_e N_a} \right) \tag{9.23}$$

Equation (9.21) confirms that the diode equation derived earlier by a less rigorous method is correct; it also provides expressions from which the saturation current density, J_0, can be calculated. Notice that for all voltages such that $V \gg kT/e$, which equals about 25 mV at room temperature, the exponential term in the diode equation dominates and the current for the forward-biased junction increases approximately exponentially with applied voltage:

$$J \simeq J_0 \exp (eV/kT) \tag{9.24}$$

9.4 Current flow in a pn junction with reverse bias

We now consider the case when the junction is reverse-biased, as illustrated in Fig. 9.8(a). With the applied voltage of the polarity shown it is evident that the effective junction voltage is now greater than the equilibrium value, V_0, by an amount equal to the applied voltage, V, and the height of the potential barrier preventing diffusion of majority carriers is correspondingly increased. This situation is illustrated in the band structure diagram of Fig. 9.8(b). The

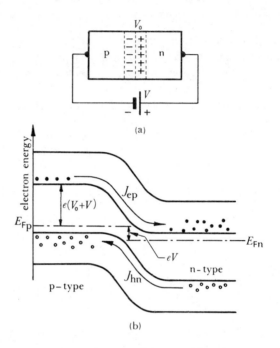

(a)

(b)

Fig. 9.8 A pn junction with reverse-bias voltage.

potential barrier is now of such a height as to inhibit almost completely the diffusion of majority carriers across the junction; J_{hp} and J_{en} are almost zero. The currents flowing due to minority carriers crossing the junction, J_{hn} and J_{ep}, are unaffected by the increased junction voltage, since, as was explained earlier, any minority carriers in the vicinity of the junction can travel freely down potential hills, as shown in Fig. 9.8(b). Thus the current flow in the reverse-biased junction, assuming positive currents to flow from p- to n-regions as before, is:

$$J \simeq -(J_{hn} + J_{ep}) = -J_0 \qquad (9.25)$$

We see that the reverse current is almost constant and is equal to the saturation current density, J_0.

Let us now consider in a little more detail the mechanism of charge transport in the reverse-biased junction. The equations derived for the forward-biased junction in section 9.3 will still be applicable provided the sign of

196

the applied voltage, V, is made negative. For instance, the diode equation is still applicable and eq. (9.12) becomes:

$$J = J_0 [\exp(-eV/kT) - 1] = -J_0 [1 - \exp(-eV/kT)] \qquad (9.26)$$

Whenever the reverse bias voltage is greater than a few tens of millivolts then the exponential term in this equation becomes negligible at room temperature and the current flowing corresponds to the saturation current density, J_0; this result is in agreement with that argued on more physical grounds in the previous paragraph.

The minority electron and hole densities just outside the depletion layer, n_{p0} and p_{n0}, can be obtained directly from eqs. (9.11) and (9.10) by replacing V by $-V$, thus:

$$n_{p0} = n_p \exp[-eV/kT] \qquad (9.27)$$

and

$$p_{n0} = p_n \exp[-eV/kT] \qquad (9.28)$$

The variation of minority carrier density as a function of distance from the depletion layer can be obtained by a similar procedure; for example, for holes, eq. (9.17) becomes:

$$p(x) = p_n [\{\exp(-eV/kT) - 1\} e^{-x/L_h} + 1] \qquad (9.29)$$

The various minority carrier densities, described by eqs. (9.27)-(9.29), are shown graphically in Fig. 9.9. The decrease in minority carrier densities below

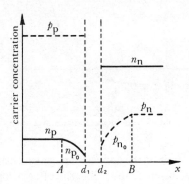

Fig. 9.9 Carrier concentrations in a reverse-biased pn junction.

their equilibrium values near to the depletion layer is a result of minority electron injection from p- to n-region and hole injection in the opposite direction, as described.

Since there is a continuous flow of minority carriers across the junction, electrons, for example, must be continually created in region d_1-A by thermal electron–hole pair generation, excess holes generated by the process drifting to the negative contact. Hence, since the junction currents are due to minority carriers generated by the intrinsic process, J_{hn}, J_{ep}, and hence the saturation current, J_0, are all relatively small and are temperature-dependent.

9.5 Current–voltage characteristics of a junction diode

The diode eq. (9.12) is, as we have seen, applicable to a junction biased in either direction. If sufficient information is known about the materials forming the junction, the saturation current density, J_0, can be estimated using eq. (9.23), say. Thus the I–V characteristic of a particular device can be predicted; it will be of the form shown in Fig. 9.10. The voltage appearing in the

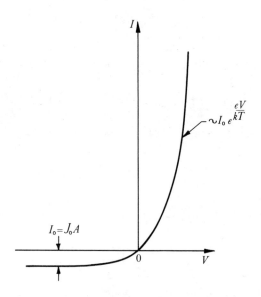

Fig. 9.10 Current–voltage characteristics of a junction diode.

diode equation is that part of the applied voltage which appears across the junction. In most circumstances there is little voltage drop across the bulk p- and n-regions because of their relatively high conductivity and the applied voltage appears almost entirely across the depletion layer. However, if the conductivity of the bulk materials is low, or for large forward currents, the voltage drops across these regions are no longer negligible but must be subtracted from the applied voltage, to give the effective voltage at the junction which is inserted in the diode equation.

198

9.6 Electron and hole injection efficiencies

It is instructive to find the relative magnitudes of hole and electron currents at the junction. This information will also be most useful for later discussions concerning more complex junction devices.

It can be seen from the diode equation (9.12) and eq. (9.23) that the ratio of hole current to electron current at the junction for either forward or reverse bias is given by:

$$\frac{J_h}{J_e} = \frac{J_{hn}}{J_{ep}} = \frac{D_h}{L_h N_d} \cdot \frac{L_e N_a}{D_e}$$

Now, for any particular temperature, Einstein's relation, eq. (6.50), applies and so:

$$\frac{J_h}{J_e} = \frac{L_e}{L_h} \cdot \frac{\mu_h N_a}{\mu_e N_d}$$

Since the conductivities at the p- and n-regions are given by eqs. (6.39) and (6.40), and since the diffusion lengths are of the same order of magnitude, the equation reduces to:

$$\frac{J_h}{J_e} \approx \frac{\sigma_p}{\sigma_n} \tag{9.30}$$

Thus, the ratio of hole current to electron current is approximately equal to the ratio of the conductivities of the p-type and n-type materials constituting the junction.

It is sometimes convenient to define electron and hole *injection efficiencies*, η_e and η_h, as the fractions of the total junction current carried by electrons and holes or

$$\eta_e = \frac{J_{ep}}{J_{hn} + J_{ep}} = \frac{1}{1 + \dfrac{J_{hn}}{J_{ep}}} \approx \frac{1}{1 + \dfrac{\sigma_p}{\sigma_n}} \tag{9.31}$$

and

$$\eta_h = \frac{J_{hn}}{J_{hn} + J_{ep}} = \frac{1}{1 + \dfrac{J_{ep}}{J_{hn}}} \approx \frac{1}{1 + \dfrac{\sigma_n}{\sigma_p}} \tag{9.32}$$

It is evident from eqs. (9.30)–(9.32) that for symmetrical junctions, when $\sigma_n = \sigma_p$, the electron and hole currents are equal but that in the asymmetrical devices the current is mostly carried across the junction by carriers which are majority carriers in the more heavily doped material. For example, for the junction where it was assumed that $\sigma_p \approx 100\sigma_n$, the current is almost entirely carried by holes, only 1% of the total current being carried by electrons.

9.7 The pn junction with finite dimensions

It has been assumed throughout this chapter that the p- and n-regions are of infinite extent, or at least that their lengths, l_p and l_n, respectively, are much longer than the diffusion lengths for minority carriers. Since this is not always the case in practice, a necessary refinement of the theory must be to consider the effects of finite dimensions on the saturation current and hence the diode equation.

We take as our starting point the expression for the minority hole density due to injected holes in the n-region of the forward-biased junction, eq. (9.15), which gives:

$$p(x) = C_1 e^{-x/L_h} + C_2 e^{x/L_h} + p_n$$

Constant C_2 can no longer be neglected since x can never become much greater than L_h, and l_n, the length of the n-region, might be less than L_h. If we assume the hole density at $x = l_n$ to be zero by virtue of there being a highly conducting metal end contact there which acts as an effective recombination site for electrons and holes, the new boundary conditions on p become:

when $\qquad x = 0, p = p_{no} = p_n \exp(eV/kT)$

and when $\qquad x = l_n, p = 0$

These conditions can be substituted in the equation to eliminate the constants C_1 and C_2 and obtain:

$$p(x) = \left[\frac{p_n \exp(-l_n/L_h) + p_{no} - p_n}{1 - \exp(-2l_n/L_h)} \right] e^{-x/L_h}$$
$$- \left[\frac{p_n \exp(-l_n/L_h) + p_{no} - p_n}{1 - \exp(-2l_n/L_h)} - (p_{no} - p_n) \right] e^{+x/L_h} + p_n$$

(9.33)

As before, the hole current is given by:

$$J_h = -e D_h \left. \frac{dp(x)}{dx} \right|_{x=0} = \frac{e D_h}{L_h} p_n \tanh \left(\frac{l_n}{L_h} \right) [e^{eV/kT} - 1] \qquad (9.34)$$

A similar expression can be derived for the electron current at the junction, so the saturation current, J_0, as defined in eq. (9.12), becomes in this case:

$$J_0 = e \left[\frac{D_h p_n}{L_h} \tanh \left(\frac{l_n}{L_h} \right) + \frac{D_e n_p}{L_e} \tanh \left(\frac{l_p}{L_e} \right) \right] \qquad (9.35)$$

which reduces to the value given by eq. (9.22) when $l_n \gg L_h$ and $l_p \gg L_e$, as was assumed originally. Since the diffusion lengths are typically of order 1 mm, eq. (9.35) should always be used to calculate the saturation current whenever

200

the thicknesses of p- and n-regions are less than this order, which is usually the case. Otherwise, the approximate expressions of eq. (9.22) are sufficient.

9.8 The geometry of the depletion layer and depletion layer capacitance

The existence of two space-charge layers of opposite sign at a pn junction, the amount of charge in each varying with bias voltage, gives rise to an effective junction capacitance, called the *depletion-layer capacitance*. It is with more than academic interest that we study the geometry of the space-charge layers and hence evaluate the junction capacitance since, for example, such capacitance is one of the factors which limits the high-frequency operation of junction devices. A further inducement is that, as we shall discover, the junction capacitance can be controlled to a large degree by the bias voltage; this voltage dependent capacitance is deliberately exploited in the *varactor diode*, an extremely useful high-frequency generating device, which will be discussed later.

We again assume an abrupt pn junction, although this time the results obtained for the capacitance will have to be modified to suit graded junctions. In thermal equilibrium, as we have seen, holes move from the p- to the n-region, leaving uncompensated negatively charged acceptors and a net negative space-charge layer in the p-region. Similarly, electrons moving from the n-region leave fixed positively charged donors and a positive space charge layer exists there. This variation of charge density across the depletion layer is indicated by the dashed line in Fig. 9.11(a). We have seen that it is justifiable to neglect

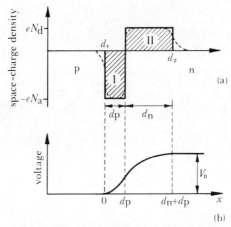

Fig. 9.11 Depletion layer in a pn junction in equilibrium with no bias voltage.

mobile charge in the depletion layer so the charge density there is approximately equal to the product of the magnitude of the impurity concentration and charge in each region. Thus the charge density in the p-region is

$$\rho_p \simeq -N_a e \qquad (9.36)$$

Similarly, the net charge density at the n- side of the junction is

$$\rho_n \simeq N_d\, e \tag{9.37}$$

We shall let the thickness of these layers be d_p and d_n and shall also assume that the space-charge density changes in the abrupt rectangular fashion, shown by the cross-hatching in Fig. 9.11(a), which can be done without too much loss in accuracy. It is convenient to take the origin of x at the junction between the depletion layer and p-region, as shown in the figure.

The potential at any position is related to the space charge via Poisson's equation:

$$\frac{\partial^2 V}{\partial x^2} = -\frac{\rho}{\epsilon}$$

Thus, in region I, for $0 \leqslant x \leqslant d_p$,

$$\frac{\partial^2 V_1}{\partial x^2} = \frac{eN_a}{\epsilon} \tag{9.38}$$

and in region II, for $d_p \leqslant x \leqslant d_p + d_n$

$$\frac{\partial^2 V_2}{\partial x^2} = -\frac{eN_d}{\epsilon} \tag{9.39}$$

We can integrate eq. (9.38) twice and if we arbitrarily choose a reference potential, $V = 0$ at $x = 0$, we get:

$$V_1(x) = \frac{eN_a\, x^2}{2\epsilon} \tag{9.40}$$

Thus, the potential in region I rises parabolically with increasing x.

We next integrate eq. (9.39) to give:

$$\frac{\partial V_2}{\partial x} = -\frac{eN_d\, x}{\epsilon} + C_1 \tag{9.41}$$

Now the electric field must be continuous across the junction at $x = d_p$ or

$$\left.\frac{\partial V_1}{\partial x}\right|_{d_p} = \left.\frac{\partial V_2}{\partial x}\right|_{d_p}$$

Therefore we can substitute in the equation from eqs. (9.40) and (9.41) to evaluate the constant C_1:

$$\frac{eN_a\, d_p}{\epsilon} = -\frac{eN_d\, d_p}{\epsilon} + C_1$$

or

$$C_1 = ed_p(N_a + N_d)/\epsilon \tag{9.42}$$

Integrating (9.41) again we obtain:

$$V_2 = -\frac{eN_d x^2}{2\epsilon} + C_1 x + C_2 \qquad (9.43)$$

Again, for continuity of V at $x = d_p$, $V_1|_{d_p} = V_2|_{d_p}$ and eqs. (9.40), (9.42), and (9.43) give:

$$\frac{eN_a d_p^2}{2\epsilon} = -\frac{eN_d d_p^2}{2\epsilon} + \frac{ed_p^2(N_a + N_d)}{\epsilon} + C_2$$

This value of C_2 can be substituted in eq. (9.43) to give:

$$V_2(x) = -\frac{eN_d x^2}{2\epsilon} + \left[\frac{ed_p(N_a + N_d)}{\epsilon}\right] x - \frac{ed_p^2(N_a + N_d)}{2\epsilon} \qquad (9.44)$$

Now, at the further extremity of the depletion layer, $x = d_n + d_p$, the electric field strength, $\mathscr{E}$, is zero, and

$$\left.\frac{\partial V_2}{\partial x}\right|_{d_n + d_p} = 0$$

or

$$0 = -\frac{eN_d}{\epsilon}(d_n + d_p) + \frac{ed_p(N_a + N_d)}{\epsilon}$$

which gives

$$\frac{d_p}{d_n} = \frac{N_d}{N_a} \qquad (9.45)$$

It can be seen that the depletion layer thicknesses are in inverse ratio to the doping concentrations, a result that can be justified on physical grounds, since we would expect there to be equality of net charge at either side of the junction in equilibrium, or $N_a d_p = N_d d_n$. We see that in an asymmetric junction the depletion layer and the potential rise occur mostly in the material which is more lightly doped; for example, in Fig. 9.11 it has been assumed that the p-type material is more heavily doped than the n-type and thus $d_p \ll d_n$.

Now, at $x = d_n + d_p$, the potential with respect to our assumed zero potential is V_0, the contact potential for the junction in equilibrium. Equation (9.44) thus gives:

$$V_2|_{d_n + d_p} = V_0 = -\frac{eN_d}{2\epsilon}(d_n + d_p)^2 + \frac{ed_p(N_a + N_d)(d_p + d_p)}{\epsilon}$$

$$-\frac{ed_p^2(N_a + N_d)}{2\epsilon}$$

We now eliminate d_n from this equation, using eq. (9.45) and rearrange to give the width of the layer in the p-region:

$$d_p = \left[\frac{2\epsilon V_0 N_d}{eN_a(N_a + N_d)} \right]^{\frac{1}{2}} \tag{9.46}$$

Finally, this equation is used in conjunction with eq. (9.45) to give the width of the depletion layer in the n-region:

$$d_n = \left[\frac{2\epsilon V_0 N_a}{eN_d(N_a + N_d)} \right]^{\frac{1}{2}} \tag{9.47}$$

The total depletion layer thicknesses is then:

$$d_p + d_n = \left[\frac{2\epsilon V_0(N_a + N_d)}{eN_a N_d} \right]^{\frac{1}{2}} \tag{9.48}$$

and the junction becomes narrower as the impurity concentration is increased.

The expressions we have derived, and in particular eqs. (9.46), (9.47), and (9.48), are still applicable to a biased junction provided the effective junction voltage is altered accordingly. For example, if a forward bias, V, is applied to the junction, V_0 in the equations is replaced by $(V_0 - V)$ and there is a decrease in the depletion layer thicknesses. On the contrary, if a reverse bias of $-V$ volts is applied the junction voltage becomes $(V_0 + V)$ and the total depletion layer thickness is increased to:

$$d_p + d_n = \left(\frac{2\epsilon(V_0 + V)(N_a + N_d)}{eN_a N_d} \right)^{\frac{1}{2}} \tag{9.49}$$

The capacitance associated with the depletion layer can be obtained by the following argument. Suppose the junction is reverse-biased and the junction voltage, $(V_0 + V)$, equals V_j. The charge stored at either side of the junction is then represented by $\pm Q_j$ in Fig. 9.12. If the junction voltage is

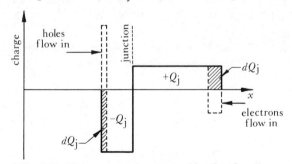

Fig. 9.12 Charge storage in a reverse-biased pn junction.

made less negative by a small amount, δV_j, there will be a reduction in the depletion layer width and a corresponding reduction, $\pm \delta Q_j$, in the charge, as indicated by the shaded regions in the figure. These changes are brought about by holes of total charge δQ_j flowing into the depletion layer from the p-region to neutralize some of the charge of the fixed exposed acceptors, and a similar negative charge flows from the n-type region as indicated by the dashed lines in the figure. Thus, if the junction voltage is changed by δV_j, this results in a flow of mobile charge δQ_j which, for small changes in δV_j, is proportional to δV_j. An incremental depletion layer capacitance, C_j, is therefore defined as:

$$C_j = \frac{dQ_j}{dV_j} \qquad (9.50)$$

Now, the magnitude of the total charge stored at either side of the junction per unit junction area is given by:

$$Q_j = eN_d \, d_n = eN_a \, d_p$$

or, using eq. (9.46) or (9.47) in which V_0 is replaced by V_j:

$$Q_j = \left[\frac{2\epsilon e V_j N_a N_d}{(N_a + N_d)} \right]^{\frac{1}{2}} \qquad (9.51)$$

This is substituted in eq. (9.50) to give the junction capacitance per unit area:

$$C_j = \frac{d}{dV_j} \left[\frac{2\epsilon e N_a N_d}{(N_a + N_d)} \right]^{\frac{1}{2}} V_j^{\frac{1}{2}} = \left[\frac{\epsilon e N_a N_d}{2(N_a + N_d)} \right]^{\frac{1}{2}} \frac{1}{V_j^{\frac{1}{2}}} \, F/m^2 \qquad (9.52)$$

We see that for an abrupt pn junction, the depletion capacitance varies as $V_j^{-\frac{1}{2}}$ where the junction voltage, V_j, is equal to $(V_0 \pm V)$, the sign depending on whether the bias is applied in the forward or reverse direction. Notice that, for large reverse bias voltages when $V \gg V_0$, C_j varies very nearly as $V^{-\frac{1}{2}}$.

The expression for C can be simplified further, using eq. (9.48), which with eq. (9.52) gives:

$$C_j = \frac{\epsilon}{(d_p + d_n)} \, F/m^2 \qquad (9.53)$$

Thus, the abrupt junction behaves as a parallel-plate capacitor, filled with dielectric of permittivity ϵ and of thickness $(d_p + d_n)$. With forward bias, $(d_p + d_n)$ is small and C_j large, whereas when the bias voltage is in the reverse direction, $(d_p + d_n)$ becomes large and C_j is correspondingly smaller.

The capacitance of graded junctions varies with reverse voltage more slowly than the abrupt junction. For instance, a linearly graded junction in reverse bias has a junction capacitance which varies as $(V_j)^{-\frac{1}{3}}$, or $(V)^{-\frac{1}{3}}$ approximately. Therefore, an abrupt junction is superior to a graded junction in a varactor, because of its larger relative capacitance change for a given bias-voltage change. High impurity concentrations are also an advantage in varactor diodes since not only is the depletion layer width reduced and hence the capacitance increased, but also the conductance of the bulk p- and n-regions in series with the capacitance is increased, which is desirable for high-frequency applications.

If the capacitance of a junction is measured as a function of the reverse bias voltage V, the information can yield experimental values for the doping levels of the p- and n-regions and also the contact potential. For example, if we assume the p-region to be the more heavily doped, such that $N_a \gg N_d$, we can rearrange eq. (9.52) to give:

$$V_j = V_0 + V \simeq \frac{1}{C_j^2}\left(\frac{\epsilon e N_d}{2}\right)^{\frac{1}{2}}$$

Thus, an experimental graph of V versus C_j^{-2} should be a straight line, with an intercept on the V-axis giving V_0 and with a slope providing a value for N_d, the impurity level on the more lightly doped n-side. The acceptor concentration can then be found from N_d and V_0 using eq. (9.8). A similar but slightly more complicated procedure can be used to find N_a and N_d when they have comparable values.

9.9 Diffusion capacitance and the small-signal equivalent circuit of a pn junction

When a junction is biased in the reverse direction its equivalent circuit will be of the form illustrated in Fig. 9.13(a). Here, r_{np} represents the resistance

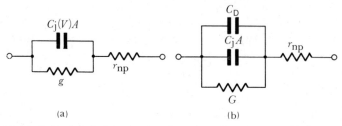

Fig. 9.13 Small-signal equivalent circuits of a pn junction, (a) reverse-biased and (b) forward-biased.

of the bulk n- and p-regions outside the depletion layer, C_j is the depletion layer capacitance per unit area, which will be a function of the reverse bias, A is the junction area and g is the conductance of the junction due to the flow of reverse current across it. Usually r_{np} is very small and can be neglected and often g can be neglected when compared to the susceptance of C_jA. Thus, in many instances, the reverse-biased junction can be represented simply by a capacitance C_jA.

206

At first sight, it might be assumed that the same equivalent circuit would be satisfactory for the forward-biased junction, provided the appropriate values for C_j and g are introduced, but this is not the case. It is true that when the diode is forward-biased, its depletion capacitance increases, but a further capacitance, called the *storage* or *diffusion* capacitance, C_D, is introduced which tends to swamp effects due to C_j. For the forward-biased junction, many minority carriers are injected into each side of the junction. It is the motion and charge storage of such carriers which give rise to the new capacitive effect. The small-signal equivalent circuit is then as shown in Fig. 9.13(b). The elements C_D and G in it can be estimated as follows:

We first assume that the steady-state forward-bias voltage, V, has superimposed on it a small alternating voltage, $V_1 e^{j\omega t}$. The injected hole density at the edge of the depletion layer, $x = 0$, is then given by eq. (9.10) and is:

$$p_{no} = p_n \exp\left[\frac{e}{kT}(V + V_1 e^{j\omega t})\right] \tag{9.54}$$

Since we have assumed small-signal conditions, $V_1 \ll V_0$ and the exponential can be approximated to the first two terms of a power series, giving

$$p_{no} = p_n \exp\left(\frac{eV}{kT}\right)\left[1 + \frac{eV_1}{kT}e^{j\omega t}\right] \tag{9.55}$$

The alternating component of the forward bias thus causes an alternating hole current to be injected into the n-region. We therefore assume that the excess minority hole concentration, δp, is given by:

$$\delta p = p(x,t) - p_n = p_0(x) + p_1(x)e^{j\omega t} - p_n \tag{9.56}$$

where $p_0(x)$ represents the steady-state hole density and $p_1(x)$ the density of the alternating component, distance x from the edge of the depletion layer. If we substitute this in the time-dependent continuity equation for holes, eq. (6.64), assuming $\mathcal{E} = 0$ as usual and retaining only a.c. components we get:

$$j\omega p_1 = \frac{-p_1}{\tau_{Lh}} + D_h \frac{\partial^2 p_1}{\partial x^2}$$

or

$$\frac{\partial^2 p_1}{\partial x^2} = \frac{(1 + j\omega\tau_{Lh})}{L_h^2}p_1$$

By comparison with eq. (9.15) this equation has a solution:

$$p_1 = C \exp\left[-\frac{(1 + j\omega\tau_{Lh})^{\frac{1}{2}}x}{L_h}\right] \tag{9.57}$$

The constant C is obtained by comparing this equation, setting $x = 0$, with the alternating part of eq. (9.55). Thus, the alternating injected hole density is:

$$p_1 = p_n \left(\frac{eV_1}{kT}\right) \exp\left(\frac{eV}{kT}\right) \exp\left[-\frac{(1 + j\omega\tau_{Lh})^{\frac{1}{2}} x}{L_h}\right] e^{j\omega t} \quad (9.58)$$

Proceeding as for the steady-state case, the alternating junction current due to injected holes is:

$$J_{h_1} = -eD_h \left.\frac{dp_1}{dx}\right|_{x=0} = \frac{(1 + j\omega\tau_{Lh})^{\frac{1}{2}} p_n D_h e^2 V_1}{L_h} \frac{}{kT} \exp\left(\frac{eV}{kT}\right) e^{j\omega t}$$

A similar expression can be derived for the alternating junction current due to electron injection into the p-region and the total a.c. junction is then

$$J_1 = \frac{e^2 V_1}{kT} \exp\left(\frac{eV}{kT}\right) \left[\frac{D_h p_n (1 + j\omega\tau_{Lh})^{\frac{1}{2}}}{L_h} + \frac{D_e n_p (1 + j\omega\tau_{Le})^{\frac{1}{2}}}{L_e}\right] e^{j\omega t}$$

This current flows on application of an alternating forward bias voltage, $V_1 e^{j\omega t}$, and the junction admittance, Y_1, is therefore:

$$Y_1 = \frac{J_1}{V_1} = \frac{e^2}{kT} \exp\left(\frac{eV}{kT}\right) \left[\frac{D_h p_n (1 + j\omega\tau_{Lh})^{\frac{1}{2}}}{L_h} + \frac{D_e n_p (1 + j\omega\tau_{Le})^{\frac{1}{2}}}{L_e}\right] \quad (9.59)$$

If the frequency is not too high, $\omega\tau \ll 1$, and the admittance expression simplifies to:

$$Y_1 \simeq \frac{e^2}{kT} \exp\left(\frac{eV}{kT}\right) \left[\frac{D_h p_n}{L_h} + \frac{D_e n_p}{L_e}\right] + \frac{j\omega e^2}{2kT}\left[\frac{D_h p_n \tau_{Lh}}{L_h} + \frac{D_e n_p \tau_{Le}}{L_e}\right]$$

Thus we see that the low-frequency admittance of the forward-biased junction can be represented by a conductance:

$$G = \frac{e^2}{kT} \exp\left(\frac{eV}{kT}\right) \left[\frac{D_h p_n}{L_h} + \frac{D_e n_p}{L_e}\right] = \frac{eI_0}{kT} \exp\left(\frac{eV}{kT}\right) \quad (9.60)$$

where I_0 is the saturation current, in parallel with a capacitance

$$C_D = \frac{e^2}{2kT}\left[\frac{D_h p_n \tau_{Lh}}{L_h} + \frac{D_e n_p \tau_{Le}}{L_e}\right] \exp\left(\frac{eV}{kT}\right)$$

or

$$C_D = \frac{e^2}{2kT} [p_n L_h + n_p L_e] \exp\left(\frac{eV}{kT}\right) \quad (9.61)$$

Notice that this diffusion capacitance increases exponentially with forward bias or, alternatively, that it is directly proportional to forward junction current.

208

9.10 Metal–semiconductor junctions

It has been assumed that electrical contacts can be made successfully to the bulk regions of the semiconductor junction diode which do not affect the electrical performance of the junction. The contacts each constitute some kind of metal–semiconductor junction which, ideally, should have a high conductance which is independent of the direction of current flow. Such a contact is said to be *ohmic*.

When a junction diode is provided with two ohmic contacts, contact potentials exist between the metal and semiconductor regions such that the algebraic sum of these and that at the pn junction is zero and there is no net voltage across the device in equilibrium. Otherwise, a current could flow in an external load connected across the diode, which clearly would violate the second law of thermodynamics.

Not all metal–semiconductor junctions are ohmic, indeed many display unidirectional current-carrying properties and are thus rectifying. Whereas rectifying contacts are an obvious disadvantage when applied to a pn junction diode, rectifying metal–semiconductor junctions have important device applications in their own right, for example, in high-frequency point-contact diodes.

Whether a particular combination of metal and semiconductor forms a rectifying or ohmic contact is dependent to some extent on the relative work functions of each and to a larger degree on the surface condition of the semiconductor, which will now be discussed in more detail. To be specific we shall firstly describe the junction formed by a metal and an n-type semiconductor. There are, of course, completely analogous arguments for the metal–p-type junction which will be briefly mentioned subsequently.

9.10.1. The junction between a metal and an n-type semiconductor.

Let us firstly consider the metal contact and semiconductor separately. Electrons in each are retained in the body of the material by a potential barrier at the surface, as discussed in chapter 4. If we assume that the work function of the metal, ϕ_m, is greater than that of the semiconductor, ϕ_s, the energy band diagrams for each are shown in Fig. 9.14(a). When contact is made between the two materials, charge is transferred from one to the other until, in equilibrium, the Fermi level is continuous across the junction, as illustrated in Fig. 9.14(b). This condition is brought about by electrons spilling over from the semiconductor into the metal, leaving a positively charged depletion layer in the semiconductor due to exposed donor atoms and producing a negative surface charge on the metal. The process continues until the electric field set up by the dipole layer is sufficiently strong to inhibit further electron diffusion. This is represented by a bending up of the band edges in the semiconductor, to form a potential energy barrier for electrons, of height $(\phi_m - \phi_s)e$, as shown. There will be some electron flow from metal to

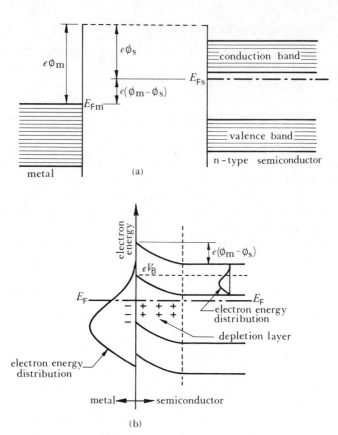

Fig. 9.14 Band structure of metal–n–type semiconductor junction, (a) before and (b) after contact, when $\phi_m > \phi_s$.

semiconductor due to thermal agitation; this is represented by the small tail of the electron distribution curve for electrons with energy greater than the barrier energy, eV_B. Similarly, a few electrons in the semiconductor will have sufficient energy to surmount the barrier and flow into the metal. In equilibrium, both electron currents will be equal and there will be net junction current.

When the semiconductor is made positive with respect to the metal by the application of an external biasing voltage, V, all energy levels in the semiconductor are lowered by an amount eV, the effective barrier height is increased, and the depletion layer becomes wider; the junction is therefore reverse-biased. Under these circumstances, electron current from semiconductor to metal is entirely prohibited by the high potential barrier, but the small electron current from metal to semiconductor is unaffected. The reverse current thus saturates at a low value independent of the reverse-bias voltage.

210

Application of a forward-bias voltage, V, by making the semiconductor negative lowers the effective junction height and reduces the width of the depletion layer. Again, the small electron current from metal to semiconductor remains constant but appreciable electron current is allowed to flow from the semiconductor into the metal contact. Minority hole injection from metal to semiconductor is now also possible since the top of the valence band is raised sufficiently for there to be appreciably more vacant energy levels in the metal than in the semiconductor at these levels.

We see that when $\phi_m > \phi_s$ the metal-semiconductor junction is rectifying, passing large currents in the forward direction and a small saturation current when biased in the reverse direction. A simple analysis of such a junction can be based on Boltzmann statistics. The electrons from metal to semiconductor have to surmount an energy barrier of height eV_B and at temperature T the electron current density from metal to semiconductor, J_{ms} is

$$J_{ms} \propto \exp\left(-eV_B/kT\right) \qquad (9.62)$$

On the other hand, the barrier to be surmounted by electrons in the semiconductor will be of height $e(V_B - V)$, which is greater or less than eV_B, depending on the direction of the applied bias and, hence, the sign of V. The electron current from semiconductor into the metal, J_{sm} is thus

$$J_{sm} \propto \exp(-e\overline{V_B - V}/kT) \qquad (9.63)$$

Thus, if we ignore minority hole injected currents for the moment, the total junction current, J, will be the difference between the two electron components or

$$J \propto \exp\left[-\frac{eV_B}{kT}\right]\left[\exp\left(\frac{eV}{kT}\right) - 1\right] \qquad (9.64)$$

Notice that this is of the same form as the rectifier equation for a pn junction, eq. (9.12), and hence the I–V characteristics will be similar to that shown in Fig. 9.10. Hole injection will have the effect of reducing the forward resistance and increasing the slope of the I–V characteristic in the forward-biased regime. A rectifying junction of this type is called a *Schottky* junction, after the original investigator.

A further point to note is that the majority electrons injected into the metal when the junction is biased in the forward direction will have energies much in excess of the Fermi energy in the metal; such electrons are called *hot electrons*. Subsequent lattice scattering reduced their energy to the average energy in the metal.

If now we consider the case when $\phi_m < \phi_s$, the band structures of metal and semiconductor before and after contact will be as shown in Figs. 9.15(a) and (b). Before contact the Fermi level in the metal, E_{Fm}, is higher than that in the semiconductor, E_{Fs}. On contact there is an exchange of charge as electrons flow from metal to semiconductor, causing a surface charge

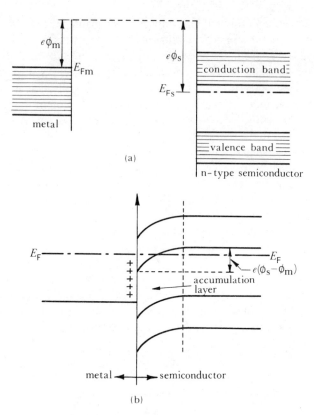

Fig. 9.15 Band structure of a metal–n-type semiconductor junction, (a) before and (b) after contact, when $\phi_m < \phi_s$.

accumulation layer to build up as shown in the figure, until the Fermi level becomes continuous in equilibrium. In the energy level diagram, such behaviour is represented by a downward bending of the bands in the semiconductor in the vicinity of the junction. It is clear that in this case there is no potential barrier formed at the junction; electrons can move across the junction in either direction, depending on the direction of the bias voltage, without much hindrance. Such a contact is thus considered ohmic.

9.10.2. Metal–p-type semiconductor junction. It is clear from arguments similar to those set out in subsection 9.10.1 that when $\phi_m < \phi_s$ and E_{Fs} is below E_{Fm}, a space-charge depletion layer is set up in the semiconductor and a barrier forms at the junction which becomes rectifying. Conversely, when $\phi_s < \phi_m$ and E_{Fm} is below E_{Fs}, no barrier is formed, holes can flow freely across the junction in either direction, and the contact is ohmic.

212

9.10.3. Surface states. It would seem that the criterion for determining whether a metal–semiconductor contact is ohmic or rectifying are (a) whether the semiconductor is n- or p-type and (b) the relative work functions of metal and semiconductor. Unfortunately, these criteria are not always successful in practice for predicting the characteristics of a given contact. For example, it is found that the characteristics of microwave point-contact diodes are largely independent of the work function of the metal. The anomalous behaviour arises because of the existence at the surface of the semiconductor of a large number of localized energy levels situated in the forbidden gap. These *surface states* arise principally because of adsorbed impurity atoms or oxide layers at the surface. The surface states behave as either electrons or hole-traps, depending on the origin of the states.

Consider, for example, electron-trapping surface states in a moderately doped n-type semiconductor. The surface states deplete electrons from the bulk material, exposing donors and setting up a depletion layer and causing a natural potential barrier to occur independent of any metal contact being made, as shown in Fig. 9.16(a). It is also possible for electrons to be removed

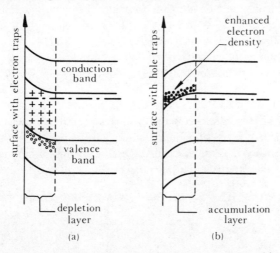

Fig. 9.16 Band structure near the surface of an n-type semiconductor, (a) with surface electron traps and (b) with surface hole traps.

from the valence band, if the electron-trap density at the surface is sufficiently high; the surface layer is then p-type in character and the Fermi level in the depletion layer is nearer the valence band, as is appropriate. Thus, a *p*-type inversion layer can be produced on the surface of an otherwise n-type crystal causing a built-in pn junction. The importance of such layers will become apparent when the insulated-gate field-effect transistor is discussed later.

It is also possible for accumulation layers to be found at the surface of a semiconductor, for example, when an n-type semiconductor has surface states which trap holes, as in Fig. 9.16(b). The hole traps are normally occupied by

213

electrons but these are given up into the conduction band to enhance the density in an accumulation layer, as shown.

Similar situations, i.e., depletion, accumulation, and inversion layers, are of course possible with p-type material, depending on the number and type of surface states.

It is evident that the nature of the contact made by a metal to such layers is strongly dependent on the surface states, and effects due to relative work function may be of secondary importance.

One practically important method of making successful ohmic contacts to a semiconductor is to alloy or interdiffuse a material which is itself of the same impurity type as that in the semiconductor to which the contact is being made. For example, the solder used to form a contact may be doped with n- or p-type impurity, whichever is appropriate; there is thus a gradual transition from metal to semiconductor and no rectifying effects will be observed.

9.11 Breakdown in pn junctions. The Zener diode

The simple theory for a pn junction leading to the diode equation predicts that under reverse-bias conditions, a small constant current, the saturation current, I_0, flows which is independent of the magnitude of the bias voltage. This prediction is not entirely correct in practical diodes, firstly because of ohmic leakage currents around the surface of the junction which result in a gradual increase of reverse current with increasing bias. Second, at some particular reverse-bias voltage, V_b, a sudden increase in reverse current can sometimes be observed which is due to some sort of *breakdown*. The reverse characteristic of a practical pn junction diode could then be of the form shown in Fig. 9.17. When breakdown occurs, the diode current is limited mostly by the resistance of the external circuit.

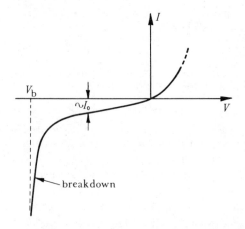

Fig. 9.17 *V-I* characteristic of a pn junction with large reverse bias voltages.

214

There are two principal cases of breakdown in the junction, Zener breakdown and avalanche breakdown. Zener breakdown is a consequence of the phenomenon of quantum-mechanical tunnelling discussed in chapter 1. It is most often encountered in thin, highly doped, abrupt junctions in which quite small reverse-bias voltages can cause large fields to exist across the narrow depletion regions. Referring to Fig. 9.18, which shows such a junction when reverse-biased, we see that electrons at, say, a in the valence band lie opposite vacant energy levels at b in the conduction band but are prevented from making this

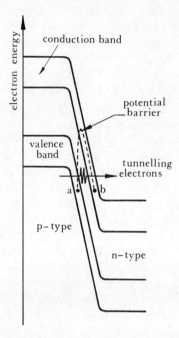

Fig. 9.18 Zener breakdown in a reverse-biased pn junction.

transition by a high potential barrier. If the junction is sufficiently abrupt or the reverse bias voltage sufficiently great, the potential barrier can become thin enough for electrons to tunnel through from valence to conduction band and large reverse currents flow.

The avalanche breakdown mechanism tends to dominate in wider junctions, for instance in a graded junction or when the doping concentration at one or both sides of the junction is only moderate. Under these circumstances, breakdown occurs if each current carrier in the depletion layer acquires on average at least enough energy between scattering collisions so as to be capable of imparting sufficient energy to the lattice when it next collides to create an electron–hole pair. Both electrons and holes produced by this process are accelerated by the field in the depletion layer, causing further hole-pair production. The process is thus a self-maintaining chain reaction which leads to very high reverse currents. If the junction temperature is increased the mean free path for phonon scattering is reduced, as we have seen earlier, and the breakdown voltage is correspondingly increased. This contrasts with Zener breakdown which, since it depends on the gap energy and barrier thickness, is largely independent of temperature.

It is possible to design a pn junction such that the reverse breakdown characteristic is both nearly vertical and accurately reproducible. Such devices are called *Zener diodes* for historical reasons although it may well be that breakdown is due to the avalanche effect. They are used as voltage reference elements in voltage regulator circuits.

Another effect which can produce rapid increases in reverse current and characteristics closely resembling breakdown is known as *punch-through*. We have seen that the reverse current in a junction is due to a small number of thermally generated minority carriers. Now, as discussed in the previous section, the ohmic contacts to the bulk regions can generate large numbers of carriers. Consider for example, the ohmic contact attached to the back-biased n-region. This will inject minority holes into the n-region, the holes being usually lost at small distances from the contact by recombination with majority electrons. However, if the n-region is relatively lightly doped, such that the depletion layer exists mostly in it, at some large reverse voltage, known as the punch-through voltage, V_{pt}, the n-region can become completely depleted of electrons and the depletion layer extend right to the end contact. Under these conditions the large number of holes generated at the end contact cannot recombine with electrons since there are none to recombine with, but they add to the thermally generated minority holes and are swept into the p-region. When this happens, the diode is punched-through and large reverse currents flow. We can estimate the punch-through voltage for an abrupt junction by using eq. (9.47), replacing the contact voltage, V_0, by the junction voltage under reverse-bias condition, $(V_0 + V)$. Then the thickness of the depletion layer in the n-region is:

$$d_n = \left[\frac{2\epsilon(V_0 + V)N_a}{eN_d(N_a + N_d)} \right]^{\frac{1}{2}}$$

If we assume that $N_a \gg N_d$, $V \gg V_0$, then the depletion layer thickness equals the length of the n-region, l_n, when

$$V = V_{pt} = \frac{eN_d l_n^2}{2\epsilon} \tag{9.65}$$

Thus, the effect is critically dependent on device dimensions, which contrasts with the other breakdown mechanisms described earlier.

9.12 The tunnel diode

Operation of this device, alternatively called an Esaki diode after its inventor, is based on the possibility of quantum-mechanical tunnelling by electrons through a potential barrier as described in chapter 1. If the p- and n-regions of a junction are extremely heavily doped, say with 10^{25} or more impurities per metre cube, the Fermi level on the p-side of the junction lies *below* the top of of the valence band and on the n-side it lies *above* the bottom of the conduction band; the materials are *degenerate*. Furthermore, the junction width becomes sufficiently narrow for tunnelling effects to become possible. Energy band diagrams for such a junction in equilibrium and with varying degrees of forward bias are shown in Fig. 9.19.

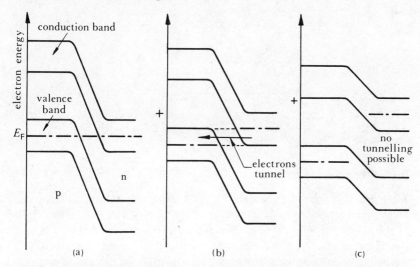

Fig. 9.19 **Band structure of a tunnel diode, (a) with zero bias voltage, (b) with a small forward-bias voltage and (c) with a large forward-bias voltage.**

In equilibrium, Fig. 9.19(a), tunnelling currents across the junction in either direction are equal and no net junction current flows. For small forward-bias voltages, Fig. 9.19(b), electrons from the conduction band in the n-type material can tunnel through the potential barrier at the junction, provided it is sufficiently thin, into vacant sites in the valence band at the p-side which have the same energy. For larger forward-bias voltages, Fig. 9.19(c), there are no longer vacant sites in the valence band in the p-region at the same level as sites occupied by electrons in the conduction band in the n-region; tunnelling is no longer possible and the current reverts to the normal forward current. For bias voltages between these two extremes, the current decreases as the voltage increases, which results in an effective negative resistance and a forward I–V characteristic of the form shown in Fig. 9.20. The positive peak in this characteristic corresponds to the condition in Fig. 9.19(b).

If the tunnel diode is incorporated in a suitable resonant circuit and biased appropriately, its negative resistance can be made to compensate for ohmic losses in the circuit and undamped oscillations can occur. Since tunnelling takes place almost instantaneously, very-high-frequency oscillators, up to say 100 GHz, can be built which utilize this effect in tunnel diodes.

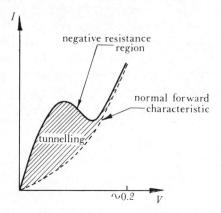

Fig. 9.20 *I–V* characteristic of a tunnel diode.

9.13 Fabrication technology

Whereas it is beyond the scope of this book to discuss in detail all the manufacturing processes involved in making pn junction devices, a brief description of the basic fabrication technology is pertinent since this will help to determine the relevance and the limitations of the various approximate theories when applied to practical diodes. The reader is referred to the extensive literature in the subject for a more comprehensive account of the technology, if this is required.

Firstly, we shall briefly discuss methods for growing and refining pure semiconductor single-crystal samples, which are a necessary ingredient of all junction devices. A procedure for growing single crystals which has found wide commercial use, known as the *Czochralski* method, employs a suitably oriented seed crystal which is partly immersed in the molten semiconductor. The melt temperature is then reduced slightly until the semiconductor begins to freeze onto the seed, which is then slowly withdrawn. If the withdrawal rate and temperature are correct, the liquid–solid interface is maintained near the suface of the melt and a single-crystal ingot is pulled from it. The process is carried out in an inert atmosphere to prevent oxidation. A further refinement is that the seed and pulled crystal are continuously rotated to stir the melt and produce a more homogeneous crystal. It is possible to produce single crystals several centimetres in diameter and tens of centimetres long by this technique.

The semiconductor used for the melt is usually purified beforehand using a technique known as *zone-refining.* In this method, a semiconductor ingot is selectively heated locally, often using an induction heating coil, so as to

218

produce a short molten section. Surface-tension forces prevent the material in the liquid state separating from the solid ingot. If the semiconductor is slowly passed through the heating coil, the liquid–solid interface passes along the ingot, and since most of the impurity atoms have an affinity for the liquid rather than the solid state, they are swept along in the liquid section. After several such passes, the unwanted impurities are nearly entirely concentrated at one end of the bar, which is cut off subsequently and discarded. It is possible to use the zone-refining technique simultaneously with crystal pulling; this leads to extremely pure single crystals, since the refined crystal has not been contaminated by a crucible.

Once the pure, single-crystal semiconductor crystal has been produced, there are many different practical methods of preparing junction devices from it. Fortunately, these can be classified into four main generic groups, according to the way in which the junction is fabricated, namely grown-junction, alloyed-junction, diffused-junction, and epitaxial diodes. The method of junction construction and the detailed device technology is governed by the application for the device as well as economic considerations.

The *grown junction* is historically most important because the first junction devices were built using this technique. A single crystal is grown from an initially n-type doped melt. After the crystal has been pulled sufficiently to ensure crystal uniformity, the melt dopant is changed to p-type by compensating with an acceptor impurity. The resulting crystal is partly n-type and partly p-type, a junction occurring at the plane of zero net impurity, as usual. Subsequent cutting of the crystal into discs each containing a pn junction can provide material for many individual diodes. The junction formed by this process is usually gradual and must be treated as a graded junction. One difficulty with the method is precise location of the junction in the crystal; this, together with further problems of lead attachment, has resulted in the process not being extensively adopted commercially.

In the *alloyed-junction* process, a small n-type single-crystal die has a dot of either a pure acceptor metal, such as indium or aluminium, or a metal heavily doped with p-type impurities placed on top of it and the unit is heated in a non-oxidizing atmosphere. When the furnace temperature is raised above the melting point of the eutectic alloy formed between the semi-conductor and metal, the metal melts and dissolves some of the n-type material forming an alloy, as in Fig. 9.21(a). The thickness of the dissolved layer is dependent on temperature and the duration of the process. On cooling, the molten region crystallizes out as a p-type compensated region with the same crystalline structure as the semiconductor. The remainder of the metal forms a convenient ohmic contact; the header to which the n-type chip is soldered forms the other contact to the diode.

The *bonded* diode, Fig. 9.21(b), uses a variation of this technique. Wire containing a p-type impurity is pressed against an n-type chip and a large current passed through the unit until the semiconductor melts at the heated wire tip. The recrystallization of the alloy on cooling again forms a p-type layer, the wire automatically becoming one lead for the diode. The bonding wire used is often gold, leading to the use of term *gold-bonded diode* to describe this device. Notice that the junction formed by this technique is rarely planar.

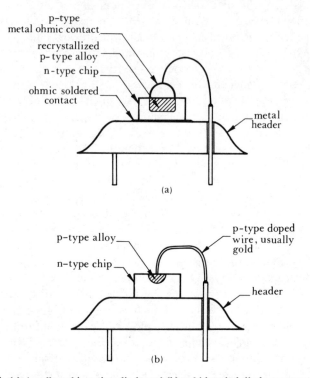

Fig. 9.21 (a) An alloyed-junction diode and (b) gold-bonded diode construction.

Diode fabrication by *diffused-junction* techniques is probably the most common manufacturing procedure at the present time. Again the basic material is homogeneous, single-crystal, n-type semiconductor. This is heated in an inert atmosphere and acceptor impurities in gaseous form, for example boron, are diffused into the surface until a compensated p-type layer results. The rate of diffusion is governed by a diffusion equation of the same form as eq. (6.47), but the impurities diffuse at a much slower rate than carriers, of course. The net p-type impurity concentration can be closely controlled by the furnace temperature and the concentration of the dopant. The area for diffusion is selected by a masking technique in which the surface of the n-type slice is oxidized by exposure to a water–oxygen mixture at elevated temperatures; windows are cut in the oxide by photo-etching techniques and diffusing only takes place where the oxide has been removed, as in Fig. 9.22(a). Ohmic contact to the p-region is usually made by an evaporated metal film. In the discrete diode structure each diode is separated from the parent slice and bonded to a suitable header, which serves as the other contact to the diode.

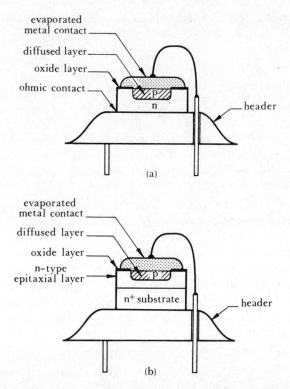

Fig. 9.22 (a) A diffused-junction diode and (b) an epitaxial diffused-junction diode.

Diodes produced by the *epitaxial* process are now being manufactured commercially on a large scale. The process involves the growing of a thin layer of single-crystal semiconductor on to a supporting slice of parent material. The basic chemical reaction which is often used to produce silicon epitaxial layers is the reduction of silicon chloride in an atmosphere of hydrogen at temperatures around 1200 °C. Doped impurity layers and even compound semiconductors can be deposited by similar techniques. For discrete diodes, the parent slice, called the substrate, is highly doped to give it a low resistivity and the epitaxial layer is lightly doped with the same impurity type. A pn junction is then formed in the layer and electrodes are deposited by the same processes that are used for diffused diodes, as shown schematically in Fig. 9.22(b). Diodes with a high breakdown voltage and a low capacitance can be fabricated in this way in the high-resistivity epitaxial layer, while the low-resistance supporting substrate reduces the series resistance of the diode.

221

Problems

1   The bulk n-type region of a particular germanium junction has a conductivity of 10^4 S/m at 300 K and that for the p-region is 10^2 S/m. Find
the voltage drop across the junction in equilibrium at 300 K, assuming
$n_i = 2.5 \times 10^{19}$ m^{-3}, $\mu_e = 0.36$ and $\mu_h = 0.17$ m^2/V. s.

    Ans. 0·36 V.

2   An ideal abrupt pn junction has the following properties:

    Doping concentration on the p-side 10^{24} m^{-3}. Doping concentration on
the n-side 10^{22} m^{-3}. Area of cross section 10^{-6} m^2. Hole mobility 0·2 m^2/V. s;
Electron mobility 0·4 m^2/V. s. Diffusion length of minority holes 2×10^{-4} m;
for minority electrons 3.10^{-4} m. Bulk relative permittivity 16; intrinsic
carrier density 10^{19} m^{-3}. Evaluate the following parameters of the diode at
room temperature:

(a) the majority and minority carrier concentration, (b) the conductivities of
each region, (c) the contact potential, (d) the diffusion constants for each
carrier type, (f) current flowing when 0·25 V is applied to the diode with the
positive terminal connected to the p-type material, (g) the current flowing
for large reverse bias voltages, (h) the battery polarity for the application of
reverse bias, (i) the width of the depletion layer when a reverse bias voltage of
10 V is applied, (j) the incremental depletion layer capacitance under the bias
conditions as for (i) and (k) the approximate ratio of hole to electron current
across the junction.

    Ans. (a) 10^{24}, 10^{22}, 10^{16}, 10^{14}, (b) 3·2 × 10^4 S/m, 6·4 10^2 S/m, (c) 0·46 V,
(d) 0·005, 0·01 m^2/s, (e) 0·04 μA, (f) 0·88 mA, (g) 0·04 μA, (h) negative
terminal to n-side, (i) 1·4 μm, (j) 100 pF, (k) 50:1.

3   The current flowing in a certain pn junction at room temperature is
2×10^{-7} A when a large reverse bias voltage is applied. Calculate the current
flowing when a forward bias of 0·1 V is applied.

    Ans. 10 μA.

4   A pn junction has an observed saturation current of 1 μA at R.T. Find
the junction voltage corresponding to forward currents of 1 and 10 mA. The
diode is constructed with p-type material of 2000 S/m and n-type of 500 S/m.
Each region is 1 mm long and 1 × 0·5 mm in cross-section. Find the applied
voltages corresponding to currents of 1 and 10 mA, including resistance drops
in the n and p regions.

5   A planar pn junction in silicon has conductivities of 1000 S/m and
20 S/m and minority carrier lifetimes of 5 μs and 1 μs for the p and n regions
respectively. Calculate the ratio of hole current to electron current in the

222

depletion layer, the saturation current density and the total current density
flowing through the junction with a forward bias of 0·3 V. Assume room
temperature, $n_i = 1\cdot4 \times 10^{16}$ m^{-3}, $\mu_e = 0\cdot12$ m^2/V. s and $\mu_h = 0\cdot05$ m^2/V. s.

Ans. 28·8 : 1, 0·5 μA/m^2, 0·081 A/m^2.

6   The reverse bias saturation current for a particular pn junction is 1 μA
at 300 K. Determine its a.c. slope-resistance at 150 mV forward bias.

Ans. 78 Ω.

7   An ideal silicon pn junction diode has a reverse saturation current of
30 μA at a temperature of 125 °C. Find the dynamic resistance of the diode
for a bias voltage of 0·2 V in (a) the forward and (b) the reverse direction.
What significance has the result?

Ans. 3·5 Ω, 380 KΩ.

8   A germanium pn junction diode has a cross-sectional area of 10^{-6} m^2
and the distance from the metallurgical junction to each ohmic contact is 0·1 mm.
The bulk resistivities and minority carrier lifetimes are 4·2 x 10^{-4} ohm-m and
75 μs for the p-type and 2·08 x 10^{-2} ohm-m and 150 μs for the n-type.
Assuming $\mu_e = 0\cdot30$ m^2/V. s and $\mu_h = 0\cdot15$ m^2/V. s and that $n_i = 2\cdot5 \times 10^{-19}$ m^{-3},
find the theoretical saturation current of the diode.

Ans. 3·82 μA.

9   The zero-voltage barrier height in an alloy germanium pn junction is
0·2 V. The concentration of acceptor atoms on the p-side, N_a, is much smaller
than that of donor atoms at the n-side and $N_a = 3 \times 10^{20}$ atom/m^3. The relative
permittivity of germanium is 16. Calculate the width of the depletion layer
for applied reverse voltages of (a) 10 V, (b) 0·1 V and a forward bias of 0·1 V.
If the cross-sectional area of the diode is 1 mm^2, evaluate the junction
capacitances corresponding to the various applied voltages. What significance
have the results?

Ans. 7·6 μm, 1·3 μm, 0·77 μm, 18·6 pF, 116 pF, 184 pF.

10. Vacuum electronic devices

10.1 Introduction

Most active electronic devices utilize some form of interaction between fields and streaming charge carriers. In vacuum valves, the carriers are electrons introduced into an evacuated region or into a low-pressure gas and their subsequent motion under the influence of electronic and magnetic fields determines the peculiar electrical properties of a particular device. Thus the characteristics of various types of valve can be systematically examined by considering in turn the basic processes of electronic emission, mutual repulsion between electrons which gives rise to space charge, and the effects of the introduction of gridded electrodes into the electron stream.

10.2 Electronic emission

It has been shown that a potential barrier exists at the surface of a solid which under normal circumstances prevents electrons in the conduction band from leaving the body of the material. A common feature of all types of emission is that sufficient energy must be transferred to such electrons that they can surmount the potential barrier at the surface and be emitted; it is only the mechanism of energy transfer to the electrons which differentiates the various emission mechanisms. For example, *photoelectric emission* occurs, as was seen earlier, when conduction electrons in a solid have their energy increased by the absorption of radiation, which may be light, X-rays, ultra-violet radiation, and so on. On the other hand, *secondary emission* can occur when energy from high-velocity electrons or ions which bombard a surface is imparted to electrons in the solid. *Field emission* relies on the presence of an intense external electric field at the surface of a solid; if the field is high enough, conduction electrons moving in the field can gain sufficient energy to escape from the surface. Finally, *thermionic emission* can occur when a solid is heated to such high temperatures that the thermal energy of some of the conduction electrons is sufficient for them to be emitted. Each of these processes will now be discussed in more detail.

10.2.1. Thermionic emission of electrons. Emission of electrons from a hot solid which is heated either directly or indirectly is by far the most common practical source; cathodes relying on this mechanism are used extensively in most commercial valves.

Since it is only the conduction electrons which are available for emission, the effective band structure of a solid including one of its surfaces can for the purposes of this discussion be simplified to the box model shown in Fig. 10.1(a). At normal temperatures most electrons occupy energy levels up to

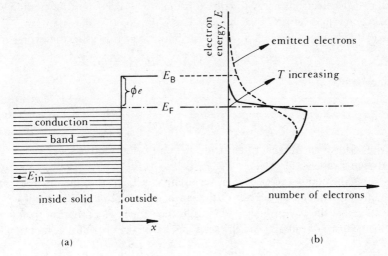

Fig. 10.1 Thermionic emission from a solid.

the Fermi level, E_F, and the small number with higher energies are represented by the tail of the solid curve in Fig. 10.1(b). To be emitted the electrons have to reach an energy level at least equal to the barrier energy, E_B, and in doing so even the most energetic electron at low temperatures must acquire energy equal to the work function, ϕ. At low temperatures the tail of the electronic energy distribution is small enough to ensure that this condition is not satisfied and no emission occurs. However, at much higher temperatures the energy tail, shown dashed in Fig. 10.1(b), is elevated until there is a small but finite number of electrons which have energies greater than E_B; it is these electrons which are emitted.

We can calculate the emission current at a particular temperature by using information about the statistical distribution of electronic energies which we have already derived. The number of electrons, dN_E, in the energy range between E and $E + dE$ is from eq. (4.19):

$$dN_E = N(E)dE = S(E)p(E)dE$$

which from eqs. (4.18) and (3.37) is

$$dN_E = \frac{8\sqrt{2}\pi m^{\frac{3}{2}}}{h^3} . E^{\frac{1}{2}} . \frac{1}{1 + \exp\left[(E - E_F)/kT\right]} dE \qquad (10.1)$$

If the surface of the emitter is assumed to be in a plane perpendicular to the x-direction, then the emitted current is dependent on the number of electrons at a given temperature with x-directed velocity, v_x, such that

$$\tfrac{1}{2}mv_x^{\ 2} > \text{barrier height, } E_B = E_F + \phi e \qquad (10.2)$$

irrespective of their y- or z-components of velocity. In order to find this number the electron energy distribution equation (10.1), must be modified to an equivalent velocity distribution. This is done in two stages. Firstly, eq. (10.1) is converted into a speed distribution function using the expression

$$E = \tfrac{1}{2}mv^2 \qquad \text{and} \qquad dE = mv\,dv$$

which gives:

$$dN_v = \frac{8\pi m^3}{h^3} \cdot \frac{v^2\,dv}{1 + \exp\left[(\tfrac{1}{2}mv^2 - E_F)/kT\right]} \qquad (10.3)$$

dN_v is clearly the number of electrons per unit volume in the speed range between v and $v + dv$.

Now, the number of electrons in a given range is equal to the distribution function multiplied by the size of the range; referring to Fig. 10.2(a), it will be clear that the size of the speed range is the volume of a spherical shell in velocity space of radius v and thickness dv; hence the distribution function is:

$$\frac{dN_v}{4\pi v^2\,dv} = \frac{2m^3}{h^3} \cdot \frac{1}{1 + \exp\left[(\tfrac{1}{2}mv^2 - E_F)/kT\right]}$$

Since the number of electrons per unit volume, $dN_{v_x v_y v_z}$, with components of velocity in the range v_x to $v_x + dv_x$, v_y to $v_y + dv_y$, and v_z to $v_z + dv_z$, is again equal to the distribution function multiplied by the size of the range which, as shown in Fig. 10.2(a), is $dv_x dv_y dv_z$, then

$$dN_{v_x v_y v_z} = \frac{2m^3}{h^3} \cdot \frac{dv_x\,dv_y\,dv_z}{1 + \exp\left[\{\tfrac{1}{2}m(v_x^2 + v_y^2 + v_z^2) - E_F\}/kT\right]} \qquad (10.4)$$

Since any electron with velocity component between v_x and $v_x + dv_x$ travels a distance v_x in the x-direction in one second, irrespective of its other velocity components, the total number of electrons with velocity v_x reaching the barrier at the emitting surface per second is equal to the volume Av_x multiplied by the number density of electrons with velocity v_x as shown in Fig. 10.2(b). Such an electron flow constitutes a current density which is (ev_x) times the number density with velocity component v_x. Now, only those electrons will be emitted which satisfy eq. (10.2), so the total emitted current density, J, is obtained by summing the contributions from all electrons with $v_x > [2(E_F + \phi e)/m]^{\frac{1}{2}}$ and with y- and z-components from $-\infty$ to $+\infty$, giving

$$J = \int_{v_x = [2(E_F + \phi e)/m]^{\frac{1}{2}}}^{\infty} \int_{v_y = -\infty}^{\infty} \int_{v_z = -\infty}^{\infty} ev_x\,dN_{v_x v_y v_z} \qquad (10.5)$$

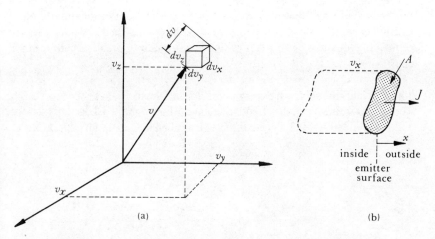

Fig. 10.2 Velocity space and a diagrammatic view of an emitter, used in thermionic emission calculation.

Substitution can now be made from eq. (10.4), which is further simplified by omitting the unity in the denominator which is negligibly small compared to the exponential term since for emission to occur the electron energy has to be much greater than E_F. Equation (10.5) then becomes:

$$J = \frac{2em^3}{h^3} \exp(E_F/kT) \int_{[2(E_F+\phi e)/m]^{\frac{1}{2}}}^{\infty} \frac{v_x \, dv_x}{\exp(mv_x^2/2kT)}$$

$$\int_{-\infty}^{\infty} \frac{dv_y}{\exp(mv_y^2/2kT)} \int_{-\infty}^{\infty} \frac{dv_z}{\exp(mv_z^2/2kT)}$$

The last two terms are standard integrals, each with value $(2\pi kT/m)^{\frac{1}{2}}$, and the first integral is solved by substituting $v_x^2 = u$, to give:

$$J = \frac{4\pi em^2 kT}{h^3} \exp(E_F/kT) \int_{2(E_F+\phi e)/m}^{\infty} \frac{du}{2\exp(mu/2kT)}$$

or

$$J = \frac{4\pi emk^2}{h^3} T^2 \exp\left(\frac{-e\phi}{kT}\right) \tag{10.6}$$

This is the *Richardson–Dushman* equation for temperature-limited electron emission from a cathode. Evaluating the constant term gives:

$$J = 1 \cdot 2 \,. \, 10^6 \,. \, T^2 \exp(-11\,600 \,\phi/T)\,\text{A/m}^2 \tag{10.7}$$

where the work function, ϕ, is in electronvolts. The relationship between J and T can be verified experimentally and while the results are in general agreement with the form of eq. (10.7) it is found that the numerical constant is

227

normally about half that predicted by theory. Apart from noting that the emitted current is a rapidly varying function of ϕ and T, a detailed discussion of the consequences of eq. (10.7) will be deferred until practical cathodes are considered later.

10.2.2. Field emission. An electron-accelerating electric field applied to a cathode can cause a reduction in the effective height of the potential barrier at its surface, as illustrated in Fig. 10.3. Before the field is applied, the restraining force on an

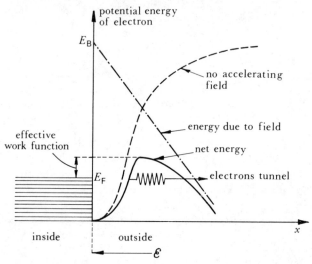

Fig. 10.3 Schottky effect and high field emission from a solid with applied electric field.

electron which has escaped a distance x from the surface is, by the method of images, $-e^2/[4\pi\epsilon_0(2x)^2]$ and its potential energy is therefore $-e^2/[16\pi\epsilon_0 x]$. When an electric field, $\mathcal{E}$, assumed uniform, is applied as shown, the electron potential energy due to the field alone is $-e\mathcal{E}x$ and when this additional term is added, the net potential energy is as shown in Fig. 10.3. The lowering of the barrier height and reduction of the effective work function of the surface, ϕ', causes emission currents which can be in excess of those predicted from eq. (10.7), which assumes no external field. The barrier height is reduced and the emission current increased with increasing field, even though the cathode temperature remains constant, an event known as the *Schottky effect*. The effect is negligibly small at low voltages and fields of the order of 10^6 V/m are necessary before significant changes in emission currents are noticed, which illustrates the large magnitude of the forces restraining electrons to the inside of a material.

The effective potential barrier at the cathode surface is still usually higher than the Fermi level for even greater applied fields and at low temperatures, by classical arguments, there is no possibility of emission for the majority of

228

electrons which have energies around E_F. However, for fields of order 10^9 V/m the barrier may become thin enough for there to be a significant statistical probability that electrons can tunnel through it, in the manner discussed in section 1.10, and thus escape from the surface, as shown in Fig. 10.3. This process is known as *field emission*. The emitted current will be a sensitive function of the width of the barrier through which electrons, mostly of energy E_F, tunnel and since the slope of the potential energy curve outside the surface is approximately $-e\mathscr{E}$, the width evaluated at the Fermi level is of order $\phi/\mathscr{E}$. From eq. (1.70) it would seem then that the emission current due to tunnelling will vary approximately as $\exp(-\phi/\mathscr{E})$, which roughly agrees with experimental findings.

10.2.3. Photoemission. As discussed briefly in chapter 1, it is possible for emission to occur from a solid which has a surface illuminated by radiation of an appropriate wavelength, λ. Referring to Fig. 10.1(a) again, since an electron at some particular energy level, E_{in}, inside the solid can only have transferred to it a maximum energy of hf from an incident photon of the radiation, and since in order to be emitted it must have energy in excess of the barrier energy E_B, then for emission to occur:

$$hf > E_F + e\phi - E_{in} \qquad (10.8)$$

The lowest frequency of incident radiation which can cause such emission, f_{min}, corresponds to a photon energy just sufficient for electrons with the highest energy possible at low temperatures, those at the Fermi level, to be emitted and

$$hf_{min} = e\phi \qquad (10.9)$$

Thus, for emission to occur at all, the incident radiation must be of wavelength less than λ_{max} given by:

$$\lambda_{max} = ch/e\phi = 1\ 240/\phi \text{ nm} \qquad (10.10)$$

For smaller-wavelength radiation the excess photon energy manifests itself as kinetic energy of the emitted electron. Equation (10.10) shows that for surfaces with a work function of a few electronvolts, the wavelengths necessary for emission are in or near to the spectrum of visible light; hence the term *photoelectric emission* which describes the effect.

10.2.4. Secondary emission. Particles incident on the surface of a material can transfer sufficient energy to an electron in the body of the material for it to be emitted. Experimentally it is found that the number of emitted or *secondary* electrons is dependent on the number of the bombarding or *primary* particles, on their velocity and angle of incidence, and, of course, on the work function and condition of the cathode surface. Since it is possible for each primary electron or ion to provide sufficient energy for the release of more than one secondary, it is usual to define a *secondary emission ratio, S*, given by

$$S = \frac{\text{number of secondary electrons}}{\text{number of primaries}}$$

S varies between 1·5 and 2 for most metals, but can be as high as 10–15 for some particular surfaces.

Whereas no simple, satisfactory theory has been developed which quantitatively explains the effect, the following qualitative description of the secondary emission mechanism accounts for some of the experimental findings. Low-energy primaries do not penetrate far into the surface and secondary electrons then have a high probability of reaching the surface without further collisions with the lattice and are emitted. Therefore, as the energy of the primaries is increased, the secondary emission ratio increases initially, but eventually S reaches a broad maximum, usually between 1 and 2, thereafter dropping slowly. This reduction in S corresponds to high-energy primaries which have a high penetration and transfer energy to electrons lying well within the body of the material: the probability of such electrons reaching the surface without collision with the lattice is lowered and a larger proportion of the primary energy is converted into increasing the level of thermal activity of the cathode.

10.3 Practical cathodes

Any of the emission mechanisms discussed in the previous section could in principle form the basis of a practical electron emitter, but the relative merits of the various cathodes would be widely diverse. For example, thermionic cathodes because of copious emission under easily produced operating conditions are almost exclusively used in vacuum valves, whereas field-effect emitters, because of the extremely high fields involved, are only used for a few specialized applications such as in electron microscopes. Indeed, some emission processes, for example secondary emission, are not only of limited use for cathodes but often have to be actively discouraged since they can cause side-effects which can degrade the performance of a particular device.

It will be noticed that the exponential term in the thermionic emission equation, (10.7), dominates and that the emission current increases rapidly as either the work function of the cathode material is reduced or its temperature increases. It would seem, then, that materials with the lowest work function might produce the best thermionic cathodes. However, since the maximum current obtainable from a cathode is also strongly dependent on its working temperature, the suitability of a particular cathode material is a function of its ability to withstand high temperatures and hence its melting point. For example, caesium has a relatively low work function of 1·8 eV but melts at 28·5 °C; this material is therefore not suitable for thermionic

230

cathodes but is preferred for photoemission or secondary-emission cathodes which operate at lower temperatures. Conversely, pure metals such as tungsten and tantalum which have high work functions (4·5 and 4·1 eV) but much higher melting-points (3380 and 3000 °C) are useful, if inefficient, emitters because of their inherent high-temperature operating capability and are used for rugged cathodes in some high-power transmitting valves.

A reduction in the effective work function of a cathode, while retaining a high-temperature operating performance, is possible when low-work-function atomic films are supported on a high-melting-point base material; for example, if a small percentage of thorium oxide is included in tungsten then, after activation, such a cathode has the mechanical properties of the tungsten but the superior emission properties of the atomic layer of thorium ($\phi = 2 \cdot 63$; m.p. 1845 °C).

One of the most efficient and widely used thermionic emitters is the oxide-coated cathode which consists of a base metal, usually oxygen-free nickel, coated with a mixture of barium, strontium, and calcium carbonates, plus a binder. The cathode is either directly heated by passing current through the nickel, which is often in the form of a hairpin, or is an indirectly heated sleeve surrounding a tungsten wire heater, as shown in Fig. 10.4(a). After

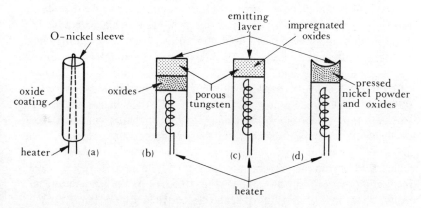

Fig. 10.4 Some thermionic emitters: (a) oxide coated, (b) Lemmon's cathode, (c) impregnated, and (d) pressed nickel cathode.

processing, when the rare-earth carbonates are reduced, the resulting effective work function of around 1 eV leads to copious emission at relatively low temperatures; for example, current densities of 10^4 A/m^2 are possible at operating temperatures of 800 °C. Such cathodes also have the advantage of long life, often in excess of 10 000 hours, but they are easily contaminated by residual gases and have a poor resistance to ion bombardment.

Various types of dispenser cathode have been devised which give saturated emission-current densities at least as high as conventional oxide-coated cathodes but which do not suffer irreversibly from contamination or ion bombardment. Several successful forms are illustrated in Fig. 10.4(a)–(d). These all consist basically of a porous metal supporting base impregnated with or backed by a reservoir of alkaline-earth carbonates. On activation an active layer is formed on the face of the cathode which is similar to that on the simpler oxide cathode, but if it is damaged in any way the layer can be renewed by reactivating more material from the large reserve behind the emitting surface. Although dispenser cathodes have many advantages, in particular extremely high emission currents and very prolonged lives, they have only been found to be economically viable in specialized valves, for example in submarine repeaters and some high-frequency valves.

10.4 The vacuum diode

The vacuum diode which consists of a thermionic cathode plus an additional electrode or anode is the simplest of all valves. If the anode is made positive with respect to the cathode, electrons emitted from the cathode are attracted to it and an electron current flows through the device and external circuit. The process is non-reversible and a negative anode voltage produces no current flow, so the diode behaves as a rectifier.

For low cathode temperatures, all electrons emitted are swept to the positive anode and a small saturation current flows which is determined by the current-emitting properties of the cathode at its particular operating temperature, as described by eq. (10.7), and which is largely insensitive to anode voltage changes. The diode is said to be *temperature-limited*.

At higher cathode temperatures the current-limiting process is very different. The cathode is now capable of larger electron emission densities and the emitted electrons produce a negative space charge which is no longer negligible but can be sufficiently great so as to depress the potential locally and lower the effective field at the cathode. The potential is lowered most where the electrons are moving most slowly and the negative space charge is maximum, that is, near the cathode (Fig. 10.5(b)). As the temperature is progressively increased still further the electric field at the cathode first reaches zero (Fig. 10.5(c)), after which the space charge produces a retarding field at the cathode and a potential minimum at a short distance from the cathode (Fig. 10.5(d)). Only those electrons which are emitted with sufficient energy to allow them to overcome the potential minimum can now reach the anode. A further increase in cathode temperature increases the space-charge density and further depresses the potential until it is just sufficient to limit the current to its previous value. Thus, the electron current flowing is no longer a function of the emission capability of the cathode but becomes dependent on the anode voltage and the valve geometry only; the diode is said to be operating in a *space-charge-limited* condition.

In order to study the problem more quantitatively we shall derive the *I–V* characteristics for the mathematically convenient one-dimensional diode

232

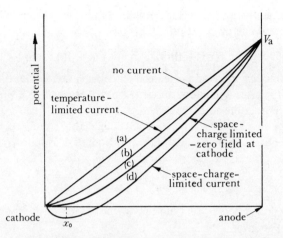

Fig. 10.5 Potential variations in a thermionic diode for different cathode temperatures.

illustrated in Fig. 10.6. The planar electrodes are assumed semi-infinite in extent to avoid edge-effects, and only variations in the x-direction need be considered. If the space-charge density at any point distance x from the cathode is $\rho(x)$ and the potential there is $V(x)$ then the two variables are related by Poisson's equation, viz:

$$\frac{d^2V}{dx^2} = \frac{-\rho}{\epsilon_0} \tag{10.11}$$

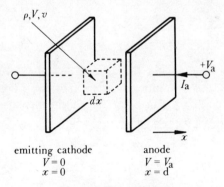

Fig. 10.6 Planar diode.

Further, the electron flow constitutes an x-directed current of density J which is independent of x and which can be expressed in terms of the electron velocity, $v(x)$ and the space-charge density, thus:

$$J = \rho v \tag{10.12}$$

233

Finally, we require a relationship between v and V which is provided by the conservation of energy equation:

$$\tfrac{1}{2}mv^2 = eV + \text{(initial kinetic energy at cathode)} \qquad (10.13)$$

Since the kinetic energy of an electron on being emitted from the cathode is of order kT, corresponding to about 0·1 eV, it is usual to neglect the bracketed term in the equation.

The three simultaneous equations, (10.11), (10.12), and (10.13), can be reduced to obtain a single equation for the potential, as follows:

$$\frac{d^2V}{dx^2} = \frac{-\rho}{\epsilon} = \frac{-J}{\epsilon_0 v} = \frac{-J}{\epsilon_0}\sqrt{\frac{m}{2eV}} \qquad (10.14)$$

This can be integrated by first multiplying both sides of the equation by $[2(dV/dx)]$ to give:

$$\left(\frac{dV}{dx}\right)^2 = \frac{-4J}{\epsilon_0}\sqrt{\frac{m}{2e}}\,V^{\frac{1}{2}} + C_1 \qquad (10.15)$$

If for the moment we restrict our attention to the simpler case of a potential variation shown in Fig. 10.5(c), when the field is zero at the cathode, then the boundary conditions are:

$$\text{at } x = 0,\ V = 0,\ \mathscr{E} = 0 \text{ and } \frac{dV}{dx} = 0$$

Thus, in this case, the integration constant in eq. (10.15), C_1, is zero. Taking the square root of the equation, integrating again, and employing the boundary conditions then yields:

$$J = \frac{-4\epsilon_0}{9}\sqrt{\frac{2e}{m}} \cdot \frac{V^{\frac{3}{2}}}{x^2} \qquad (10.16)$$

The negative sign arises because the assumed flow of electrons in the positive x-direction results in a conventional current flow in the opposite direction. Since, at the anode, $V = V_a$ and $x = d$, then, if the total anode current is I_a and the area of the electrode is A:

$$I_a = -JA = KV_a^{\frac{3}{2}} \qquad (10.17)$$

where

$$K = \frac{4\epsilon_0 A}{9d^2}\sqrt{\frac{2e}{m}} \qquad (10.18)$$

which is called the *perveance* of the diode. Equation (10.17) is known as the *Child–Langmuir law* for space-charge-limited flow. It is alternatively known as the *three-halves power law* since, as shown in eq. (10.17), for fixed electrode geometry the anode current is proportional to $V_a^{\frac{3}{2}}$.

234

More generally, the field is not zero at the cathode as has been assumed, but there is a potential minimum and zero field at some point slightly removed from the cathode, at x_0 in Fig. 10.5(d). The potential variation in this situation is still given by eq. (10.15) and the current density by eq. (10.16), provided a new origin is taken at $x = x_0$, which is consequently called the *virtual cathode*.

Finally, the planar geometry assumed for mathematical convenience is not often encountered in practice, and a cylindrical geometry is much more common. However, it is found that the three-halves power law as expressed by eq. (10.17) is still applicable, provided the perveance K, given by eq. (10.18), for the planar diode is modified to suit the different electrode configuration.

It follows from the previous discussions that the shape of the $V_a - I_a$ characteristics of a vacuum diode are dependent on both the emission properties of its cathode and the electronic space charge developed in the valve. A typical set of characteristics is shown in Fig. 10.7. For low anode

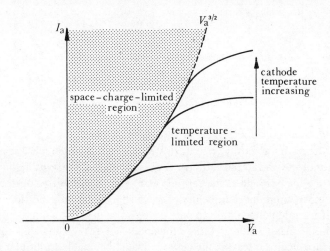

Fig. 10.7 *V-I* characteristics of a vacuum diode.

voltages the diode is always space-charge-limited and the anode current is determined by the anode voltage alone, via the three-halves power law. As the anode voltage is increased, the anode current becomes limited to the saturation current that the cathode is capable of supplying at its particular operating temperature, which is determined by the Dushman equation; the diode becomes temperature-limited and the anode current tends to remain constant and largely independent of further increases in V_a. The slight increase in current with voltage in the temperature-limited regime is due to Schottky emission from the cathode. Of course, the onset of the temperature-limited condition occurs at higher anode voltage and current values as the operating temperature of the cathode is increased, as shown in the figure. It should be emphasized that the vacuum diode is usually operated space-charge-limited, since the anode current is then largely insensitive to changes in cathode emission brought about by variations in heater current or ageing.

10.5 The vacuum triode and other multielectrode valves

The construction of the vacuum triode is similar to that of the diode but an additional wire grid electrode is introduced between cathode and anode. A triode of cylindrical geometry is shown in cross-section in Fig. 10.8(a). In

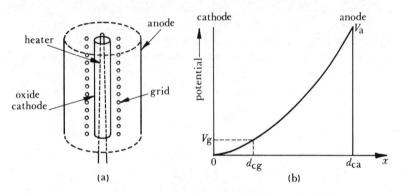

Fig. 10.8 (a) Cylindrical vacuum triode, (b) potential variation in a planar triode.

operation, the grid is usually held at a negative potential, V_g, and does not collect appreciable electron current. However, because of the relatively close proximity of the grid to the cathode, the grid voltage is most influential in determining the net field at the cathode and in this way largely controls the current drawn from the cathode under space-charge-limited conditions. Of course, if the grid voltage were to create a uniform negative equipotential surface in the plane of the grid, then the anode current would be completely cut off since electrons leaving the cathode would be unable to surmount the potential barrier. However, because of the permeable nature of the grid some of the field caused by the anode voltage is able to penetrate it and some electrons can reach the anode via paths through the grid apertures where the overall field is not retarding. Thus although the anode voltage has some influence on the cathode current flowing, it will be appreciated that the grid voltage plays a more dominant role. The effective voltage in the triode is therefore $(V_g + V_a/\mu)$ where μ, *the amplification factor,* is a dimensionless constant of order 10–100 which is a function of valve geometry and which can be estimated from electrostatic considerations. This expression demonstrates the relative effectiveness of the grid voltage in controlling the anode current.

Now, since the triode is usually operated space-charge-limited it is to be anticipated that the anode current again obeys a three-halves power law with

236

effective voltage. The voltage–current relationship would then be of the form

$$J_a = K_t(V_g + V_a/\mu)^{\frac{3}{2}} \qquad (10.19)$$

where K_t is again a constant known as the perveance. The validity of this expression has been demonstrated experimentally but no rigorous theoretical derivation has yet been found possible, even for the simplest of geometries.

In order to estimate perveance K_t in eq. (10.19) let us consider a *planar* triode geometry with electrode spacings d_{cg} and d_{ca}. If the cathode-anode diode is considered first, with the grid assumed absent, then the potential distribution again for the special case of zero field at the cathode is as shown in Fig. 10.8(b) and the anode voltage as given by eq. (10.17) is

$$V_a = \frac{I_a^{\frac{2}{3}} d_{ca}^{\frac{4}{3}}}{\left(\dfrac{4\epsilon_0 A}{9}\sqrt{\dfrac{2e}{m}}\right)^{\frac{2}{3}}} \qquad (10.20)$$

If the grid is now inserted at $x = d_{cg}$ at such a potential as not to disturb the potential distribution, then V_g must be so chosen that

$$V_g = \frac{I_a^{\frac{2}{3}} d_{cg}^{\frac{4}{3}}}{\left(\dfrac{4\epsilon_0 A}{9}\sqrt{\dfrac{2e}{m}}\right)^{\frac{2}{3}}} \qquad (10.21)$$

Substitution of expressions (10.20) and (10.21) into eq. (10.19) gives the required expression for K_t and the current is then:

$$I_a = \frac{\dfrac{4\epsilon_0 A}{9}\sqrt{\dfrac{2e}{m}}\left(V_g + \dfrac{V_a}{\mu}\right)^{\frac{3}{2}}}{d_{cg}^2\left[1 + \dfrac{1}{\mu}\left(\dfrac{d_{ca}}{d_{cg}}\right)^{\frac{4}{3}}\right]^{\frac{3}{2}}} \qquad (10.22)$$

Briefly, the amplifying properties of a triode rely on the superposition of the small alternating signal voltage which is to be amplified on the negative d.c. grid-bias voltage; this causes a sympathetic modulation of the anode current which produces an amplified voltage swing across a load resistor placed in series with the anode circuit. Because the grid always remains negative and draws little current, it presents an extremely high impedance, typically several megohms, to the signal source and so draws almost negligible current from it. The triode thus exhibits power gain.

237

The *mutual conductance,* g_m, of a triode describes the change in anode current, ∂I_a, which results in a change in grid voltage, ∂V_g, for a constant anode voltage and is by definition:

$$g_m = \frac{\partial I_a}{\partial V_g} = \frac{dI_a}{dV_g}\bigg|_{V_a \text{ const.}} \qquad (10.23)$$

By performing this differentiation on eq. (10.22) it can be seen that for the planar triode that:

$$g_m \propto I_a^{\frac{1}{3}}$$

Thus, the mutual conductance is only constant in the small-signal limit; in all other cases the device is non-linear and g_m is a function of I_a, V_g, and V_a. The performance of the triode is then most conveniently described in terms of a set of experimentally obtained characteristic curves.

The high-frequency performance of a triode is restricted by interelectrode capacitance; in particular, owing to feedback effects, the grid–anode capacitance is most troublesome. To overcome this difficulty, the *tetrode* valve was devised which has an additional electrode consisting of a coarse wire grid, called a *screen grid,* which is interposed between grid and anode. This grid effectively screens the anode from the control grid and reduces feedback capacitance effects. As well as extending the high-frequency operating range in this way, the introduction of a screen grid also increases the amplification factor, since the controlling effect of the anode voltage on the current relative to the control-grid voltage is reduced. However, if the screen-grid voltage is ever allowed to exceed the anode voltage, secondary electrons liberated at the anode are attracted back to the screen causing the net anode current to fall; this effect limits the permissible anode voltage swings in a tetrode amplifying stage. The addition of another grid between screen grid and anode which is held at cathode potential and called a *suppressor grid* eliminates unwanted secondary emission effects. The resulting valve, the *pentode,* is the most extensively used amplifying valve.

Since multielectrode valves are essentially non-linear devices and because a space-charge theory with realistic electrode geometries is as yet incomplete, reliance is normally placed on experimental characteristic curves to describe their behaviour. Reference should be made to the more specialized literature for more information on this topic.

Problems

1   An oxide-coated cathode gives a saturated emission current of 100 mA at 1000 K. If $\phi = 1 \cdot 1$ eV, what temperature is required for an emission current of 110 mA?

Ans. 1007 K.

2   A thermionic cathode provides saturation emission currents of 95 mA
at 1050 K and 275 mA at 1150 K. What is the work function of the cathode?

   Ans. 0·92 eV.

3   The tungsten cathode of a diode is 20 mm long and 0·05 mm diameter.
The saturation current I_0 is measured at different cathode temperatures, T.
The graph of $\log{(I_0/T^2)}$ against T^{-1} is a straight line of slope $1·16 \times 10^4$
and the intercept at $T^{-1} = 0$ is $2·26 \times 10^{-3}$. Evaluate the constants in the
Richardson–Dushman equation:

$$I_0 = AT^2 \exp{(-e\phi/kT)}$$

and compare with equation (10.7).

   Ans. $7·2 \times 10^5$ A/m^2, 4·52 eV.

4   A tungsten wire cathode 10 mm long is to provide an emission current
of 100 mA at 2650 K. Calculate the wire diameter required, assuming the
constants in the Richardson-Dushman equation are 6×10^5 A/m^2 and $\phi = 4·5$
eV.

   Ans. 0·27 mm.

5   If the emission from a certain cathode is 10 000 times as great at
2000 K as at 1500 K what is the work function of its surface.

   Ans. 4·45 eV.

6   The work function of the cathode of a photocell is 3·5 eV. What is the
maximum velocity of the emitted electrons when the cell is irradiated with
light of wavelength 600 nm?

   Ans. $8·5 \times 10^6$ m/s.

7   The cathode of a photocell is illuminated by light of wavelength 600 nm.
An anode potential of −1 V is found to be just sufficient to prevent electrons
from reaching the anode. What is the work function of the cathode? If the
anode is made positive, what is the maximum wavelength of radiation which
will produce a current in the photocell?

   Ans. 1·07 eV, 1 160 nm.

8   A tungsten-filament cathode 100 mm long and 2 mm diameter is con-
centric with a cylindrical molybdenum anode. An anode current of 150 mA
flows when the anode voltage is 100 V and the filament temperature is 2400 K.
What are the anode currents corresponding to anode voltages of 200 and 400
V? Neglect end-effects and assume $\phi = 4·54$ eV.

   Ans. 0·425 A, 0·728 A.

9   A certain vacuum diode requires an anode voltage of 30 V for a current of 120 mA to flow under space-charge limited conditions. What voltage produces a current of 95 mA? What is the maximum current possible if the anode dissipation is not to exceed 3·2 W? Are these results dependent on the geometry of the diode?

   Ans. 25·4 V, 113 mA.

10   A diode with plane parallel electrodes is operated under space-charge limited conditions. The anode current is 10 mA when the anode voltage is 100 V. What anode voltage is required to double this current? What current flows if the anode voltage is doubled (i.e. 200 V)? If another diode is constructed with half the cathode–anode spacing and twice the electrode area, what current will be obtained if 100 V is applied to its anode?

   Ans. 159 V, 28·3 mA, 80 mA.

11   Assuming that the electrons in a planar space-charge limited diode are emitted with zero velocity, show that the transit time from cathode to anode, τ, is given by

$$\tau = \frac{3d}{(2e/m)^{\frac{1}{2}} V_a^{\frac{1}{2}}}$$

where d is the electrode spacing and V_a is the anode voltage. What is the significance of the result?

12   Show that the transit time of an electron in a space-charge limited planar diode is one and a half times the transit time in a diode of the same geometry with the same anode voltage applied but in which space-charge is negligible.

240

11. The bipolar junction transistor

11.1 Introduction

The physical processes which determine the electrical behaviour of bipolar junction transistors will be discussed in this chapter. It will become evident that the operation of transistors in this class depends on the interaction of both majority and minority carriers, and because two carrier types are essential such devices are classified as *bipolar*. This term serves to differentiate the devices discussed here from another main class, unipolar transistors, in which the current is transported by majority carriers only and which will be discussed later.

11.2 Phenomenological description of current transport in the abrupt-junction bipolar transistor

The bipolar junction transistor consists essentially of a single-crystal semiconductor, most often of silicon or germanium, which contains a narrow central region of opposite conductivity type to that of the rest of the material. For example, an npn transistor contains a narrow p-type layer sandwiched between two n-type layers with ohmic contacts made to each region, as shown diagrammatically in Fig. 11.1(a). Now, the physical construction of a modern

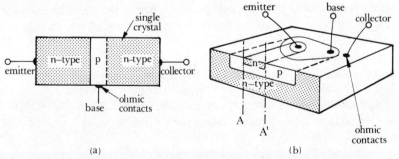

Fig. 11.1 (a) Model of an npn transistor, (b) a planar transistor structure.

241

transistor, which will be discussed in more detail later, may well be very different in appearance from the simple model shown; for example, a planar version of a discrete transistor structure may be as shown in Fig. 11.1(b). However, it will be seen that sections at A, A' encompass an npn sandwich not unlike the model and for the moment at least the simple model will be sufficient to help understand the basic transistor action.

The transistor thus consists of two-back-to back pn junctions closely coupled electrically by a narrow region of material common to both. In normal operation, one of the junctions is forward-biased and the other reverse-biased, as shown in Fig. 11.2. Briefly, what happens is that minority

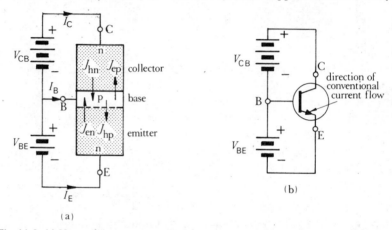

Fig. 11.2 (a) Normal biasing arrangement for an npn transistor, (b) circuit element representation.

carriers are injected from the *emitter* into the *base* region as a consequence of the forward bias appearing across the emitter–base junction and, because the base is deliberately made very thin, nearly all the injected carriers reach the reverse-biased base collector junction, eventually determining the *collector* current. Although these physical processes have resulted in convenient labels for the various regions not too much significance should be attached to the names, since in some applications a particular part of the transistor may not behave as its name suggests; for instance, the collector may be emitting rather than collecting electrons.

Of course, transistor action will also be possible if the conductivity type of emitter, base, and collector regions is reversed so as to produce a pnp device. This will behave in a similar way to the npn transistor, provided the polarities of the bias voltages are reversed, so for simplicity we shall initially restrict our attention to the npn device, assuming that parallel arguments can easily be developed for the complimentary device.

In most modern transistors, transport of carriers across the base is by diffusion and drift in the presence of density gradients of carriers and of an

242

electric field. It will be convenient to consider these two processes independently so that initially the base region will be considered field free, thus ensuring that transport of minority carriers across it is exclusively by diffusion. It will also be simpler at first to assume that the junctions are abrupt by virtue of a doping profile which changes rapidly with distance, as discussed in chapter 9. The alloyed-junction transistor, the construction of which will be discussed later, satisfies both these initial assumptions.

The band structure of an unbiased, symetrically doped npn structure in equilibrium will be as shown in Fig. 11.3(a). The relative widths of base and

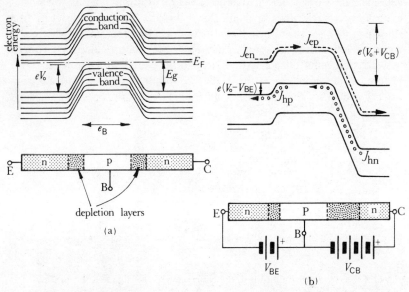

Fig. 11.3 Band structure of an npn transistor, (a) with no bias applied and (b) with external bias voltages.

depletion regions are much exaggerated for clarity. As a result of the necessary continuity in the Fermi level through the transistor in equilibrium, contact potentials and potential barriers are established at the emitter–base and base–collector junctions which prevent diffusion of majority carriers across the junctions, as described earlier. When the correct d.c. bias voltages are applied the band structure is modified to that shown in Fig. 11.3(b). The potential barrier between emitter and base is reduced by virtue of the forward bias to $e(V_0 - V_{BE})$ and an electron current is injected from emitter into base region, J_{en}, and a hole current in the reverse direction, J_{hp}. We shall see later that efficient transistor operation is achieved if most of the current across this junction is carried by carriers originating in the emitter; i.e., $J_{en} \gg J_{hp}$. This is achieved by doping the emitter to a higher degree than the base. The reverse bias at the collector–base junction causes an increase in barrier height to $e(V_0 + V_{CB})$; as a consequence, there is no majority carrier diffusion and the only current flow across the junction is due to the motion of minority carriers. Thus a very small saturation current, I_{co}, called the collector leakage current, flows across the collector–base junction which has contributions J_{ep} and J_{hn} from minority carriers in the base and collector regions.

Turning our attention now to the base region let us first assume that its width l_B is longer than the diffusion length for minority carriers L_e and L_h. The density of minority electrons in the p-type base will be increased above the equilibrium value near the emitter–base junction because of the presence there of electrons injected from the base. This excess of electrons decays exponentially away from the junction because of recombination with majority holes, reaching the equilibrium value at a distance of order L_e from the junction. Near the reverse-biased base–collector junction the electron density is lower than the equilibrium value since minority electrons from the base are swept into the collector, but again the equilibrium density is restored at distances greater than about L_e from the junction. The electron density profile for the thick base transistor is then as shown in Fig. 11.4(a).

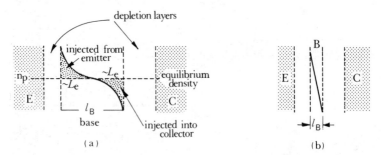

Fig. 11.4 Electron density profile in the base region for (a) a wide base and (b) a narrow base.

This situation is artificial in that an essential property of the base region for efficient transistor operation is that it is very narrow and made of high-life-time material, such that its length is much smaller than the diffusion length for minority electrons, or $l_B \ll L_e$. The minority carrier concentration in the base region is then as shown in Fig. 11.4(b). Under these circumstances there is little recombination in the base region and nearly all the electrons injected from the emitter diffuse across the base because of the steep electron density gradient existing in it and are eventually swept across the base–collector junction down the potential hill and into the collector. If, as is usually the case, the emitter is more heavily doped than the base, so that the majority of the current across the emitter–base junction is transported by electrons, then the collector current, I_C, is only slightly less than the emitter current, I_E.

It will be noticed that the electron current flowing into the collector is largely independent of V_{CB}, provided this is large enough to prevent majority carrier diffusion across the junction; as a consequence, the collector circuit

244

has a high impedance. This is in contrast to the emitter circuit which has a very low impedance because small voltage changes at the emitter–base junction cause large changes in the current flowing across it. Since the collector current is nearly equal to the emitter current, as explained, the large difference in impedance level between collector and emitter circuits can result in potentially high power amplification. Incidentally, this description of the action of the device in terms of the transfer of current from a low- to a high-impedance circuit accounts for its original name, transfer-resistor, which was subsequently contracted to transistor.

If we now consider the base current, I_B, it can be seen from Fig. 11.5 that

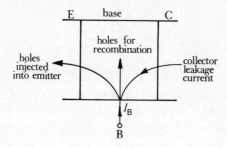

Fig. 11.5 Components of the base current in a transistor.

it is comprised of three components, (a) the hole current flowing across the base emitter junction, J_{hp}, which is made as small as possible by high emitter doping (b) the collector leakage current I_{co}, and (c) a hole current flowing into the base to replace holes which are lost by recombination with electrons flowing across it; this current can be made very small by reducing recombination to a minimum by ensuring that the base is thin and that the lifetime of minority electrons in it is high. Thus the base current is normally much smaller than either collector or emitter currents.

11.3 Gain parameters of the bipolar transistor

Let us assume initially that the external circuit of the transistor is as shown in Fig. 11.2; this arrangement is the *common-base* connection, since the base contact is common to both collector and emitter circuits. If the emitter current is changed by increment ΔI_E, there will be a corresponding incremental change in collector current, ΔI_C, and the relative change is described in terms of a gain parameter which is defined by:

$$\frac{\text{change in collector current}}{\text{change in emitter current}} = \frac{-\Delta I_C}{\Delta I_E}\bigg|_{V_{CB} \text{ const.}} = \alpha_B \qquad (11.1)$$

where α_B is the *common-base current gain*. Since by previous arguments a change in emitter currents results in a change in collector current which is only marginally smaller, $\Delta I_C \simeq \Delta I_E$ and α_B is only slightly less than unity, typical values being in the range 0·900–0·999.

Although it has been convenient to discuss the common-base operation of a transistor first, it is far more usual for the device to be operated in the *common-emitter* circuit configuration shown in Fig. 11.6, in which the

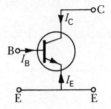

Fig. 11.6 Common-emitter configuration.

emitter connection is common to input and output circuits. Arguing as before, a change in base current, ΔI_B, produces a corresponding change in collector current, ΔI_C, and a *common-emitter current gain*, α_E, is then defined by

$$\alpha_E = \frac{\Delta I_C}{\Delta I_B}\Bigg|_{V_{CE}\text{const.}} \tag{11.2}$$

Since by Kirchhoff's law:

$$I_B + I_C + I_E = 0$$

then

$$\Delta I_B = -(\Delta I_C + \Delta I_E)$$

using eq. (11.1) to eliminate ΔI_E gives:

$$\Delta I_B = \Delta I_C \left(1 - \frac{1}{\alpha_B}\right)$$

and finally

$$\frac{\Delta I_C}{\Delta I_B} = \alpha_E = \frac{\alpha_B}{1 - \alpha_B} \tag{11.3}$$

Thus, we arrive at a relationship between the common-base and common-emitter current gains. Since α_B is usually very nearly unity, it is evident from eq. (11.3) that α_E is much greater than unity, typically being in the range 10–1000.

It is possible to estimate the value of the gain parameter α_B, and hence α_E, through eq. (11.3), in terms of the physical processes occurring in the

246

transistor, its structure, and its composition. It is evident that α_B will be dependent on (a) the number of electrons injected from the emitter into the base and (b) the proportion of these which diffuses across the base without recombination, to the collector. It is therefore convenient to subdivide the gain parameter, α_B, into two components, thus:

$$\alpha_B = \eta_E \beta \tag{11.4}$$

where η_E, the *injection efficiency*, is the ratio of the electron current injected into the base from the emitter to the total emitter–base junction current and β, the *base transport factor*, is the ratio of the electron current at the collector junction to that at the emitter junction. Current transport in an npn transistor in terms of these components of α_B is shown schematically in Fig. 11.7. Since the current flowing into the base to replace holes lost by

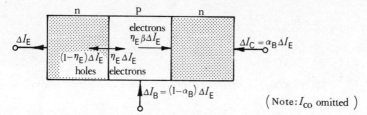

Fig. 11.7 Current transport in an npn transistor.

recombination is $\eta_E \Delta I_E(1 - \beta)$, and the base current flowing to provide the hole current across the emitter junction is $\Delta I_E(1 - \eta_E)$, then, ignoring the collector leakage current, the total base current is

$$\Delta I_B = \eta_E \Delta I_E(1 - \beta) + \Delta I_E(1 - \eta_E) = \Delta I_E(1 - \alpha_B)$$

which is the same as that required to satisfy Kirchhoff's law.

We now consider the components of α_B in more quantitative detail.

11.3.1. Emitter injection efficiency, η_E.

From the definition given above and by referring to Fig. 11.2(a) it follows that the emitter injection efficiency can be written:

$$\eta_E = \frac{J_{en}}{J_{en} + J_{hp}} \tag{11.5}$$

It is tempting to use the arguments outlined in section 9.6 and assume that the ratio of electron to hole currents at the junction is approximately equal to the ratio of emitter to base conductivities but this would apply only if the base and emitter widths were substantially longer than the minority carrier diffusion lengths, which we know is not usually the case in a transistor. A rigorous derivation of η_E would follow the analysis for the pn junction with finite

247

dimensions, which is outlined in section 9.7, but the following approximate approach will be sufficient for our purposes.

Consider first the density variation of minority carriers to the base as illustrated in Fig. 11.8. Electrons injected from the emitter raise the local

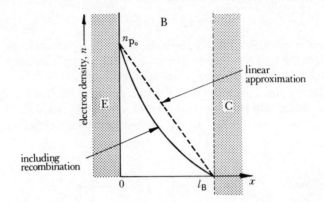

Fig. 11.8 Minority carrier density in the base of an npn transistor.

electron density just inside the base from n_p, the equilibrium value, to n_{po}, given by eq. (9.11) as:

$$n_{po} = n_p \exp{(eV_{BE}/kT)} \qquad (11.6)$$

At the collector end of the base region the electron density is depressed below the equilibrium value by virtue of the reverse bias there, to a value $n_p \exp{(-eV_{BC}/kT)}$ which can be assumed zero since $V_{BC} \gg kT$ usually. Since the length of the base, $l_B \ll L_e$, the diffusion length for minority carriers, there will be little recombination in the base and the minority carrier density falls off almost linearly with distance. Assuming such a constant density gradient, the electron diffusion current is:

$$J_{en} = eD_e n_{po}/l_B \qquad (11.7)$$

On comparing this equation with (9.20) for the electron current flow in a wider n-type region of a pn junction it will be noticed that the difference between the two expressions is that l_B in eq. (11.7) replaces L_e in the earlier equation. It follows that eq. (9.22) is applicable to the thin-base, thin-emitter junction provided that L_e and L_h are replaced by l_B and l_E, respectively. Using this modified equation and applying similar arguments to those used in section 9.6 gives:

$$\frac{J_{en}}{J_{hp}} \simeq \frac{D_e n_p}{l_B} \div \frac{D_h P_n}{l_E} \simeq \frac{\sigma_E}{\sigma_B} \cdot \frac{l_E}{l_B} \qquad (11.8)$$

248

Substituting this expression in eq. (11.5) gives the emitter injection efficiency:

$$\eta_E \simeq \left(1 + \frac{\sigma_B}{\sigma_E} \cdot \frac{l_B}{l_E}\right)^{-1} \simeq 1 - \frac{\sigma_B}{\sigma_E} \frac{l_B}{l_E} \tag{11.9}$$

Thus, the emitter efficiency is largely controlled by the relative doping of base-emitter regions but it is also influenced by the ratio of the lengths of such regions. For example, if the conductivity of the emitter is made, say, one hundred times that of the base then provided the base length is less than the emitter length, which is usually the case, η_E is in excess of 99% and such values can be achieved in practice.

11.3.2. Base transport factor, β. The base transport factor gives the efficiency with which minority carriers are transported across the base region and for the particular case of an npn transistor

$$\beta = \frac{J_e|_{\text{collector junction}}}{J_e|_{\text{emitter junction}}} \tag{11.10}$$

Since in this expression the numerator is only slightly less than the denominator because of the usually slight recombination which takes place in the base, a more accurate method for determining J_e is required than that described in the previous section; the linear approximation to the electron density profile in the base region is no longer good enough to calculate the electron current, and the lower curve of Fig. 11.8 is now applicable. The shape of this curve can be found by applying the continuity equation for excess electrons in the base region, δn, which gives:

$$\frac{d^2}{dx^2}(\delta n) = \frac{\delta n}{L_e^2}$$

which, we have seen, has the general solution

$$\delta n = C_1 \exp(-x/L_e) + C_2 \exp(+x/L_e) \tag{11.11}$$

The constants C_1 and C_2 can be determined from the boundary conditions, which are:

at $\qquad x = 0 \qquad \delta n = n_{po} - n_p$

and at $\qquad x = l_B \qquad \delta n = -n_p \simeq 0$ since $n_p \ll n_{po}$

Applying these boundary conditions to eq. (11.11) gives

$$\delta n = \frac{n_{po} - n_p}{1 - \exp(2l_B/L_e)} [\exp(x/L_e) - \exp(2l_B/L_e)\exp(-x/L_e)] \tag{11.12}$$

249

Now, since the electron diffusion current is proportional to the gradient of the electron density given by eq. (11.12), performing the differentiation and substituting in eq. (11.10) gives:

$$\beta = \frac{J_e|_{x=l_B}}{J_e|_{x=0}} = \frac{\dfrac{d}{dx}(\delta n)|_{x=l_B}}{\dfrac{d}{dx}(\delta n)|_{x=0}} = \frac{2\exp(l_B/L_e)}{1 + \exp(2l_B/L_e)}$$

Since $l_B \ll L_e$ usually, this expression simplifies to:

$$\beta = \left[1 + \tfrac{1}{2}\left(\frac{l_B}{L_e}\right)^2\right]^{-1} \simeq 1 - \tfrac{1}{2}\left(\frac{l_B}{L_e}\right)^2 \tag{11.13}$$

Thus, for high base transport factors giving current gains as near to unity as possible the lifetime of minority electrons in the base region must be high so as to make L_e large. An advantage of Si or Ge in this respect is that relatively high lifetimes in the range 1–100 μs are realizable; for base widths of 1–5 μm, which are readily fabricated using modern technology, transport factors in the range 0·95 to in excess of 0·99 can result.

11.4 Non-ideal transistor structures

Although the model used so far is satisfactory for explaining basic transistor mechanisms, it needs considerable modification before it is applicable to physically realizable transistors. Some of the additional effects which occur in real transistors and the manner in which these limit their electrical performance will now be discussed.

11.4.1. Avalanche breakdown and multiplication. An upper limit is set on the collector voltage V_{CB} by avalanche breakdown in the reverse-biased collector–base junction, as discussed previously in section 9.11. Fields of order 10^6 V/m are required in the depletion layer for breakdown to occur, which usually limits V_{CB} to a maximum of several tens of volts.

For collector voltages lower than that necessary for the onset of avalanche breakdown, V_B, there is a voltage range in which minority electrons in the base–collector depletion layer are accelerated sufficiently to cause electron-hole pair production by ionizing collisions with the lattice, but the holes produced by the process are not sufficiently energetic when accelerated in the field to produce the secondary ionization which is essential to maintain a self-sustained breakdown. In this voltage range, although no complete breakdown occurs, there is some electron multiplication and the number of electrons collected is greater than the number arriving at the base–collector layer edge. Under these conditions the current gain, α_B, is increased by a factor, η_c,

250

called the *collector efficiency*, which has been found to be given empirically by:

$$\eta_c = (1 - V_{CB}/V_B)^{-n} \tag{11.14}$$

where n is usually in the range 2-4. It is thus possible for the effective current gain which includes this additional factor due to avalanche multiplication to exceed unity; the emitter circuit may then display negative resistance effects which can lead to undesirable instabilities.

11.4.2. Base-width modulation and punch-through. It has been tacitly assumed that the base width, l_B, is always constant, but in a real device the effective width of the base, $l_{B\,eff}$, is dependent on V_{CB} and to a lesser extent on V_{BE}. This is because the boundaries which delineate the extent of the base are the edges of the depletion layers at the junction, which vary in position with changing bias voltages. For example, the assumed almost-zero minority carrier concentration occurs at the edge of the collector–base depletion layer, which in turn is dependent on the collector voltage V_{CB}. If the base is relatively lightly doped, the collector–base depletion layer extends mostly into the base and the effective base width, using eq. (9.49), is given approximately by

$$l_{B\,eff} \simeq l_B - \left(\frac{2\epsilon V_{BC}}{eN_a}\right)^{\frac{1}{2}} \tag{11.15}$$

where l_B is now the distance between the metallurgical junctions and N_a is the acceptor concentration in the base. Therefore, as V_{CB} is increased, the effective base width is reduced; there is a corresponding increase in the slope of the minority carrier density profile as shown in Fig. 11.9, which leads to

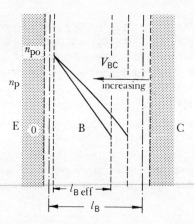

Fig. 11.9 Variation of effective base width with collector voltage V_{BC}.

a higher collector current. It follows that the emitter efficiency, the base transport factor, and current gains α_B and α_E are dependent in a non-linear way on the voltage V_{CB}.

The variation of collector current with changing V_{CB}, an effect known as *base-width modulation*, also affects the output characteristics of a transistor since the I_C-V_{BC} curves are no longer horizontal but take on a positive slope indicating that the device has a finite output impedance which is voltage-dependent. The input characteristics are also affected; since the input circuit behaves as a forward-biased diode and the input current is given by

$$I \simeq I_0 \exp(eV_{BE}/kT)$$

where I_0 is dependent on the effective base width, the input impedance is then to some extent influenced by V_{CB}.

At high collector voltages or for low doping concentrations in the base, it is possible for the collector–base depletion layer to extend completely across the base region, thus effectively short-circuiting the collector to the emitter. The minimum voltage for this *punch-through* effect to occur can be obtained by letting $l_{B \ eff}$ go to zero in eq. (11.15), which gives:

$$V_{BC}|_{max} = \frac{eN_a l_B^2}{2\epsilon} \tag{11.16}$$

Punch-through may thus set an upper limit to the permissible collector voltage but in many transistors the maximum value of V_{BC} is set by the onset of avalanche breakdown, which often occurs at lower voltages. It is of course possible to raise the punch-through voltage by increasing the doping concentration in the base, but since this automatically reduces the emitter efficiency, η_E, the particular choice of N_a is an engineering compromise.

11.4.3. Base resistance. It has been assumed in the simple transistor model that all externally applied voltages appear across the relatively high-resistance depletion layers and that voltages dropped across the bulk semiconductor regions are negligible. While it is usually permissible to ignore the resistance of collector and emitter regions in this way, the base region is relatively lightly doped in modern transistors and effects due to its finite resistance must normally be taken into account. Consider, for example, the planar transistor shown in Fig. 11.1(b) and in section in Fig. 11.10. Base current, I_B, flowing to the active base region, passes through a region which can have a significantly high resistance, which is represented by a lumped resistance, r_B, in the diagram. As a consequence, the effective emitter–base voltage is given by:

$$V_{BE \ eff} = V_{BE} - I_B r_B \tag{11.17}$$

252

Unfortunately, the situation is more complicated than is suggested by eq. (11.17), since I_B itself is dependent on $V_{BE\ eff}$.

It should be noted that the arguments so far are also applicable to a.c. signals; indeed, whereas it is often possible to omit r_B when calculating biasing conditions, it is usually necessary to include an effective base resistance in the small signal-equivalent circuit.

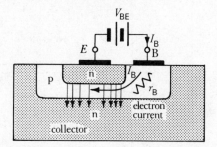

Fig. 11.10 Base resistance and emission crowding in a real transistor.

A more serious consequence of a finite base resistance is that it causes *emission crowding* in the base. This arises because the base current which is moving laterally in the active base region, i.e., perpendicular to the minority electron flow, causes a voltage drop across the face of the emitter which is in such a direction as to reduce the effective forward bias voltage in the centre of the emitter relative to that at the edges. Electron current from the emitter thus tends to concentrate towards the periphery of the emitter, as shown diagrammatically in Fig. 11.10. Under high-current conditions irreversible damage can be caused by excessive current densities at emitter edges. At more modest current levels, emission crowding is not so serious and can be accounted for by inclusion of an additional resistance in the effective lumped base resistance.

11.4.4. Graded-base or drift transistors. The transistors discussed so far have been assumed to possess a uniformly doped base in which negligible electric fields exist; minority electron transport in this case is predominantly determined by diffusion effects. However, many modern transistors, particularly those made by the diffusion process, have an inherently non-uniform base doping profile. For many applications this is advantageous and in some devices, for example, high-frequency and switching transistors, such a doping profile is introduced deliberately. Devices with a non-uniform impurity concentration in the base are known as minority carrier *graded-base* or *drift* transistors; the latter name arises since an electric field always exists in the base which causes the minority carrier current in it to have a drift component.

The origins of the built-in electric field in the base of a drift transistor can be explained with reference to the typical doping profile and band structure

253

of an npn device shown in Figs. 11.11(a) and (b). It will be noticed that the net acceptor level in the base has its largest value, N_{aE}, next to the emitter and falls to zero at the base–collector junction. The corresponding negative

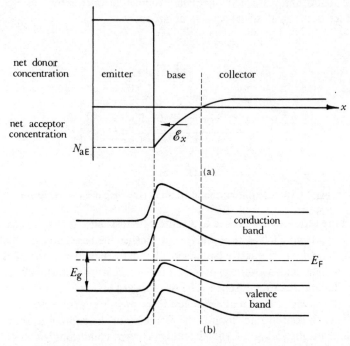

Fig. 11.11 (a) Idealized doping profile and (b) equilibrium band structure of a drift transistor.

gradient in majority hole density causes holes to move towards the collector, thus exposing fixed ionized acceptors and creating negative space charge. The resulting electric field is in such a direction as to oppose further migration of holes and so maintains the net hole current due to drift and diffusion at zero. The base current due to majority holes will, in the absence of recombination, be given by eq. (6.52):

$$J_h = e\mu_h p \mathscr{E}_x - eD_h \frac{dp}{dx} \tag{11.18}$$

For low-level injection, the hole density at any point in the base, p, is approximately equal to the acceptor concentration there, so, for zero hole current, eq. (11.18) yields:

$$\mathscr{E}_x = \frac{D_h}{\mu_h N_a} \cdot \frac{dN_a(x)}{dx} = \frac{kT}{e} \cdot \frac{1}{N_a} \frac{dN_a}{dx} \tag{11.19}$$

254

Since the impurity gradient is negative, $\mathscr{E}_x$ is directed towards the emitter as expected. Now, this built-in field, which prevents diffusion of majority carriers, is in such a direction as to cause electrons injected into the base to drift under the influence of the field towards the collector, and the net electron current in the base is given by

$$J_e = ne\mu_e \mathscr{E}_x + eD_e \frac{dn}{dx} \qquad (11.20)$$

Further, since carriers usually drift with faster velocities than they diffuse, the transit time of electrons across the base is very much lower in a drift transistor than in a corresponding diffusion transistor in which $\mathscr{E}_x$ is assumed zero. This property has enabled drift transistors to be operated at frequencies in the GHz range.

It is desirable for some applications that the doping gradient be arranged such that the built-in field in the base is everywhere uniform. If the transistor is constructed so that the doping profile is exponential and of the form:

$$N_a(x) = N_{aE} \exp(-Cx)$$

then eq. (11.19) gives:

$$\mathscr{E}_x = \frac{kT}{e} \cdot \frac{1}{N_a} \cdot (-C) N_a = - \frac{kTC}{e}$$

which satisfies the condition that $\mathscr{E}_x$ is constant and independent of position.

11.4.5. Geometrical effects. The flow of minority carriers through the base of a transistor has been assumed to be one-dimensional. Of course, in real transistors this is not so and the minority carrier current flow from the emitter spreads out laterally to some extent in the base, before it arrives at the collector. The proportion of the current from the emitter which is collected thus depends in some part on the geometry of the transistor. For example, if the base region is thin and the area of the collector is made much greater than the area of the emitter, then the base transport factor approximates to the ideal value found for the one-dimensional model.

11.4.6. High-frequency response. Gain parameters for a diffusion transistor have been determined in earlier sections assuming near-equilibrium conditions and are only applicable to low-frequency or slowly varying signals. The expressions obtained are modified when the transistor is operated at high frequencies. For example, the current gain in the grounded-base connection, α_B, is not constant but falls off with increasing frequency in the manner shown in Fig. 11.12. The fall-off in gain arises because of the finite time taken for minority carriers to diffuse across the base; when the transit time becomes comparable to the periodic time of an applied signal, the minority carriers

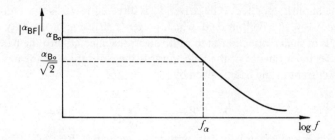

Fig. 11.12 High-frequency common-base gain of a diffusion transistor.

can no longer respond fast enough and the gain falls to zero. The α-*cut-off frequency*, f_α, is defined as that frequency at which the magnitude of the current gain, α_{BF}, falls by 3 db to $1/\sqrt{2}$ of its low-frequency value, α_{B0}. The value of f_α can be estimated by considering the continuity equation for minority electrons in the base, assuming no electric field exists there, which is, from eq. 6.63:

$$\frac{\partial}{\partial t}(\delta n) = -\frac{\delta n}{\tau_{Le}} + D_e \frac{\partial^2}{\partial x^2}(\delta n) \tag{11.21}$$

The term on the left-hand side of the equation, which was neglected in the time-independent solution, must be retained when discussing high-frequency effects. If small sinusoidal alternating signals of angular frequency ω are superimposed on the d.c. currents flowing in the base under equilibrium conditions, the solution to the continuity equation is expected to be of the form:

$$\delta n(x, t) = \delta n(x) \exp j(\omega t + \phi) \tag{11.22}$$

Substituting this trial solution into eq. (11.21) gives:

$$0 = -\delta n \frac{(1 + j\omega\tau_{Le})}{\tau_{Le}} + D_e \frac{\partial^2}{\partial x^2}(\delta n)$$

or

$$\frac{\partial^2}{\partial x^2}(\delta n) = \frac{\delta n(1 + j\omega\tau_{Le})}{L_e^2} \tag{11.23}$$

Comparing this equation with that given in section 11.3.2 it will be noticed that L_e^2 in the d.c. continuity equation has to be replaced by $L_e^2/(1 + j\omega\tau_{Le})$ to give the a.c. version of the equation. Equation (11.13) will therefore still be valid for the base transport factor in the a.c. case, provided L_e^2 is replaced by $L_e^2/(1 + j\omega\tau_{Le})$. Thus, the gain at high frequencies, α_{BF}, neglecting

256

the frequency dependence of the emitter efficiency and assuming it to be near unity, becomes:

$$\alpha_{BF} \simeq \beta_F = \left[1 + \frac{1}{2} \frac{l^2{}_B(1 + j\omega\tau_{Le})}{L_e{}^2} \right]^{-1} \tag{11.24}$$

This equation, together with the corresponding low-frequency equation derived from eq. (11.13), gives:

$$\frac{\alpha_{BF}}{\alpha_{B0}} = \frac{1}{1 + j\dfrac{\omega}{\omega_c}} \tag{11.25}$$

where

$$\omega_c = \frac{2L_e{}^2 + l_B{}^2}{\tau_{Le}\, l_B{}^2} \simeq \frac{2L_e{}^2}{\tau_{Le}\, l_B{}^2} = \frac{2D_e}{l_B{}^2} \tag{11.26}$$

It is evident from eq. (11.25) that $|\alpha_{BF}|$ falls to $\alpha_{B0}/\sqrt{2}$ when $\omega = \omega_c$ and, hence, from (11.26):

$$f_\alpha = \frac{\omega_c}{2\pi} \simeq \frac{D_e}{\pi l_B{}^2} \tag{11.27}$$

Although a transistor can be operated at higher frequencies, eq. (11.27) gives an indication of the frequency at which the gain is falling off rapidly and at which phase-shift distortion becomes apparent. It will be noticed that, according to the approximate analysis presented, the α-cut-off frequency is dependent only on the diffusion coefficient in and the width of the base. A thin base is again advantageous for good high-frequency performance and there is also some advantage in using npn transistor structures because the diffusion rate for minority electrons is higher than for holes. However, there are physical limitations to the reduction in base width and a more useful* method of reducing the transit time, and hence increasing the high-frequency operating capabilities of a transistor, is to introduce a drift field in the base region by means of some degree of impurity grading, as discussed in sub-section 11.4.4.

11.5 Small-signal equivalent circuit

Although the bipolar transistor is inherently non-linear for large-amplitude signal variations, it may be considered to behave in a linear manner over a limited range of its operating characteristics and a small-signal equivalent circuit can be derived to represent its electrical performance. Strictly, such a circuit will only therefore be applicable to small-amplitude a.c. or incremental d.c. signals. Many different equivalent circuits have been proposed; an equivalent circuit based on our discussions of the physical processes which

257

take place in a transistor in the grounded emitter configuration will be derived as an example. The parameters of the circuit will then be compared with those of a more usually encountered, more generally applicable circuit which is based on a four-terminal network, 'black-box' approach.

Consider the base–emitter current of an npn bipolar transistor in the common-emitter connection (see, for example, Fig. 11.5). In the normal operating mode of the transistor, the base–emitter junction will be forward-biased and the small-signal input voltage, v_i, will be applied in series with the d.c. bias voltage V_{BE}. The input impedance presented to the signal includes the effective dynamic resistance of the forward-biased junction. Since:

$$I_b \simeq I_0 \exp(eV/kT)$$

and

$$\frac{\partial I_b}{\partial V} = \frac{e}{kT} I_b$$

it follows that the dynamic resistance is given by

$$r = \frac{kT}{eI_b} \tag{11.28}$$

which is a low resistance at room temperature and normal bias voltage. The input circuit also includes the bulk resistance of the base region and this is usually lumped together with the dynamic resistance to give an effective input resistance, r_{BE}.

Turning now to the output circuit, a large dynamic impedance will exist at the collector–base junction by virtue of the reverse d.c. bias across it and this results in a high value for the output resistance, r_{CE}, which is the resistance looking back into the collector–emitter terminals.

The signal current in the base, i_B, will be amplified and appear in the collector circuit as a current $\alpha_E i_B$, where α_E is the common-emitter current gain. Therefore, a simple, low-frequency, small-signal equivalent circuit based on the physical processes discussed so far might be of the form shown in Fig. 11.13(a), where a current generator $\alpha_E i_B$ is included in the collector circuit.

The simple equivalent circuit shown in Fig. 11.13(a) is highly idealized and can be refined somewhat so as to include base-width modulation effects by the addition of an extra component in the circuit to account for the built-in feedback between output and input circuits. The feedback arises because a change in output voltage changes the effective width of the base width, resulting in changes in collector, emitter, and hence base currents. The sign of the change is such that an increase in v_0 leads to a decrease in i_B. The

258

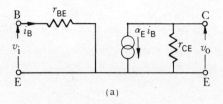

(a)

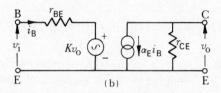

(b)

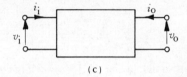

(c)

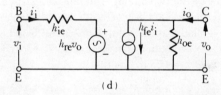

(d)

Fig. 11.13 Possible low-frequency, small-signal equivalent circuits for a bipolar transistor.

effect is accounted for in the more comprehensive equivalent circuit shown in Fig. 11.13(b) by including a voltage generator proportional to the output voltage in the base circuit, which is of such a polarity as to cause a reduction in the base current when the output voltage is increasing.

It is sometimes more convenient to treat the transistor as a two-port active network, as shown in Fig. 11.13(c), and develop an equivalent circuit from measurements which can be made at the two ports, rather than devising a circuit based on the physical processes occurring in a particular device. Again, there are several different forms for the defining equations of the equivalent circuit, depending on which set of terminal characteristics is considered. As an example, one possible set of measured parameters might be:

259

the *i*nput impedance with output short-circuited, $h_{ie} = \dfrac{v_i}{i_i}\bigg|_{v_o=0}$

the *re*verse open-circuit voltage amplification, $h_{re} = \dfrac{v_i}{v_o}\bigg|_{i_i=0}$

the *fo*rward current gain with output short-circuited, $h_{fe} = \dfrac{i_o}{i_i}\bigg|_{v_o=0}$

and the *o*utput conductance with input open-circuited, $h_{oe} = \dfrac{i_o}{v_o}\bigg|_{i_i=0}$

These are the *hybrid parameters* of a transistor, so called because they do not all have the same dimensions. The additional subscript is added to designate the circuit configuration, in this example common *e*mitter. It follows that the small-signal voltages and currents at the input and output terminals of the equivalent circuit are then related by the equations:

$$\left.\begin{aligned}
v_i &= h_{ie}\,i_i + h_{re}\,v_o \\
i_o &= h_{fe}\,i_i + h_{oe}\,v_o
\end{aligned}\right\}
\tag{11.29}$$

The equivalent circuit shown in Fig. 11.13(c) used in conjunction with eq. (11.29) can be used to define the small-signal performance of a transistor completely when it is included in a particular circuit.

The equivalence of the two circuit representations discussed can be seen by noting that eqs. (11.29) are also valid for the circuit shown in Fig. 11.13(d). This has obvious similarity to the equivalent circuit based on the internal physical processes occurring in a transistor, Fig. 11.13(b), and it follows by direct comparison of the two circuits that

$$h_{ie} \equiv r_{BE},\, h_{re} \equiv K,\, h_{fe} \equiv \alpha_E,\quad \text{and} \quad h_{oe} \equiv 1/r_{CE}.$$

11.6 Fabrication of junction transistors

Transistors have been made using all the basic junction-forming techniques discussed in chapter 9, namely grown junction, alloyed junction, diffused junction, epitaxial diffused junction, and by various combinations of these processes.

Grown transistors, shown in Fig. 11.14(a), which are produced by compensation doping of the melt from which the semiconductor ingot is pulled with alternate amounts of opposite polarity impurities, have historical significance; however, the process has little practical importance today because of difficulties of locating the junction and of attaching leads to the narrow grown base region.

260

The alloying process is used extensively to make general-purpose, low-frequency transistors. A thin wafer of, say, n-type parent material has small dots of either pure p-type impurity, for example indium, or another metal heavily doped with p-type impurities, alloyed to either side of it as shown in Fig. 11.14(b). The alloyed sections have the twofold purpose of providing both the correctly doped collector and emitter regions and making ohmic contacts to them. Transistors made using this technique usually have a poor high-frequency performance because of high junction capacitances and

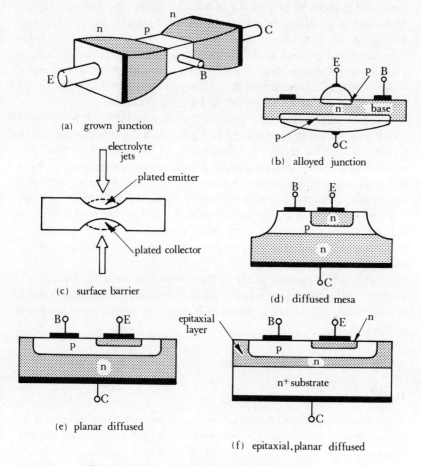

(a) grown junction

(b) alloyed junction

(c) surface barrier

(d) diffused mesa

(e) planar diffused

(f) epitaxial, planar diffused

Fig. 11.14. Construction of some transistor types.

because of the difficulty of controlling the process sufficiently to produce very thin base regions. The *surface-barrier* alloyed-junction transistor shown in Fig. 11.14(c) is fabricated by an alternative process which produces a reduced base thickness, thus extending the transistor's high-frequency operating range to above 100 MHz. In this process the base region is formed by

261

etching away the parent semiconductor using jets of etching solution which is subsequently employed as the electrolyte used to electroplate alloying contacts on to either side of the base.

The *diffusion* process for fabricating transistors has many advantages and is now most prevalent. A p-type impurity to form the transistor base is diffused into the top face of an n-type semiconductor slice, followed by a shallower, more highly concentrated n-type diffusion which forms the emitter and delineates the narrow base region. Ohmic contacts are made to the various regions by evaporation of metallic conductors. In the *mesa* version, shown in Fig. 11.14(d), the area of the collector junction is formed by an etching process which leaves the active portions of the transistor isolated on a tapered plateau or mesa. In the *planar* diffused-junction transistor shown in Fig. 11.14(e), the geometry of collector, base, emitter, and ohmic contacts is determined by an oxide masking technique before each successive stage of manufacture, similar to that described for the planar diode.

A disadvantage of the diffusion process is that the lightly doped collector region provides a high resistance path in series with the collector circuit. The *epitaxial* fabrication technique shown in Fig. 11.14(f) is used to overcome this difficulty. In this process a highly doped, low-resistance substrate has a higher-resistivity epitaxial layer grown from the vapour phase on to it to form a composite collector. The base and emitter layers are diffused in the usual way into the high-resistivity epitaxial layer. The substrate provides the required low-resistance path to the collector terminals. Epitaxial diffused transistors have the additional advantages of reduced collector capacitance and higher breakdown voltages.

In all types of transistor made by the diffusion process, any grading of the impurity in the base layer to produce a drift field in it is readily obtained by controlling the diffusion conditions so as to form a predetermined impurity profile.

Problems

1   A certain pnp transistor has an effective base width of 20 μm under certain biasing conditions. The thickness of the emitter region is 5 μm and its resistivity is 50×10^{-6} ohm-m. The effective base lifetime is 20 μs and $D_h = 0.0047 \text{ m}^2\text{s}^{-1}$. Estimate the common emitter current gain of the device.

Ans. 81.

2   Draw a diagram showing the division of electron and hole currents in the various regions of a pnp transistor and confirm that the sum of the base current components is $I_E (1 - \alpha) - I_{co}$.

3   When the collector voltage of a transistor is sufficiently high it is possible for the collector-base depletion layer to extend right across the base region. This condition, called *punch-through*, is achieved in a particular npn germanium transistor when the collector voltage is 30 V. Assuming that the collector doping density is very much greater than that of the base, which contains 10^{21} atoms per m^3 and that $\epsilon_r = 16$, estimate the base width with no bias voltages applied.

Ans. 7·3 μm.

4   The transistor of question 3 has a quoted low frequency current gain α_E of 30. Estimate the lifetime of minority electrons in the base of the transistor. Assume an emitter efficiency of 100% and $D_e = 0.0093$ m^{2}s^{-1}.

Ans. 0·09 μs.

12. Field-effect devices

12.1 General properties and types of field-effect transistor

This class of transistor may be distinguished from solid-state devices discussed so far by several features which are common to all members of the class. Firstly, the flow of carriers in a particular device is controlled by the application of an electric field which permeates into the main conduction path in a semiconductor; this gives rise to the term *field effect*. Secondly, current flow along this main conduction path is almost entirely due to the motion of majority carriers. Injection of minority carriers, a mechanism which is essential for the operation of the bipolar transistor as described in chapter 11, is not a necessary requirement in field-effect devices. The generic term *unipolar* is therefore used as an alternative to field-effect to describe the devices since they rely only on one type of carrier for current transport.

Before going on to describe the various types of field-effect transistor, it will be useful to list some further properties which distinguish them as a class from bipolar transistors. Firstly, they have extremely high input impedances, ranging from 10^{10} to 10^{15} ohms depending on the type, often with lower noise levels than bipolar devices. The performance of bipolar transistors is degraded by neutron radiation because of the reduction in minority carrier lifetime, whereas field-effect transistors can tolerate a much higher level of radiation since they do not rely on minority carriers for their operation. Field-effect devices are particularly attractive for use in integrated circuits because of their relatively small area and hence high packing density, their lack of need for additional isolation, and their ability to be directly coupled. Finally, their performance is relatively unaffected by ambient temperature changes.

The field-effect transistor (FET) consists essentially of a semiconducting path whose resistance is controlled by the application of a transverse electric field. There are two main categories for such devices, *junction* field-effect transistors and *insulated-gate* field-effect transistors. In the former the resistance of the main current path is modulated by the application of a bias voltage to pn junctions adjacent to the path, while in the latter type there are no junctions and the controlling electric field is applied to the conducting path via an insulating layer.

264

There are two further subcategories into which a particular unipolar device can be classified. In a *depletion* device, the controlling electric field reduces the number of majority carriers available for conduction, whereas in the *enhancement* device, application of electric field causes an increase in the majority carrier density in the conducting regions of the transistor. The various field-effect transistors will now be discussed in more detail and some of these introductory points will be substantiated.

12.2 The junction field-effect transistor (JFET)

The junction field-effect transistor exists in several practically realizable geometries. For example, Fig. 12.1(a) shows a cylindrical version sometimes

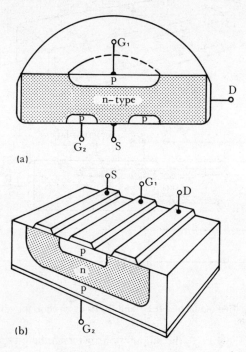

Fig. 12.1 Construction of a junction field-effect transistor: (a) cylindrical and (b) planar geometry.

used for discrete transistor manufacture and Fig. 12.1(b) shows the planar form which is most suitable for inclusion in integrated circuits. However, in order to investigate the basic general characteristics of such devices without added complications due to complex device geometry, we shall consider the most rudimentary configuration consisting of an n-type, single-crystal, semi-conducting bar with ohmic contacts at either end and two p-type contacts on opposite sides, as shown in Fig. 12.2(a).

If the two p-type regions, called *gates*, G_1 and G_2, are shorted to the left-hand end contact of the bar, called the *source*, S, and a small positive voltage, V_d, is applied to the right-hand contact, the *drain*, D, as in Fig. 12.2(b), a current I_d flows in the external circuit, as shown. Since the bulk of the material is n-type, the current is transported in the semiconductor by majority electrons flowing from source to drain; the left-hand contact is thus an electron source and the right-hand contact drains electrons out. Since the bar has ohmic resistance, the flow of current in it produces an *IR* drop and the potential at any point in the bar increases from the source to the drain end, becoming more positive towards the drain. Therefore, since the gates have

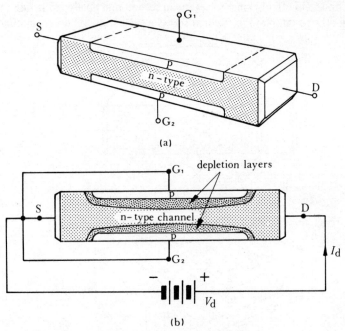

Fig. 12.2 (a) Simplified model of a JFET and (b) its connection for grounded-gate operation.

been shorted to the source, the pn junctions between the p-type gates and the n-type bar are reverse-biased, becoming progressively more so towards the drain end. Now, we have seen that the thickness of the depletion layer of a reverse biased pn junction varies approximately as the square root of the bias voltage, the layer becoming wider as the reverse voltage increases. Thus, the depletion layers between gates and bar become wider towards the drain end, as shown in Fig. 12.2(b). Further, the ratio of the thickness of the depletion layer in a p-type gate, d_p, to that in the *n*-type bar, d_n, at any point is given by eq. (9.45) as:

$$\frac{d_p}{d_n} = \frac{N_d}{N_a}$$

where N_a and N_d are the doping concentrations in the two regions. Therefore, if, as is usually the case, the p-type gates are much more heavily doped than the n-type conducting path, i.e., $N_a \gg N_d$ and $d_p \ll d_n$, most of the depletion layer thickness occurs in the n-type region. As a consequence, current flow in the device is confined to the wedge-shaped region or *channel*, shown in Fig. 12.2(b), since there are no free carriers in the depletion layers.

As the voltage V_d is increased the thickness of the conducting channel is reduced because of the widening of the gate depletion layers as the reverse bias is automatically increased. The source to drain resistance is increased correspondingly until at some voltage $V_d = V_p$, called the *pinch-off voltage*, the space-charge regions from the gates meet; the channel is then said to be pinched-off. At drain voltages beyond pinch-off the drain current becomes essentially saturated and remains at some value I_{do}. The $I_d - V_d$ or drain characteristic therefore has the form shown in Fig. 12.3(a), the particular curve applying to the bias conditions discussed being labelled $V_g = 0$.

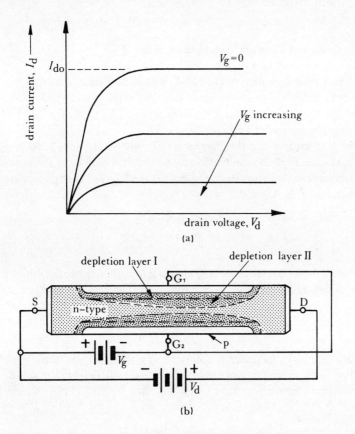

Fig. 12.3 (a) Form of the drain characteristics of a JFET, (b) the JFET with reverse-bias voltage applied to its gates.

267

If now an additional fixed reverse-bias voltage, V_g, is applied to the gates G_1 and G_2 in parallel, as shown in Fig. 12.3(b), in the absence of drain current the space-charge layers would extend uniformly into the channel, region I in the drawing. When drain current flows due to the application of a drain voltage, V_d, the characteristic wedge-shaped depletion layers, region II, are superposed on top of the uniform layers due to V_g alone, as shown. Under these conditions the IR drop and hence the value of V_d required to produce pinch-off is smaller and current saturation occurs at lower drain voltages. This results in a family of drain characteristics as shown in Fig. 12.3(a). Thus, application of a reverse voltage to the gates governs the effective width of the depletion layers, which in turn changes the effective channel dimensions, modulates the channel resistance, and hence controls the drain current. When operating in this fashion the JFET behaves as a depletion mode device, since the channel current is reduced as the gate voltage is increased. In the succeeding section we will consider the operation of a JFET more quantitatively with a view to characterizing its d.c. and a.c. performance.

12.3 Drain and transfer characteristics of the JFET

12.3.1. Linear operation of the JFET. Let us firstly consider the situation when the drain voltage, V_d, is small enough for the conduction channel to be substantially uniform. This case is illustrated in Fig. 12.4(a), which includes relevant dimensions and coordinate system.

We shall assume that the channel is relatively lightly doped compared with the gates, i.e., $N_a \gg N_d$, so that nearly all the depletion layer thickness occurs in the n-region. In these circumstances the thickness of the space-charge layer is given by eq. (9.47) and

$$d_n = a - b \simeq \left[\frac{2\epsilon(V_0 + V_g)}{eN_d} \right]^{\frac{1}{2}} \tag{12.1}$$

where V_0 is the contact potential between n- and p-regions, as usual. This equation can be rearranged to give the channel half-thickness, b:

$$b = a - \left[\frac{2\epsilon(V_0 + V_g)}{eN_d} \right]^{\frac{1}{2}} \tag{12.2}$$

Notice that as V_g increases, b decreases, as was argued qualitatively earlier.

Pinch-off occurs when the gate voltage is just sufficient to make the conduction channel width zero, or $b = 0$ when $V_g = V_p$, the pinch-off voltage. Then

$$a^2 = \frac{2\epsilon(V_0 + V_p)}{eN_d}$$

or

$$V_p = \frac{eN_d a^2}{2\epsilon} - V_0 \tag{12.3}$$

The half-channel thickness can then be expressed in terms of the pinch-off voltage by substituting eq. (12.3) in (12.2) to give:

$$b = a\left[1 - \left(\frac{V_0 + V_g}{V_0 + V_p}\right)^{\frac{1}{2}}\right] \tag{12.4}$$

Now, the conducting channel has conductance G where:

$$G = \frac{\sigma_n \cdot 2b \cdot w}{l} = eN_d \mu_e \cdot \frac{2bw}{l} \tag{12.5}$$

where w is the gate width and μ_e the electron mobility. Thus, the drain current, I_d, flowing when a small drain voltage, V_d, is applied is given by:

$$I_d = V_d G = eN_d \mu_e \frac{2bw}{l} \cdot V_d = \frac{eN_d \cdot \mu_e 2wa}{l}\left[1 - \left(\frac{V_0 + V_g}{V_0 + V_p}\right)^{\frac{1}{2}}\right]V_d \tag{12.6}$$

It is convenient to write the drain current in terms of the channel conductance when zero gate–bias voltage is applied, G_0, where:

$$G_0 = \frac{\sigma_n \cdot 2aw}{l} = \frac{eN_d \mu_e \cdot 2aw}{l} \tag{12.7}$$

which can be substituted in eq. (12.6) to give:

$$I_d = G_0\left[1 - \left(\frac{V_0 + V_g}{V_0 + V_p}\right)^{\frac{1}{2}}\right]V_d \tag{12.8}$$

Further simplifications are possible since, at all but the lowest gate voltages, $V_g \gg V_0$ and in all cases except for very thin, high-resistivity channels, $V_p \gg V_0$. The drain current then becomes:

$$I_d \simeq G_0\left[1 - \left(\frac{V_g}{V_p}\right)^{\frac{1}{2}}\right]V_d \tag{12.9}$$

This relationship between drain current and voltage is only valid for $|V_g| < |V_p|$, that is, before pinch-off. The equation shows that for small drain voltages and fixed gate voltages, the drain current varies linearly with drain voltage. Hence, the device acts as a voltage-controlled resistor whose resistance can be altered by altering the gate voltage, as shown in the characteristics of Fig. 12.4(b). JFETs in this linear resistive mode have applications in voltage-controllable attenuator and variable phase-shift networks.

269

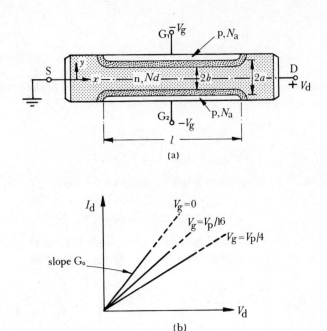

Fig. 12.4 Operation of a JFET with low-drain voltages: (a) mathematical model and (b) the linear drain characteristics.

12.3.2. Operation as far as pinch-off. We now turn our attention to the more usual case of larger drain voltages which cause a not insignificant axial electric field, $\mathscr{E}_x$, to exist. Since such a component of electric field is now present, there exists a corresponding change in potential along the channel. Thus, the net reverse bias voltage between the channel and the gate varies with distance along the channel, x, and the space-charge depletion layers take on their characteristic wedge shape, converging towards the drain end, as explained in section 12.2.

This situation can be treated by assuming that the depletion layer converges in a gradual manner. A typical configuration might then be as shown in Fig. 12.5(a). If we now consider an element of thickness, δx, situated at x along the axis as shown, and let the voltage at x be V_x, then, if the voltage at $x + \delta x$ is $V_{x + \delta x}$, the voltage drop across the element is given by:

$$V_{x+\delta x} - V_x = \left(V_x + \frac{dV_x}{dx}\delta x\right) - V_x = \frac{dV_x}{dx}.\delta x \qquad (12.10)$$

We further assume that the gate junctions can be treated as equipotentials by virtue of the relatively high gate conductivity. Then, if the gate voltage is V_g, the total reverse bias at the element is $V_x + V_g$. Equation (12.6) will still be

270

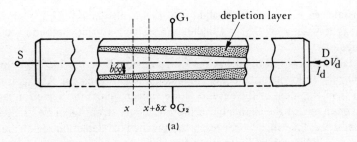

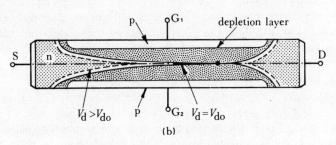

Fig. 12.5 Operation of the JFET with high-drain voltages: (a) mathematical model and (b) conditions after pinch-off.

applicable to the element, provided l is replaced by δx, V_d by $(dV_x/dx)\,\delta x$, and V_g by $V_x + V_g$, and this gives:

$$I_d = \frac{eN_d\,\mu_e\,2wa}{\delta x}\left[1 - \left(\frac{V_x + V_g}{V_p}\right)^{\frac{1}{2}}\right]\frac{dV_x}{dx}.\,\delta x \qquad (12.11)$$

Notice that we have again assumed that the contact voltage, V_0, is negligibly small. We next rearrange the equation and integrate over the length of the gate, l, as follows:

$$\frac{I_d}{2eN_d\,\mu_e\,wa}\int_0^l dx = \int_0^{V_d}\left[1 - \left(\frac{V_x + V_g}{V_p}\right)^{\frac{1}{2}}\right]dV_x \qquad (12.12)$$

which, using eq. (12.7), gives:

$$I_d = G_0\left[V_d - \frac{2}{3}\left(\frac{V_d + V_g}{V_p}\right)^{\frac{3}{2}}V_p + \frac{2}{3}\left(\frac{V_g}{V_p}\right)^{\frac{3}{2}}V_p\right] \qquad (12.13)$$

This equation can be rewritten in terms of the drain–gate voltage V_{dg}, which equals $V_d + V_g$, to give:

$$I_d = G_0\left[V_{dg}\left\{1 - \frac{2}{3}\left(\frac{V_{dg}}{V_p}\right)^{\frac{1}{2}}\right\} - V_g\left\{1 - \frac{2}{3}\left(\frac{V_g}{V_p}\right)^{\frac{1}{2}}\right\}\right] \qquad (12.14)$$

271

It must be remembered that these equations are only valid for $V_{dg} = (V_d + V_g)$ $< V_p$; otherwise, when $V_{dg} = V_p$, the channel has zero thickness and becomes pinched-off.

Detailed analysis of the behaviour of the device above pinch-off is complex but the following qualitative explanation might be useful. As V_{dg} is made bigger than V_p, most of the excess voltage appears across the depletion layers at the drain end of the channel, causing a relatively strong axial electric field to exist there. Electrons which reach this pinched-off depletion region are therefore rapidly removed into the drain. The effect of further increasing V_{dg} or V_d is to move the position where pinch-off occurs nearer to the source, as shown diagrammatically in Fig. 12.5(b). However, since large drain voltage changes cause only slight movement of the pinch-off position, there is a tendency for the drain current to saturate and increases in drain voltage above pinch-off cause only small increases in drain current.

The drain characteristics or I_d-V_d curves, derived from eq. (12.13) or (12.14), and assuming that current saturation occurs after pinch-off, are then as shown in Fig. 12.6(a). The current in the saturation region for a particular gate voltage, I_{ds}, can be obtained from eq. (12.14) by letting $V_{dg} = V_p$. Thus:

$$I_{ds} = G_0\left[\frac{V_p}{3} - V_g\left\{1 - \frac{2}{3}\left(\frac{V_g}{V_p}\right)^{\frac{1}{2}}\right\}\right] \tag{12.15}$$

and the saturated drain current for the particular case of zero gate voltage, I_{do}, is from this equation:

$$I_{do} = \frac{G_0 V_p}{3} \tag{12.16}$$

Finally, eq. (12.15) and (12.16) can be rearranged to give the saturated drain current at any particular gate voltage in terms of the current at zero gate voltage, to yield:

$$I_{ds} = I_{do}\left[1 - \frac{3V_g}{V_p} + 2\left(\frac{V_g}{V_p}\right)^{\frac{3}{2}}\right] \tag{12.17}$$

The transfer characteristics of the device, or the variation of drain current with gate voltage in the pinch-off region, can be predicted using this equation and is of the form shown in Fig. 12.6(b). The incremental mutual conductance of the device beyond pinch-off, g_m, is also obtained from eq. (12.17), as follows:

$$g_m = \frac{\partial I_{ds}}{\partial V_g}\bigg|_{V_d} = \frac{\partial}{\partial V_g}\left[I_{do}\left\{1 - \frac{3V_g}{V_g + V_d} + 2\left(\frac{V_g}{V_g + V_d}\right)^{\frac{3}{2}}\right\}\right]$$

$$= -I_{do}\frac{3V_d}{V_p{}^2}\left[1 - \left(\frac{V_g}{V_p}\right)^{\frac{1}{2}}\right] \tag{12.18}$$

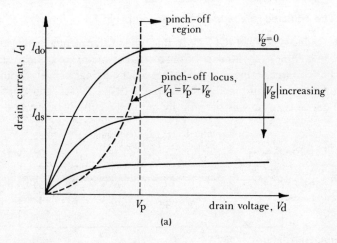

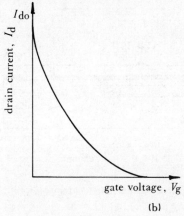

Fig. 12.6 Drain and transfer characteristics of the JFET.

The maximum transconductance g_{mo} occurs at $V_g = 0$ and is therefore:

$$g_{mo} = -\frac{3I_{d0}}{V_p} = -G_0 \qquad (12.19)$$

We see that the maximum transconductance equals the conductance of the channel with zero gate voltage. The transconductance at any other gate voltage is then given approximately by:

$$g_m \simeq g_{mo}\left[1 - \left(\frac{V_g}{V_p}\right)^{\frac{1}{2}}\right] \qquad (12.20)$$

273

12.4 The insulated-gate field-effect transistor (IGFET)

12.4.1. Induced-channel IGFET. In this type of transistor a metal gate electrode is completely insulated from a semiconductor by a thin insulating layer, but voltages on the gate can induce a conducting channel within the semiconductor and also modulates its conductivity. Typical construction of a planar device is as shown schematically in Fig. 12.7(a). Two heavily doped

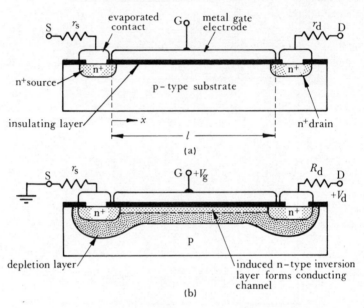

Fig. 12.7 (a) The induced-channel insulated-gate field-effect transistor, (b) with positive gate voltage applied.

n^+ stripes are diffused into a p-type substrate by the photo-masking techniques described in section 9.13 and form the source and drain electrodes. An oxide layer of order $0\cdot1\ \mu$ thick is thermally grown on the surface of the slice and etched away so that it just overlaps the n^+-regions, as shown. Finally, a metal gate electrode and metal connections to source and drain regions are evaporated on. Very often the device is fabricated using silicon technology and it is then known particularly as a metal-oxide–silicon transistor, or MOST.

In order to understand the operation of this transistor, we will firstly assume for simplicity that no surface traps exist at the boundary between the substrate and the oxide layer. This approximation is often quite valid since it has been shown that thermally grown silicon dioxide on a silicon surface can so passivate the surface as to substantially reduce the number of deep traps to such an extent that for many devices they can be neglected. Under these conditions and with no gate voltage applied, no current can flow between source and drain contacts because of the existence of back-to-back pn junction diodes between them.

274

If, now, a small positive gate voltage, V_g, is applied, positive and negative charges are established at either side of the oxide layer, and the transverse electric field which is set up is terminated on negative charges which are induced in the p-type substrate. For small gate voltage, the necessary negative charges in the semiconductor are provided by holes being depleted from the channel, exposing negatively charged ionized acceptor impurities which just balance the positive charge on the gate electrode; a depletion layer is formed in this manner and the band edges near the surface of the semiconductor begin to bend down as described in section 9.10. As the gate voltage is further increased, conduction electrons are drawn to the surface of the semiconductor to provide the additional negative charge necessary to balance the extra positive charge placed on the gate electrode. Thus, as the gate voltage is increased the channel changes from p-type to intrinsic and finally to an n-type induced layer, as shown in Fig. 12.7(b).

The energy band diagram after the induced channel has been formed is as shown in Fig. 12.8. Its evolution can be explained as follows. For small positive gate voltages a depletion layer is formed in the semiconductor as explained and the bands begin to bend down near to the surface, as discussed in chapter 9, the amount of bending corresponding to the potential drop across the layer. As the gate voltage increases, the depletion layer widens, the potential across the layer increases, and the bands bend down further. Eventually when the gate voltage is sufficiently high, the band edges bend down to such an extent that the Fermi level, which is necessarily constant throughout the semiconductor in equilibrium, approaches the bottom of the conduction band, as shown in Fig. 12.8. The band structure of the material near to the surface then corresponds to that for an n-type semiconductor and an inversion layer is formed.

Immediately the n-type layer is induced, ohmic conduction from source to drain becomes possible. Further increases in V_g cause more mobile electrons to be introduced into the induced channel with a corresponding increase in the channel conductivity and drain current. The device therefore operates in an enhancement mode, since the number of mobile carriers and hence the drain current increases with increasing gate voltage; consequently it is sometimes known as an induced-channel enhancement transistor.

The form of the characteristics of the enhancement mode device can be derived as follows. At some distance x along the channel the voltage is assumed to be $V(x)$, which is a function of distance because of the IR drop along the channel and ranges from V_s at the source to V_d at the drain end. The voltage across the oxide layer at this point is then $V_g - V(x)$. If we assume the oxide layer to have thickness t_o, neglecting fringing fields and assuming that the oxide is relatively thick compared with the shallow conducting channel the electric field in the oxide, $\mathscr{E}(x)$ is then:

$$\mathscr{E}(x) = [V_g - V(x)]/t_o \qquad (12.21)$$

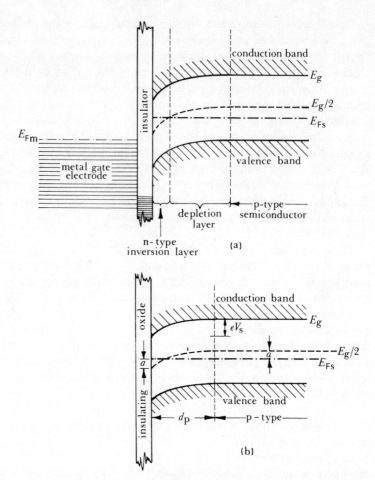

Fig. 12.8 Band structure of the induced-channel IGFET (a) when the induced channel is fully formed and (b) just at the onset of inversion layer formation, when $V_g = V_T$.

The surface-charge density, ρ_i, induced in the channel at x, is related to the electric field by Gauss's law and is given by:

$$\rho_i(x) = \epsilon \mathscr{E}(x) = \epsilon_o \, \epsilon_{ro} \left[\frac{V_g - V(x)}{t_o} \right] \text{C/m}^2 \qquad (12.22)$$

where ϵ_{ro} is the relative permittivity of the oxide layer.

Not all of this charge is available for conduction in the channel, since at low gate voltages a depletion layer but no inversion layer is formed. However, if a characteristic voltage, V_T, known as the *turn-on voltage*, is defined as that voltage across the oxide which just causes the mobile charge concentration in the channel to go to zero, then voltages in excess of V_T induce the inversion layer necessary for conduction. The excess mobile carrier density in the

276

inverted channel, Δn, can then be related to an effective voltage across the oxide $[V_g - V(x)] - V_T$ and the mobile surface charge density is given by:

$$e\Delta n(x) = \epsilon_o \epsilon_{ro}[V_g - V(x) - V_T]/t_o \text{C/m}^2 \tag{12.23}$$

Now the gate-electrode-insulator-semiconductor combination behaves as a capacitor of capacitance C_g, which is given approximately by the parallel plate expression and is thus:

$$C_g = \frac{\epsilon_o \epsilon_{ro} \, lw}{t_o} \text{ F} \tag{12.24}$$

where w is the width of the gate electrode. Equation (12.23) can now be rewritten in terms of the gate capacitance to yield:

$$e\Delta n(x) = \frac{C_g}{lw}\left[\frac{V_g - V(x) - V_T}{t_o}\right] \text{ for } (V_g - V(x)) > V_T$$

$$= 0 \qquad\qquad \text{for } (V_g - V(x)) < V_T \tag{12.25}$$

Now let us consider a portion of the assumed infinitesimally thin channel of length dx, and width w. This has conductance, $G(x)$, given by

$$G(x) = \sigma(x) \, w/dx \tag{12.26}$$

where $\sigma(x)$ is the surface conductance per metre square of channel. The conductance of the elemental channel length is then:

$$G(x) = e\Delta n(x)\mu_e \frac{w}{dx} = \frac{\mu_e C_g}{l\,dx}(V_g - V(x) - V_T) \tag{12.27}$$

where μ_e is the mobility of electrons in the channel. The channel or drain current, I_d, is then given by Ohm's law:

$$I_d = G(x) \, dV$$

where dV is the voltage across the incremental length of channel, dx.
Substituting from eq. (12.27) and taking to the limit then yields:

$$I_d = \frac{\mu_e C_g}{l}(V_g - V(x) - V_T)\frac{dV}{dx} \tag{12.28}$$

This equation can be integrated over the length of the channel, l, to give:

$$\int_0^l I_d \, dx = \frac{\mu_e C_g}{l} \int_0^{V_d} (V_g - V(x) - V_T) \, dV \tag{12.29}$$

Here, for simplicity, we have assumed the parasitic series resistances of source and drain, r_s and r_d in Fig. 12.7, to be negligibly small because of the relatively high doping level, but these could be included without too much additional complication. Carrying out the integration yields:

$$I_d = \frac{\mu_e C_g}{l^2}\left[V_g - V_T - \frac{V_d}{2}\right]V_d \tag{12.30}$$

277

Note that this equation is only valid when the net voltage across the oxide layer at any point exceeds the turn-on voltage, or $(V_g - V(x)) > V_T$. Thus, for any particular gate voltage, V_{g1} say, the equation is only valid for drain voltages in the range $0 \leqslant V_d \leqslant (V_{g1} - V_T)$. This upper limit for the drain voltage is physically explainable as that voltage which is just sufficient to prevent the formation of an inversion layer at the drain end. When the drain voltage is increased above this limit, the drain current saturates at some maximum value, I_{ds}, found by putting $V_d = V_g - V_T$ in eq. (12.30) to give:

$$I_{ds} = \frac{\mu_e C_g}{l^2} \cdot \frac{(V_g - V_T)^2}{2} \tag{12.31}$$

The drain characteristics of an IGFET operating in the enhancement mode are derivable from expressions (12.30) and (12.31) and are therefore typically of the form shown in Fig. 12.9. Notice that, except for the direction of

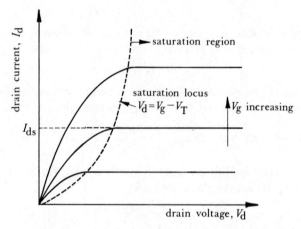

Fig. 12.9 **Drain characteristics of the induced-channel insulated-gate field effect transistor.**

increasing V_g, these characteristics are similar in form to those shown for the JFET operated in the depletion mode, shown in Fig. 12.6(a).

The transconductance of the IGFET when operated in the saturated region, g_m, is obtained from eq. (12.30), which gives:

$$g_m = \left. \frac{\partial I_d}{\partial V_g} \right|_{V_d} = \frac{\mu_e C_g V_d}{l^2} = \frac{\mu_e C_g (V_g - V_T)}{l^2} \tag{12.32}$$

Measured transconductances are somewhat lower than would be predicted by this equation, partly because the parasitic resistances r_s and r_d have been neglected and partly because of the lowering of the mobility in the thin channel below that of the bulk material because of scattering at the oxide surfac

278

Since the turn-on voltage, V_T, appears in all the derived expressions it will be useful to estimate its value. By definition, when the turn-on voltage is applied across the oxide layer, an inversion layer is about to be formed but meanwhile the negative charge of the fixed ionized acceptors in an induced depletion layer just balance the positive charge supplied to the gate electrode. This onset of an inversion layer corresponds to the condition that the electron concentration at the surface of the semiconductor is approximately equal to the acceptor concentration, $n = N_a$. For this to apply, it will be seen from eqs. (6.13) and (6.18) and the band structure shown in Fig. 12.8(b) that the Fermi level at the surface must be below the bottom of the conduction band by as much as it is above the top of the valence band in the bulk material, if the density of states in each band is assumed to be approximately equal or $N_C \simeq N_V$. It follows that if the energy bands bend down a total amount eV_s then, from Fig. 12.8(b):

$$eV_s = 2a = 2(E_g/2 - E_{Fs}) = E_g - 2E_{Fs} \tag{12.33}$$

The corresponding depletion layer width can be obtained by integrating Poisson's equation across the depletion layer to give:

$$d_p = \sqrt{\frac{2\epsilon V_s}{eN_a}} \tag{12.34}$$

Now, assuming no contact voltage exists between oxide and semiconductor, the turn-on voltage is divided between the oxide and the depletion layer and

$$V_T = V_{ox} + V_s \tag{12.35}$$

where V_{ox} is the voltage across the oxide. Further, if the depletion layer thickness is assumed to be much less than that of the oxide, so that the charge in the layer can be considered as a surface charge, then for the continuity of electric displacement across the interface

$$\frac{\epsilon_{ox} V_{ox}}{t_o} = eN_a d_p$$

or

$$V_{ox} = \frac{wl}{C_g} \cdot eN_a d_p \tag{12.36}$$

Finally, substitution of eqs. (12.33), (12.34), and (12.36) into (12.35) gives the required expression for estimating the turn-on voltage:

$$V_T = \frac{wl}{C_g} \sqrt{2\epsilon_s N_a(E_g - 2E_{Fs})} + \frac{E_g - 2E_{Fs}}{e} \tag{12.37}$$

12.4.2 Diffused-channel IGFET. The diffused-channel IGFET has similar constructed features to the induced channel type, with the important difference that a thin channel of the same conductivity type as the source and drain is diffused into the surface of the semiconductor during manufacture, as shown in Fig. 12.10. The device can be operated in depletion or enhancement modes. If the gate has a negative bias voltage applied to it, the resulting

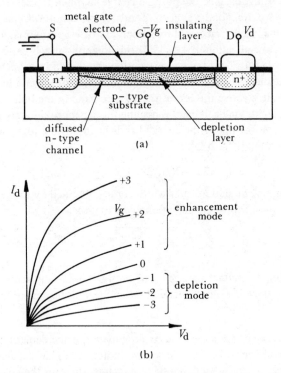

Fig. 12.10 (a) A diffused-n-channel IGFET operating in the depletion mode (b) drain characteristics of the diffused-channel IGFET.

transverse field must terminate on positive charges which are induced in the n-type channel. In order to achieve this condition, majority electrons move away from the semiconductor surface to expose positively charged fixed ionized donors and so produce a depletion layer, as shown in Fig. 12.10. The channel conductance is reduced by the application of the bias voltage to the gate electrode, in much the same manner as for a JFET, and maximum drain current flows for zero gate voltages.

On the other hand, if the polarity of the gate voltage is reversed so as to apply forward bias, i.e., the gate is made positive, electrons are drawn into the channel to enhance the number of mobile carriers there, with a corresponding increase in the conductivity of the channel and hence the drain current. This enhancement mode of operation is possible because the complete isolation of the insulating layer results in negligibly small gate currents whatever the polarity of the gate voltage, but it is prohibited in a JFET, since forward biasing of the

280

gate–channel junctions causes large gate currents to flow. A typical set of drain characteristics for the device is shown in Fig. 12.10(b).

It is not always possible to ignore the existence of surface states at the semiconductor–insulator interface, as has been assumed so far. If surface states exist there will be curvature of the band edges in the semiconductor even when the applied gate voltage is zero in an induced-channel device, (see section 9.10.3). If the surface states act as donor impurities, there will be a tendency for an inversion layer to form, even when $V_g = 0$, and the turn-on voltage will be much lower than with no traps present. In the extreme case, when the surface trap density is very high. it is possible for an n-type inversion layer to be fully developed before any gate voltage is applied. The unit then operates in depletion or enhancement modes in a manner exactly similar to the operation of the depletion-type IGFET with an n-type doped channel, and its drain characteristics are similar in form to those shown in Fig. 12.10(b).

A further point to note is that although n-channel devices have been discussed throughout this chapter, this does not preclude the possibility of devices being constructed with p-type channels. Our earlier discussions are readily extended to describe such units by interchanging p- and n-type and the polarity of the bias voltages throughout.

12.5 The small-signal equivalent circuit and frequency response of FETs

The normal symbolic representations of the JFET and the MOST, each with n-type channel, are shown in Figs. 12.11(a) and (b). For a p-type channel the direction of the arrow on the gate connection is reversed.

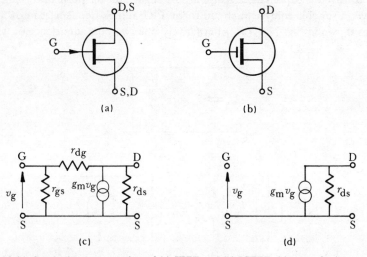

Fig. 12.11 Symbolic representation of (a) JFET and (b) IGFET, (c) a low-frequency equivalent circuit of a field-effect transistor, (d) approximate low-frequency equivalent circuit.

281

Field-effect transistors have input characteristics which in no way resemble those of bipolar transistors. In the junction FET the gate-channel junctions are reverse-biased; the gate current flowing corresponds to the very small saturation current of a reverse-biased pn junction, and the input impedance in the common-source configuration is usually many megohms. The insulated-gate FET by virtue of the electrical isolation of the gate electrode by the oxide layer has even lower gate currents, typically a few nanoamperes, and its input impedance can be of order of many thousands of megohms. On the other hand, the bipolar transistor in common emitter configuration has a low input impedance corresponding to the forward-biased base–emitter junction. In this respect, therefore, the FET is a voltage-controlled device more nearly resembling the vacuum devices discussed in chapter 10 than the bipolar transistor which is current-controlled.

A convenient low-frequency equivalent circuit for an FET in common-source connection, based on its observed and calculated characteristics, is shown in Fig. 12.11(c). As we have just discussed, the input impedance is very high and the feedback resistance r_{dg}, by similar reasoning, is of the same order, so both r_{gs} and r_{dg} can normally be omitted to give the simple low-frequency equivalent circuit shown in Fig. 12.11(d).

At high frequencies, interterminal capacitances must also be included in the equivalent circuit. For instance, associated with the reverse-biased junction gate of a JFET is an input capacitance of several tens of picofarads, typically, although this can be made considerably smaller for the IGFET. Similarly, the gate–drain capacitance cannot be neglected at high frequencies. Both are at least partly depletion layer capacitances and hence are voltage-dependent but usually the capacitance change is only slight over the normal working range. A suitable equivalent circuit for an FET at high frequencies might then be as shown in Fig. 12.12(a). Alternatively, the two-port admittance or 'y'

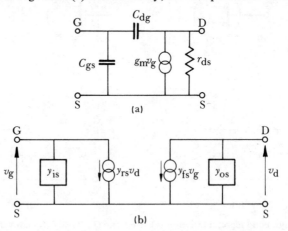

Fig. 12.12 (a) A high-frequency equivalent circuit of the FET and (b) an alternative high-frequency equivalent circuit.

282

parameters are sometimes found convenient to characterize the FET for small-signal and high-frequency use, as shown in the equivalent circuit of Fig. 12.12(b).

As we have seen, current in a field-effect transistor is carried by majority carriers drifting under the influence of an electric field, whereas in the bipolar transistor, current is transported by means of diffusing minority carriers. Since drift velocities in semiconductors are usually very much higher than diffusion velocities, carrier transit times are much shorter in FETs than in bipolar transistors. For this reason, we might expect FETs to have a much more extended high-frequency range than bipolar devices.

A limitation to the high-frequency performance or the switching speed of an FET is the gate-channel capacitance, which must be charged via the channel resistance. The resulting time constant determines the upper limit of the frequency response. The gain–bandwidth product, which can be derived from the equivalent circuit and which equals $g_m/2\pi C_g$, is normally taken as a figure of merit which indicates the high-frequency response of a particular device. Thus, ideally, for good high-frequency performance, the transconductance should be as large as possible and the total gate capacitance C_g should be as small as possible, both of which require the channel length to be short. Using this criterion it is possible for an IGFET to have a higher g_m/C_g ratio and hence a higher high-frequency cut-off than a JFET because of the shorter gates which are more easily fabricated with insulated gate technology.

The g_m/C_g ratio for an IGFET can be found from eq. (12.32), which gives:

$$g_m/C_g = \mu_e(V_g - V_T)/l^2 \qquad (12.38)$$

Since the average field in the channel is $(V_g - V_T)/l$, and since the carrier velocity is the product of μ_e and this field, eq. (12.38) shows that g/C_g is also approximately equal to the reciprocal of the transit time of majority carriers from source to drain.

12.6 Other field-effect devices

Although lack of space precludes a detailed discussion, a brief description of various other devices which rely for their operations on the field effects will be useful.

The so-called field-effect *current limiter* is not, in fact, a different device but is an FET with gates permanently strapped to the source contact. The *V-I* characteristic of this arrangement is the same as the $V_g = 0$ curve in Fig. 12.3(a); as the drain voltage increases the drain current increases until it saturates and remains sensibly constant. Its much smaller bulk for a high dynamic resistance and the lower dissipation make this device more suitable for integrated circuit use than the conventional lumped limiting resistors, as we shall see.

Whereas an obvious aim in the design of the majority of FETs is to obtain a high value of g_m together with a low pinch-off voltage, for certain circuit applications it is desirable to have a device with a high pinch-off voltage but which still retains the high g_m at low gate voltages which is usually associated with FETs with low pinch-off voltages. The *remote-cut-off* (or variable-μ) JFET satisfies these dual requirements. It has a transfer characteristic as shown in the full line of Fig. 12.13(a). The device consists essentially of a JFET

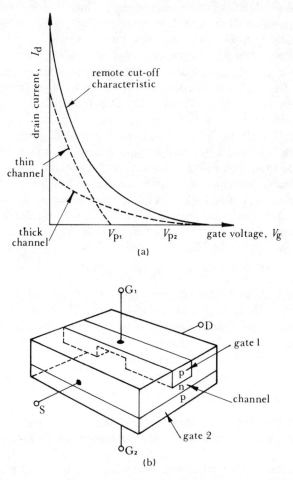

Fig. 12.13 Remote cut-off JFET, (a) typical transfer characteristic and (b) possible construction.

containing two channels of different thicknesses and widths in parallel in one unit, as shown schematically for a planar device in Fig. 12.13(b). Reference to eqs. (12.7) and (12.19) will confirm that the channel transconductance for zero gate voltage is largely determined by the thinner, wider channel portion

284

of the device, whereas eq. (12.3) shows that the thicker channel primarily determines the pinch-off voltage, V_{p2}. The combined transfer characteristics resulting from two such channel regions in parallel can then be synthesized as shown in Fig. 12.13(a).

The *field-effect tetrode* is a four-terminal device which consists of two conducting channels of opposite conductivity types placed side by side in one unit so as to have a common junction. The four terminals are connected to the sources and drains of each channel as shown in Fig. 12.14(a). No gate connections are necessary since each channel in effect behaves as a gate for the other. While the device has several applications, one of the most interesting is its use as a linear, high-frequency, electronically variable resistor whose resistance can be varied up to several megohms. The basic circuit is as shown in Fig. 12.14(a). The signal voltage to be controlled, v_i, is applied in series with

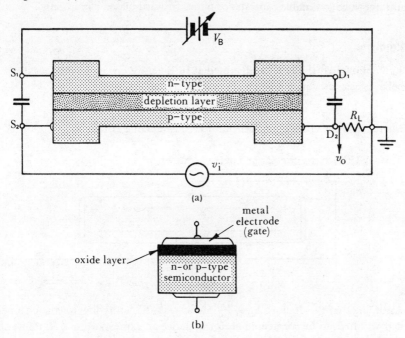

(a)

(b)

Fig. 12.14 (a) A field-effect tetrode used as an electronically variable resistor, (b) MOS capacitor.

the channels and a resistance R_L. The capacitors have a low enough reactance to ensure that the signal voltage does not appear across the junction and modulate the channel resistance. The variable reverse-bias voltage V_B controls the depletion layer width, hence the resistance of the two channels in parallel which in turn determines the output voltage, v_o.

The *MOS capacitor*, as its name suggests, consists of an extrinsic semiconductor with a thin insulating oxide layer on one surface, surmounted by a metal electrode, often called a 'gate' by analogy with a MOST. It is shown diagrammatically in Fig. 12.14(b). The total capacitance of the device is a series combination of the capacitance of the oxide layer and that of the semiconductor surface, which includes the depletion layer capacitance and a capacitance due to surface states. Such capacitors are constructed as research vehicles to study the technology and physics of semiconductor surfaces. They are also useful in their own right as integrated circuit components. At high frequencies the surface states are unable to follow alterations of the field and capacitance due to their effect can be ignored; the surface capacitance is then analogous to that of one half of an abrupt-junction diode. However, an essential difference is that the dielectric layer in the MOS capacitor prevents forward conduction when forward bias is applied. The MOS capacitor thus has attractive possibilities as a high-frequency varactor, since advantage can be taken of its large voltage variable capacitance under forward-biased conditions.

Problems

1   Show that if a JFET is operated at sufficiently low drain voltages it behaves as a resistance R given approximately by

$$R = R_0 [1 - (V_g/V_p)^{\frac{1}{2}}]^{-1}$$

where R_0 is the channel resistance for zero gate voltages.

2   A JFET has a circular geometry as shown

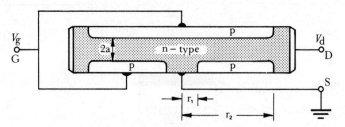

Assuming that the drain voltage, V_d, is always sufficiently low for the channel half width, b, to be considered uniform, derive an expression for b in terms of V_g, the contact potential V_0 and a pinch-off voltage V_p. Hence show that the channel resistance is given by

$$R = R_0 \left[1 - \left(\frac{V_0 + V_g}{V_0 + V_p} \right)^{\frac{1}{2}} \right]^{-1}$$

where R_0 is the channel resistance when $V_g = 0$.

286

13. Integrated circuits

13.1 Introduction

Although a detailed discussion of the intricate and complex new technology associated with integrated circuits is not possible here, because of their extreme importance at present and their potential for the future, a brief description of their types and processes used for their manufacture will now be given.

An integrated circuit is a complete electronic circuit containing both active and passive components which is fabricated in one small chip of semiconductor, usually silicon, complete with metallic interconnections. Consider, for example, the circuit shown schematically in Fig. 13.1(a). Although the circuit is artificial in that it has been chosen so that the interconnections are more easily represented, a discussion of its realization in integrated form will be useful. It is evident that each of the circuit elements shown can be made using semiconductor material, with or without junctions, provided the component values are within prescribed limits. As a first step, the active devices might take the form of the discrete versions mentioned in the relevant earlier chapters, resistors could be rods of suitably doped semiconductor of a particular geometry to suit the resistance required, and capacitors may be comprised, for example, of the junction capacitance of a reverse-biased junction of suitable geometry, as shown in the figure. It will be noticed that each component type can be fabricated from, say, an npn sandwich of semiconductor, although not all would utilize all three layers. It seems a reasonable conception, therefore, that each circuit element might be fabricated on the same semiconductor slice, using diffusion techniques, say, with metal circuit connections deposited on one face of the slice. Such an integrated circuit unit, as shown in section in Fig. 13.1(b), will have obvious advantages of high packing density, reliability, robustness, reproducibility, and so on.

There are several difficulties to be overcome before a particular electronic circuit can be realized in integrated form as envisaged. Firstly, every circuit component must be so designed that all electrical connections can be made at one surface of the semiconductor from which they are formed. Second, since each circuit element is to be fabricated in close proximity to its neighbours in the same slice of semiconductor, which is itself a conducting medium,

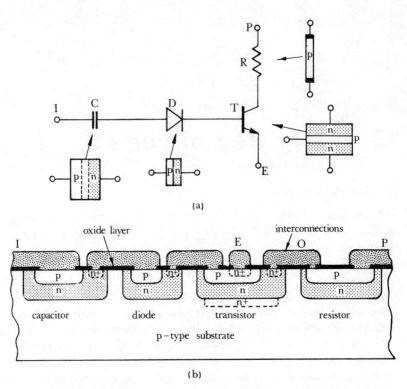

Fig. 13.1 (a) Hypothetical electronic circuit, (b) possible integrated-circuit realisation.

some means of electrical isolation between elements must be introduced. This ensures that there is no unintentional coupling between components and that the only conducting paths joining them together are metallic interconnections.

A description of various possible isolation techniques follows.

13.2 Methods of isolation

Electrical isolation of integrated circuit components has been achieved in several different ways. By far the most common technique is that of *diode isolation*. In this process, each component is formed in an island of, say, n-type semiconductor surrounded by bulk p-type, as shown for example in Fig. 13.1(b). In operation, the pn junction so formed is reverse-biased by making the p-type bulk material more negative than any other part of the integrated circuit; this provides a very high resistance between components and effectively isolates them electrically. An obvious disadvantage of the method is that additional parasitic capacitances are introduced as a consequence of the reverse-biased isolating junctions.

Integrated circuits with a higher degree of isolation can be fabricated using the *beam-lead* method. After the components have been formed in the

288

semiconductor slice, to provide a circuit similar to that shown in Fig. 13.1(b), an especially thick metallizing layer is deposited to produce mechanically strong interconnections. The bulk p-type semiconductor is then completely removed by applying a suitable etch to the back face of the slice, to leave each component completely isolated from all others and only supported by relatively massive interconnections, as shown in Fig. 13.2(a). The leads act

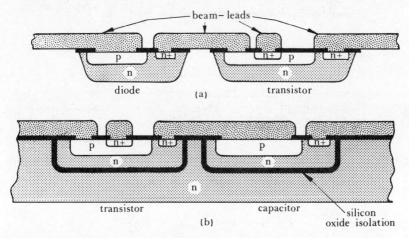

Fig. 13.2 Other possible isolation techniques, (a) beam-lead and (b) oxide isolation.

as cantilever beams; hence their name. It is usual to add additional mechanical rigidity by potting the complete circuit in a thermosetting plastic.

A further possible isolation process is that of *dielectric isolation* in which a thick insulating layer of dielectric, often silicon oxide, completely surrounds each component and effectively isolates it electrically from its neighbours, as shown in Fig. 13.2(b). The process has the advantages of much-reduced parasitic capacitance, provided the insulating layer is thick enough. It also affords an opportunity for fabricating npn and pnp complimentary transistor pairs on a single slice, which can be advantageous. The choice of a particular isolation technique is governed by economic considerations and depends on the degree of isolation required.

13.3 Integrated circuit elements

Before going on to describe the fabrication of a complete integrated circuit, it will be useful to discuss the various possibilities for its constituent components.

13.3.1. Resistors for integrated circuits.
Diffused planar resistors for integrated circuits can be formed by a p-type diffusion into an n-type isolating layer, as shown in Fig. 13.3(a). For effective diode isolation the

resistor must be given a negative potential relative to the isolating n-type material. The resistance value is determined by the resistivity and geometry of the p-type diffused layer. Since in an integrated circuit this layer is formed by the same diffusion as that used to form transistor bases, see for example Fig. 13.1(b), its thickness is usually prescribed. It is therefore

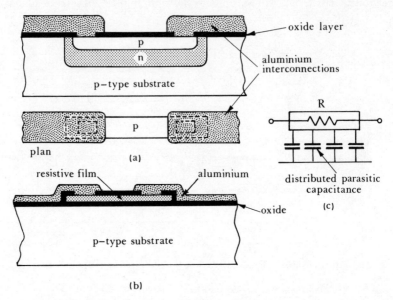

Fig. 13.3 Integrated circuit resistors: (a) diffused, (b) thin-film, and (c) a simple equivalent circuit.

convenient to quote its resistance per unit square of surface area, a typical value for such a *sheet resistance* being 100 Ω/square. For example, a resistor stripe 0·01 mm wide has a resistance of 100 Ω per 0·01 mm run of its length, giving, say, 1 kΩ for a length of 0·1 mm. By correct choice of dimensions resistances in the range of 10–20 kΩ are currently possible using this method. Lower values can be obtained if the n^+-emitter diffusion is used as the resistive medium; this has a typical sheet resistance of around 1 Ω/square. It should be noted that because of difficulties in controlling the process, the tolerance held on nominally identical resistors on different slices in only ±10%, but this can be reduced to relative values of around ±1% for resistors which are side by side on the same slice.

Resistors made by thin-film techniques can also form compatible parts of intergrated circuits. A thin film of resistive metal or semiconducting material is deposited directly on top of the protective oxide layer formed on the semi-conducting slice which incorporates other circuit components, as shown in Fig. 13.3(b). Resistive films which have been used are tin oxide, tantalum, nichrome, and aluminium for low resistance values. The desired geometry

290

for a particular resistor is determined by a masking and etching process. An additional protective oxide layer is then applied and interconnections are deposited on top of this, as shown. Typical sheet resistances of 10–400 Ω/square are achieved with nichrome, resulting in a possible resistance range of 20–50 kΩ. Since parasitics are reduced by the construction process, thin-film resistors can have a superior high-frequency performance to their diffused counterparts.

13.3.2. Integrated circuit capacitors. Probably the easiest capacitor to produce for integrated circuit application is the diffused junction type as shown in Fig. 13.4(a), which utilizes the capacitance of a reverse-biased pn junction.

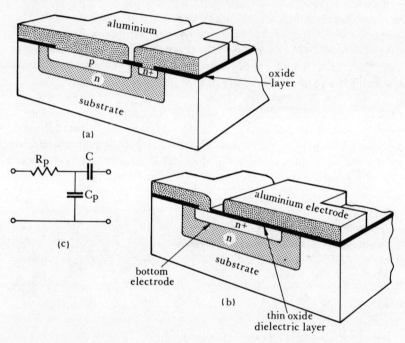

Fig. 13.4 Integrated circuit capacitors: (a) diffused-junction, (b) MOS, and (c) an equivalent circuit.

Its principle advantage is that it can be formed as one of the intermediate steps in the manufacture of a complete circuit as we shall see, the n-type half of the capacitor being diffused at the same time as transistor collectors and the p-type along with base diffusions. Since aluminium used for inter-connections is an acceptor impurity in silicon, the area immediately below the contact to the n-type region is heavily doped n^+ to ensure that no pn junction is formed there and that the connection is ohmic. Capacitances up to about 200 pF with ±5 per cent tolerance are possible. Diffused-junction

291

capacitors have the disadvantages that their capacitance is dependent on the reverse bias voltage and they also do not behave as pure capacitances but have parasitic resistance, R_p, and capacitance to the substrate, C_p, built in. These can be accounted for by the simple equivalent circuit shown in Fig. 13.4(c).

Thin-film capacitors which are compatible with integrated circuits have the advantages of not requiring or having their capacitance determined by a bias voltage and of being non-polar. They consist essentially of a parallel plate capacitor with a dielectric filling of silicon dioxide, tantalum oxide, or alumina. A metal-oxide–silicon (MOS) capacitor is shown in Fig. 13.4(b). The n^+-diffusion, which is put down at the same time as emitter diffusions, forms one electrode of the capacitor. On top of this is grown a layer of SiO_2 of controlled thickness, typically 50 nm. The top electrode is usually aluminium which is deposited concurrently with the interconnections. Capacitances of up to about 500 pF are possible with lower parasitic resistances than the diffused type, but since the MOS capacitor requires additional processing it is more expensive to produce.

13.3.3. Transistors for integrated circuits. Bipolar planar transistors for inclusion in integrated circuits are basically similar to the discrete versions described in chapter 11. An obvious difference is that the collector lead has to be accessible at the top surface of the slice. This is achieved as shown in Fig. 13.5(a), which shows a cross-section of an integrated planar transistor

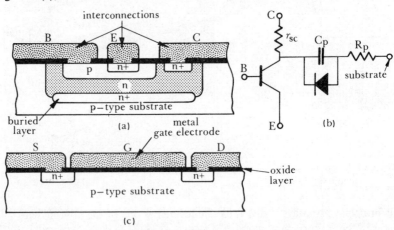

Fig. 13.5 (a) Bipolar planar integrated-circuit transistor and (b) its equivalent circuit, (c) MOS n-channel integrated transistor.

with diode isolation. The n^+-diffusion near the collector contact ensures that a low-resistance ohmic connection is made to the collector region. Since the collector contact is now made to the top surface, collector current is constrained to flow transversely to the active part of the transistor via a longer path than in the discrete version, with a corresponding increase in the series resistance of the collector, r_{sc}. This effect is often counteracted by a buried layer of n^+-material which is formed during processing underneath the collector diffusion, as shown, which provides a low resistance path for the collector current and effectively minimises r_{sc}. A possible equivalent circuit of the transistor plus parasitic components due to the isolation is shown in Fig. 13.5(b).

Insulated-gate field-effect transistors and in particular MOSTs offer some advantages for integrated circuits application. The cross-section of a typical n-channel enhancement-mode integrated circuit mode MOST is shown in Fig. 13.5(c). No additional isolation is required, since source and drain are self-isolating because the n^+-regions form reverse-biased junctions with the substrate; the gate is isolated by the insulating layer under it and the induced n-type channel by the pn junction which appears simultaneously. This elimination of isolation islands leads to a higher packing density per slice and a reduced cost per transistor.

MOST structures can be used as resistors, provided gate and drain are strapped together, ensuring that the bias is such that a conducting channel is formed. The resistance value is dependent on drain voltage and is approximately equal to the reciprocal of the device transconductance, g_m^{-1}. High resistance values, typically up to 100 kΩ, are possible with this arrangement, with the additional advantage of a much lower surface area requirement than for diffused resistors. MOS resistors and transistors are compatible and complete integrated circuits using MOS components alone are possible. The advantages of relatively high packing density afforded by MOS integrated circuits is offset to some extent by their lower switching speed and by a poorer high-frequency performance.

13.3.4. Integrated circuit diodes. General-purpose diffused diodes for incorporation in integrated circuits can be made by the same processes which are used for the bipolar transistor but omitting the emitter diffusion, to produce the device shown in cross-section in Fig. 13.6(a). Alternatively, a

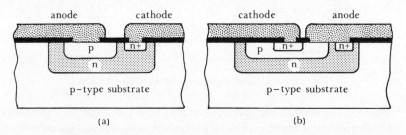

Fig. 13.6 (a) Collector–base diode, (b) emitter–base diode.

293

diode can be formed using a complete transistor structure in which the collector and base are strapped together at the same time that the metallized connections are formed, as shown in Fig. 13.6(b). The resulting diode has the advantage of a fast response, but its reverse voltage is limited by the low breakdown voltage of the base–emitter junction.

13.4 Monolithic integrated circuits

A *monolithic* (Greek: single-stone) integrated circuit is so called because all passive and active circuit components are formed in one small chip of single-crystal semiconductor, usually silicon, using planar diffusion techniques, the metallic interconnecting matrix being incorporated on one face of the chip. Various other types of integrated circuit are possible, however. For example, *thin-film* integrated circuits have a pattern of passive components and interconnections deposited on to a ceramic insulating substrate by evaporation techniques; the active semiconductor devices are made by a separate process and are subsequently bonded and connected to the thin film circuit. *Thick-film* circuits use a variant of this technique in that the passive components and interconnecting pattern are produced on the substrate by a silk-screen printing process. Although film microcircuits have been used extensively, monolithic circuits have many advantages, not least of which is a considerable potential for large-scale integration, and it is becoming apparent that they will supersede film circuits for many applications. For this reason, our attention will mostly be devoted to monolithic integrated circuits in silicon.

Monolithic circuits are made using essentially the same processes of masking, diffusion, and evaporation which are employed to make discrete planar devices, as discussed for example with reference to diodes in chapter 10. Because of the extremely small size of the components and of each complete circuit, many identical integrated circuits are made simultaneously on the same slice of silicon. An idea of the sizes involved can be obtained from Fig. 13.7. It will be seen that a 30 mm diameter slice can contain up to about

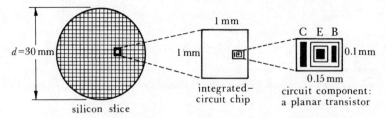

Fig. 13.7 Typical slice and integrated circuit geometry.

600 integrated circuits, each typically occupying a 1 mm square chip. Since a bipolar transistor covers an area of order 0·15 x 0·1 mm and the other circuit components are often smaller, around fifty circuit elements per

294

individual circuit are possible. Since all components in each circuit are designed to be constructed by compatible planar diffusion processes, they are all formed at the same time by a sequence of masking and diffusion steps.

The fabrication of epitaxial monolithic integrated circuits starts with the preparation of a slice of single crystal, p-type silicon. The slice, which is typically 150 μm thick and 20–50 mm in diameter, is cut from an ingot of extrinsic silicon, prepared as described earlier, and is then lapped and polished. The top surface of the slice then has an oxide layer about 1 μm thick formed on it by heating it, together with many other such slices, in an oxidizing atmosphere of oxygen and steam at 1150 °C. The steam serves to accelerate the oxidization. The next and subsequent processing steps involve cutting *windows* at appropriate places in the oxide so that the layer forms a mask through which diffusion and later selective etching can take place. Since the process of making openings in the oxide layer is common to all stages of production, it will now be discussed in more detail.

13.4.1. Photolithographic masking. A predetermined pattern of windows in an oxide layer can be prepared by a photolithographic process, the basic steps of which are shown in Fig. 13.8. The oxide is first coated by a spinning

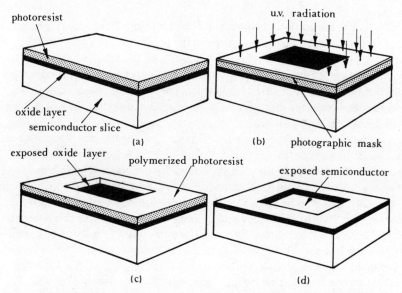

Fig. 13.8 Cutting of *windows* in the oxide layer: (a) oxidized slice coated with photo-resist, (b) mask applied and exposed to u.v., (c) photoresist developed and hardened, (d) oxide selectively etched and resist removed.

technique with a thin uniform laquer of photoresist material, typically 1 mm thick, as shown in Fig. 13.8(a). This photosensitive emulsion has the property of becoming insoluble in certain developers wherever it has been polymerized by exposure to ultra-violet light. A photographic mask is therefore prepared which is opaque to ultra-violet light at locations where the oxide has to be removed for a particular diffusion and is transparent elsewhere. The mask is placed in contact with the coated oxide layer and is exposed to the ultra-violet radiation, as shown in Fig. 13.8(b), followed by the removal of the unpolymerized film with a suitable solvent, for example trichloroethylene, as shown in Fig. 13.8(c). The remaining photoresist is hardened and since it is then insoluble in an etchant containing hydrofluoric acid which attacks the oxide, it acts as a convenient mask through which the oxide layer can be etched away to expose areas of semiconductor underneath, as shown in Fig. 13.8(d). In practice, a different photographic mask is made for each stage of the manufacture of a complete circuit, which determines the location of all openings in the oxide and hence the areas over which the particular diffusion step is effective. Each mask is reproduced from a large black-and-white replica of the appropriate masking scheme for the entire circuit, which is reduced photographically in several stages to the actual size required. A master photographic mask is prepared at the same time as the final reduction stage by step-and-repeat printing, to produce a composite matrix of masks, each corresponding to one set for an individual circuit, which is of sufficient area to cover the entire slice.

13.4.2. The fabrication of epitaxial-diffused integrated circuits.

It is now possible to describe the various stages in the production of a complete integrated circuit. We take as a simple example of the processes involved the portion of an integrated circuit shown in Fig. 13.9(a). This has the advantage that its interconnections are easily depicted in two dimensions whereas in a more complex circuit they may be in any direction on the surface of the semiconductor wafer.

A single crystal p-type slice with an oxide layer formed on its top surface as described earlier provides the basic material from which the circuit is constructed. Windows are cut in the oxide layer by the masking and photoetching described in the previous section, so as to locate areas through which an n^+-diffusion is to be carried out to form the buried layers of all transistors, Fig. 13.9(b). Arsenic is usually chosen as the donor for this operation because it has a lower rate of diffusion in silicon than phosphorus or boron, which are used for subsequent diffusions; this ensures that the buried layers remain in the same position during succeeding processing stages. A doping concentration in excess of $10^{25}/m^3$ provides the low resistance required for the buried layer.

After removal of the oxide layer, an n-type epitaxial layer, typically 20 μm thick, is grown over the p-type substrate and n^+ buried layers by heating the wafer at 1200 °C in an atmosphere of silicon tetrachloride and phosphine using an induction furnace, Fig. 13.9(c). This n-type material has a typical donor concentration of about $10^{22}/m^3$ and a corresponding

296

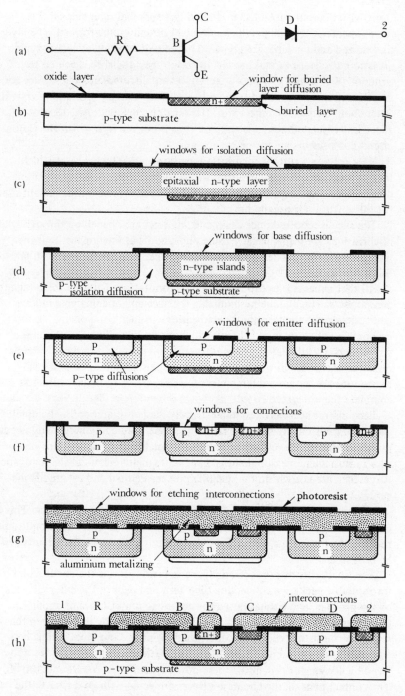

(a)

(b) oxide layer | window for buried layer diffusion | n+ | buried layer | p-type substrate

(c) windows for isolation diffusion | epitaxial n-type layer

(d) windows for base diffusion | n-type islands | p-type isolation diffusion | p-type substrate

(e) windows for emitter diffusion | p | p | p | p-type diffusions | n | n | n

(f) windows for connections | p | n+ | n+ | p | p | n | n | n

(g) windows for etching interconnections | photoresist | p | p | p | aluminium metalizing | n | n | n

(h) 1 R B E C interconnections D 2 | p | p | n+ | p | n | n | n | p-type substrate

Fig. 13.9 Fabrication of a monolithic integrated circuit.

297

resistivity of around 0·004 Ω m. It is in this epitaxial layer that all the components of the integrated circuit are eventually to be formed. The layer is oxidized and openings are prepared in the oxide through which p-type isolation diffusions can take place. In this process the slice is heated to around 1000 °C and phosphorus acceptors are diffused into the surface for a sufficient length of time for the p-type diffusion to penetrate the expitaxial layer completely and connect with the substrate below it, Fig. 13.9(d). Electrically isolated n-type islands are thus produced into which the various circuit components are formed.

Next follows a further oxidization, masking, and etching stage which locates areas for a p-type diffusion which forms transistor bases, resistors, diode anodes, and capacitor electrodes, Fig. 13.9(e). The p-type dopant used for this diffusion is usually boron.

The slice is oxidized once again and windows are opened up through which n^+-diffusions are made, usually using phosphorus as the dopant, to form transistor emitters, collector contacts, diode cathode contacts, and so on, Fig. 13.9(f).

All that remains is to produce the interconnections between the integrated components. This is done by oxidizing the slice and opening up windows which determine the location of connections to each component. Vacuum evaporation of aluminium follows, which produces a film of metal on the entire slice. This is coated with photoresist and exposed through a suitable mask to provide windows through which surplus aluminium is etched away, to produce the required interconnection pattern and terminal pads and so complete the integrated circuit, as shown in section in Fig. 13.9(h).

Each circuit is usually tested electrically while it is still on the complete slice, along with many similar circuits. A probe head containing many needle probes is lowered on to the aluminium terminal pads of each circuit on the slice in turn and a measurement is made of its major electrical characteristics. Any which are not within the specification are marked and eventually discarded.

The next stage is to separate individual circuit chips from the slice. This is done by scribing lines on the slice between the circuits with a diamond-tipped tool, in much the same way as for cutting glass, after which the circuits can be broken apart.

The final series of production processes involve fixing the circuit chips into suitable packages, connecting their terminal pads to the external leads of the package, and encapsulating the complete unit. Choice of circuit package is dependent on the final application but usually lies between the multipin transistor-type T05 header, the 'flat-pack', and 'dual-in-line' configuration, shown in Fig. 13.10. In each case, the circuit chips are securely fixed by alloying or cementing them down at temperatures around 300 °C. The contact pads on the circuit are then connected with gold wire to the external leads by a bonding technique which has basic steps as shown in

Fig. 13.11. A 20 μm diameter gold wire is fed down a capilliary tube and has a gold ball about 100 μm in diameter formed on its end by melting in a hydrogen flame, Fig. 13.11(a). The ball is pressed on to a circuit pad which has been heated to 300 °C, so making a permanent electrical connection to the circuit, Fig. 13.11(b). The capilliary tube is raised, while at the same time more wire is released, and moved to the header post, where the wire is once again pressure-welded to the heated post, Fig. 13.11(c).

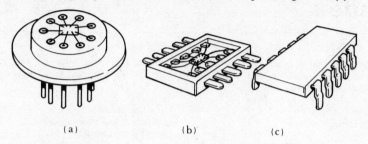

Fig. 13.10 Various integrated-circuit packages: (a) transistor type, (b) flat-pack, and (c) dual-in-line.

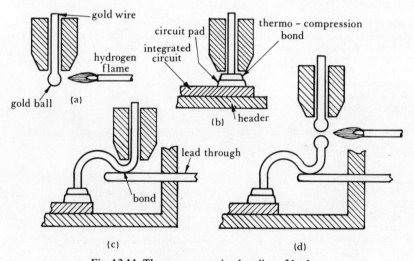

Fig. 13.11 Thermocompression bonding of leads.

Finally, the tube is raised and the wire is cut using a hydrogen flame, which simultaneously forms the gold ball required for the next wire bond. After all connections have been made in this way, the package is either hermetically sealed in an atmosphere of dry nitrogen or is completely encapsulated in a plastic material, to produce an end-product which has evolved through many complex, intricate, and exacting stages of production.

Index

300

Printed in Great Britain by Spottiswoode Ballantyne Ltd, Colchester and London